ANDIAMO FULL CIRCLE

A Round-the-World Motorcycle Adventure

by Bob Dolven

Copyright © 2020 Robert Dolven,
World Betterment Coalition WBC LLC
All rights reserved.

Cover design:
The cover is a picture created by a mosaic of over 5,000 pictures I have taken on "The Ride". If we have taken a picture together, it is likely somewhere on the cover. I want to share these adventures like you are on the back of the bike with me.
"Let's Go"
(In Italian- "Andiamo")

Dedication:

I'd like to dedicate this book to <u>YOU</u>, the reader. My compensation for writing it will be you saying; "Hey Bob, I enjoyed reading your book".

Table of Contents

Foreword 1

North America 5
    Kindness Quest 7

Central America 15
    Mexico 17
    Belize 23
    Guatemala 27
    El Salvador 30
    Honduras 34
    Nicaragua 36
    Costa Rica 40
    Panama 46

South America 51
    Colombia 53
    Ecuador 57
    Peru 61
    Bolivia 70
    Chile 81
    Argentina 87

United Kingdom 93
    England 95

Scandinavia 99
    Denmark 101
    Sweden 103

Norway 105

Europe 111
Germany 113
Switzerland 116
Monaco 118
France 119
Spain 122
Portugal 126

Africa 131
Morocco 133
Algeria 141
Tunisia 149

Europe 155
Sicily 157

Eastern Europe 161
Italy 163
Albania 167
Montenegro 169
Croatia 175
Bosnia 178
Macedonia 180
Greece 183

Near East 187
Turkey 189
Cyprus 195
Lebanon 197

Eastern Europe 203
Bulgaria 205

Romania 231
Moldova 236
Transnistria 238
Ukraine 241
Russia 246
Georgia 260

Asia 265
Azerbaijan 267
Kazakhstan 276
Uzbekistan 282
Mongolia 297
South Korea 300
North Korea 302
Japan 312

Southeast Asia 321
Malaysia 323
Thailand 329
Cambodia 337
Laos 346

Oceania 359
Indonesia 361
Australia 383
New Zealand 402

Extras 413
COVID-19 415
Gear Guide 417
Airlines Flown 420
Parking Spots 423
Common Questions 425

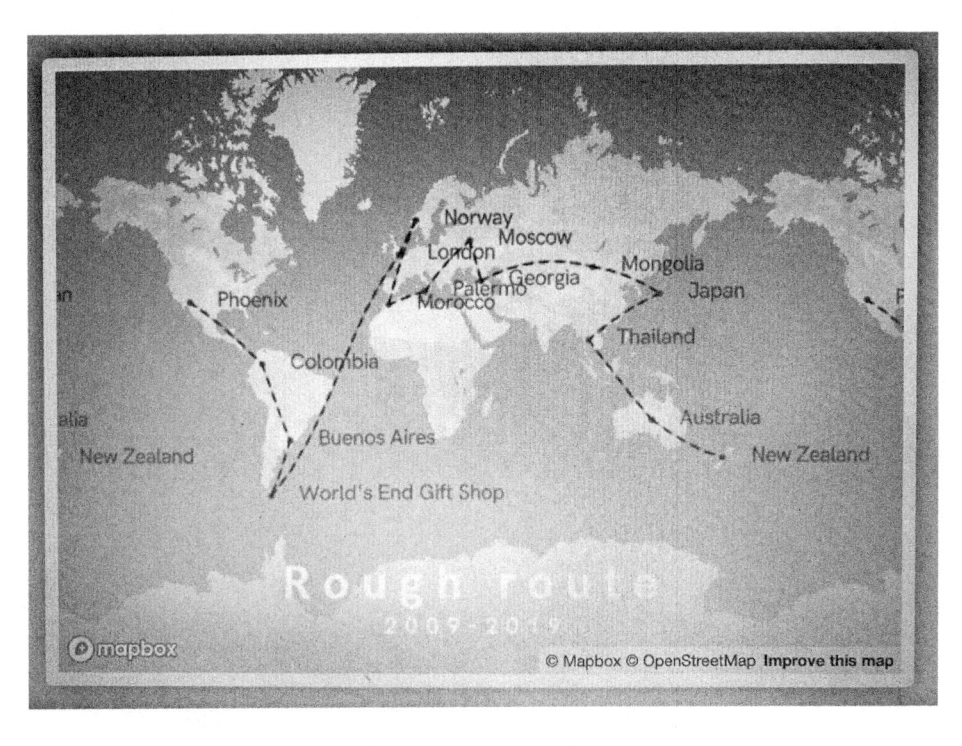

A basic overview of my route

Foreword

by David Aller

For what is sure to become a must-read book in any adventure rider's library, *Andiamo Full Circle* follows the incredible travels and exploits of Captain Robert "Bob" Dolven, airline pilot turned long-distance motorcycle rider.

When Captain Bob started his adventure, his plan was not to circumnavigate the globe on a motorcycle. But as with most great endeavors, it started out as something much less grandiose.

Having been grounded from flying for two months due to a trivial infraction involving the betrayal of a former friend and colleague, Bob felt himself becoming disillusioned with the human condition. Not willing to allow this event to turn him bitter, he made a conscious and deliberate decision to find good in the world, thus embarking on a "Kindness Quest."

Combining his love of riding motorcycle's with a genuine desire to make a difference in the world, he envisaged and embarked on a trip to ride the contiguous lower forty-eight states doing random acts of kindness, thus "paying forward" cosmic karma to anyone in his way!

This experience was enough to serve as a catalyst to something much bigger that eventually consumed the next ten years and every waking moment of his life.

Astride a 2004 BMW 1150GS motorcycle, Bob departed south from his residence in Phoenix, Arizona, with no real destination in mind. Because, you see, for the true adventure rider, it is only "the ride" that matters, not the destination. It's about the people you come in contact with either by chance or necessity, thus weaving the fabric of their lives into your own.

Country after country, Bob puts close calls and dangerous situations into his memoirs like children put seashells into a bucket. From being nearly pulled off his bike in the jungles of Nicaragua during a botched robbery attempt to being stranded on a cargo ship in the Caspian Sea, Bob shows firsthand how life is not about what happens to you, but rather how you *deal* with what happens to you.

With enough miles logged to circumnavigate the earth three and a half times, Bob uses his unique writing style to introduce you to many colorful characters in countless exotic locals, affording you a brief glimpse into his epic adventure.

In an amazing story of man and his machine, "the ride," as it became known to him over the years, took him across vast expanses of the globe, testing his personal limits of both mental fortitude and physical stamina. With no support crew and with no one to depend on except himself and his trusted (if not loved) motorcycle Andiamo, he becomes known over the years as "the motorcycle guy," a term of endearment reaching near-legend status in some circles.

Whereas some people attack life with a scorched-earth mentality, Bob's approach is always to see the good in every person and situation. As a result, good karma is always just around the next corner ready to lend a helping hand.

Whether it be a night in the Kazakhstan desert repelling wolves with a Soviet-era shotgun or choosing to sleep in a mountaintop jail cell in Bolivia for lack of a safer option, the stories told never disappoint and never cease to amaze.

Bob's charismatic personality, fueled by his perpetual travel and lust for human connection, takes him not only to the far corners of the globe but into the hearts of everyone he encounters along the way.

Perhaps one day Bob's adventures will have come to an end, and he will have no more miles left to ride and no more mountains left to climb, and no words left to write. I can only hope that at that very moment, somewhere in the world a young person will be putting down this book, and it will have somehow inspired them to travel beyond the confines of their own shallow view of the world—and they will choose to embrace the human condition in its raw, pure, imperfect, unadulterated state and leave the world a better place.

Only then can we all say we have truly gone full circle with Bob and Andiamo.

North America

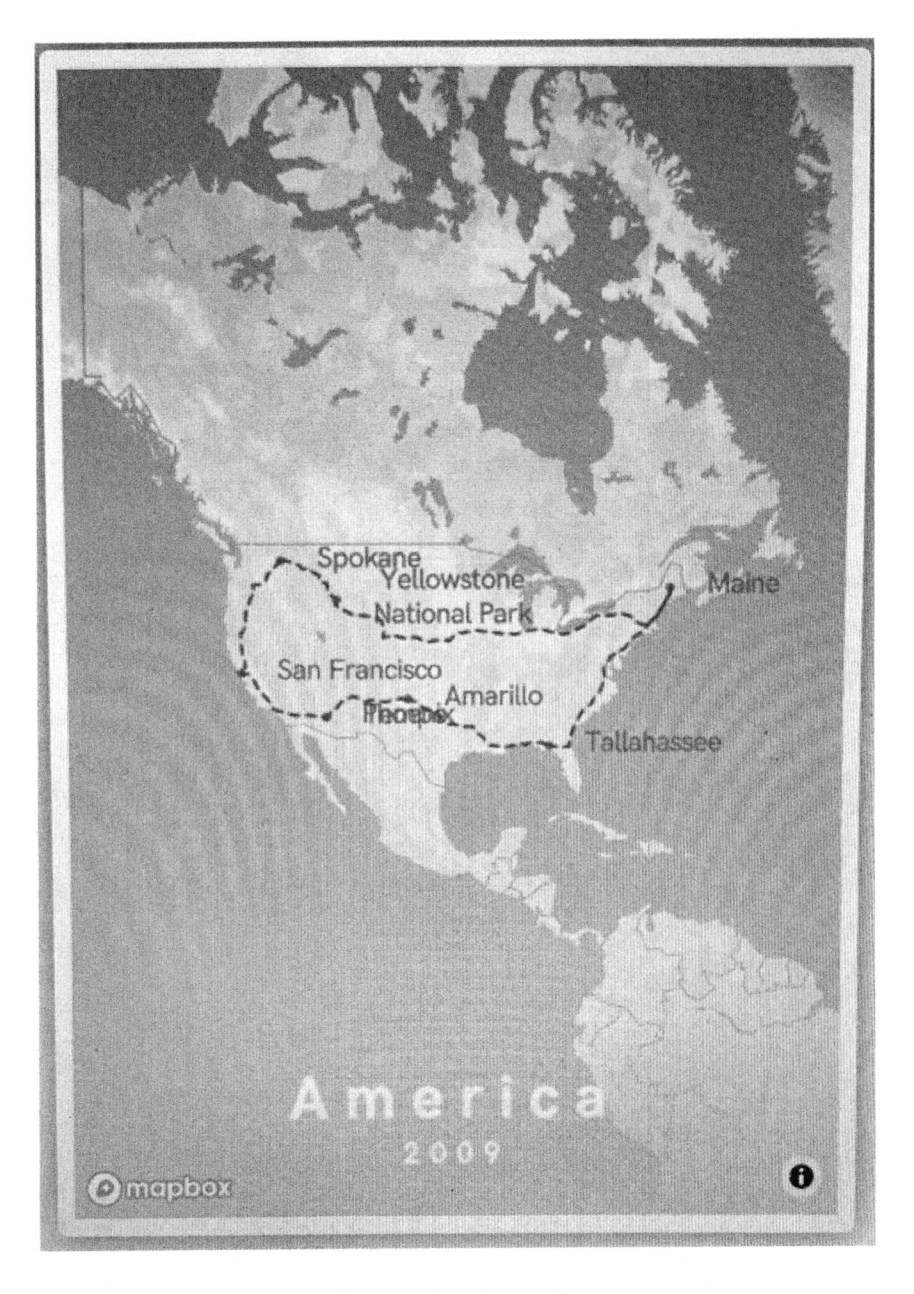

Approximate route

Kindness Quest

2009

Mileage: 6,000

This decade-long odyssey began with a two-month suspension from flying for not wearing a required mask. It finishes with a two-month leave of absence and masks required for a different reason. These coincidences inspired the title *Full Circle*.

In 2009, I was battling tough times. I needed "to turn lemons into lemonade." IMHO, my lemon was a senseless betrayal by my former chief pilot. He turned me in to the Federal Aviation Administration (FAA) for an obscure and antiquated regulation. The regulation was FAR 121.333, which stated that when one pilot leaves his duty station, the remaining pilot must put on an oxygen mask. Not complying is similar to motorists exceeding the speed limit. Pilots frequently overlooked this regulation, and it has since been removed from the Federal Aviation Regulations.

On a flight from Los Angeles to Denver, while my first officer was in the lavatory, this regulation required me to wear an oxygen mask. One of my flight attendants was in the cockpit. I had a conversation with this flight attendant, who had caused disturbances and disruptions on several flights. With the company's best interests in mind, I chose to write a report detailing her inappropriate behavior.

The next week, my chief pilot read my report and called me with a question. "How did you have a conversation with your oxygen mask on?"

I told him the truth. "My mask was in my lap so I could communicate clearly."

"I'm self-disclosing this to the FAA and conducting an investigation," he said, then hung up.

During the ensuing year-long battle, my lawyer subpoenaed his phone records. From the time the chief pilot hung up after talking to me to when he made his call to the FAA was four minutes. He gave four minutes of consideration to my career.

I had known him thirty years, since we began our careers at a smaller airline. He had always been a cool guy. When I'd walk by his office, he would invite me in to talk about motorcycles. I enjoyed his sense of humor, although risqué in mixed company. If he hadn't voluntarily self-disclosed to the FAA, they would have never known. My intentions were to ensure our passengers received the kind friendly family spirit of our airline however; this turned on me.

I received a letter from the FAA the following week requesting my side of the story. Again, I told the truth.

"Since you were honest and told the truth, admitting to not wearing your oxygen mask, there is nothing I can do," my lawyer told me.

I fought the fight for a year, spending tens of thousands of dollars, but there was nothing I could do to stop the FAA from finding me in violation of their antiquated regulation. I conceded and was grounded for two months.

How would I spend sixty days off work? I needed to turn this situation around. Turn this lemon into lemonade. Take the high road. Be a better person. Not harbor anger for he who betrayed me. Create something bigger to overshadow this negative event in my life. I resolved to be kind.

I had several ideas. In the spirit of "pay it forward," I planned to ride my motorcycle around the forty-eight states, doing random acts of kindness. To legitimize this, I started a 501(c)(3) corporation called the "Kindness Quest."

On May 1, 2009, I started the two-month endeavor, immersing myself in performing random acts of kindness. This was my attempt to turn everything around. The "Great Recession" was in full swing. My friends had lost their jobs, lost their homes, lost their lives. I wanted to travel our country telling people, "The tough times will get better."

All preparations completed, I rode my motorcycle eastbound out of Phoenix, Arizona. I handed out envelopes with dollar coins in them. At tollbooths, I paid for the car behind me. I bought coffee for the people in line at coffee shops. I handed out bottles of cold water to people in need. At a laundromat, I did laundry for an elderly woman. I landscaped an entire yard for an underprivileged family. The list goes on.

I carried a stack of envelopes with three Susan B. Anthony dollar coins in them. One morning at a coffee shop in Amarillo, Texas, I noticed a Susan B. Anthony coin in the tip jar. I asked the barista about it.

"Oh my God, what a cool story," she said. "A customer told me about a guy riding his motorcycle around the country doing random acts of kindness. The customer said, 'This motorcycle guy gave me an envelope with three one-dollar coins in it. I intend to pay them forward, so here's one for your tip jar.'"

"I'm that motorcycle guy," I told her.

"This is a cosmic coincidence," the barista said, a big smile on her face.

I left an envelope in her tip jar. This story validated my kindness "pay it forward" motive and that I was in a small way making our world a better place. It confirmed my idea was effective, motivating me further to carry out my ambition.

The next day, I sat down by a good-looking blonde at a Kinko's in East Texas, who introduced herself as Chanda. She had a golden retriever with her. I love goldens. The beautiful girl and I got into a long conversation.

"I suffered a gunshot wound to my neck at age nine and needed special therapy not covered by insurance," she said, "so I started a foundation to benefit people in similar situations." She created the Chanda Plan Foundation, an organization to benefit physically disabled persons. From her shoulders up, she was a thirty-year-old woman with thick hair and kind eyes. The area below her shoulders had been frozen at age nine.

Her hands clutched her phone to show me her interview on the *Today* show, which had aired the previous month. Inspired by her perseverance, I wrote her a check for $1,000.

"This money will be paid forward to my foundation and be distributed to those in need," Chanda said. She had tears in her eyes.

I wanted to learn more about her. I wasn't ready to say goodbye.

She was very gracious, but she had to leave abruptly because of physiological needs. Her dog led the way out. I helped her into her van, and we said goodbye.

Dear Chanda,

I've seen the accomplishments of your foundation and how successful you have become. You've helped thousands in need and should feel wonderful about the positive things you've done for the world. I hope all is well with you.

Sincerely,
Bob

As I rode eastbound into Pensacola, Florida, I kept spreading my own kindness, trying to convince people the world would get better. I stopped at a flower shop named Flowerama, where Delores, the kind owner, assisted me with preparing a dozen vases of flowers that I planned to distribute to nursing home residents. Delores phoned a local facility, where the head nurse was ecstatic about someone visiting to brighten her residents' day.

At the facility, I arranged the vases on a pushcart at the central nursing station, then walked the tiled hallways, introducing myself and presenting flowers to sweet elderly folks. Some of them had family present. Some hadn't seen family for years. Either way, each individual appreciated the small gesture. I listened to their stories of lives lived. I gave them flowers. They gave me happy fulfillment.

Nearby in Tallahassee, Florida, a local news station did a feature on me and the Kindness Quest. After the filming, my motorcycle needed service, since it had been running poorly. I pulled into BMW Tallahassee for repairs. The owner, Paul, greeted me with a firm handshake and a smile. A southern-mannered gentleman with a wonderful sense of humor, Paul introduced me to his wife, Kathy, a hard-working, kind soul. While the mechanic diagnosed the problems with my motorcycle, Paul, Kathy, and I got to know each other in the comfortable waiting area. They would become an important inspiration to me.

Kathy trained hybrid foxhunting horses. It's big business in those parts. Some of the plantations are massive dog- and horse-training facilities. When people go out on a fox hunt, they wear traditional attire with the red coat, white pants, black gloves, and helmet. From what I learned, dressing seemed as important as the hunt itself. Paul showed me pictures of him and Kathy attending charitable foxhunting events, formally dressed. Kathy and Paul were at the heart of all the pageantry.

The mechanic interrupted our conversation to inform me that the motorcycle had bigger problems than originally thought. "This could take two weeks to repair," he said.

Disappointing news, but I decided to continue the spirit of the Kindness Quest while I waited. Paul and Kathy invited me to spend the two weeks on their plantation in the carriage house, which was a cozy cabin formerly used by servants. I couldn't have been more fortunate with this unfortunate setback.

Kathy and Paul made a feast that evening. At their massive dinner table used for entertaining guests, Kathy and I brainstormed kind things to do.

"Paul and I gave an acre of land to a family," she said. "Recently, the husband and wife both have been laid off from their teaching jobs. We could see what they need."

The next morning, Kathy and I drove to the family. She introduced me to Melvin and Mareta in front of their mobile home on the acre of land. Melvin and Mareta had soft, timid demeanors and said they didn't need anything. Cameron, their twelve-year-old son, had just won a first-place medal for marksmanship from his Boy Scout group. While Kathy told them my story, I quietly asked Cameron what he would do with twenty dollars.

"Mr. Bob, I'd save it for something special," he said.

I pressed further to see what he needed.

"I'd spend three dollars on ammo for my .22 rifle and save the rest."

Cameron was a smart, well-behaved kid. I snuck him a twenty-dollar bill and watched his face light up.

As Kathy and I were leaving, I overheard Cameron whisper to his father, "Hey, Dad, how much does grass seed cost?"

It was a dirt yard, and they couldn't afford landscaping. Cameron wanted to help his family.

"We have our random act of kindness for today," I told Kathy. "We're going to Lowe's to plan, then deliver landscaping for this sweet family."

She agreed it was a great idea, and we set out for a Lowe's Home Improvement. At a display table in the garden center, Kathy and I drew up our plans: a circular driveway lined with paving bricks, three large ficus trees, geraniums and decorative rock in the middle, flowers bordering the entrance, grass seed, and a welcome-home doormat.

Paul met us back at Melvin and Mareta's house with his backhoe to help excavate and spread the rock. Paul's son and a few friends also pitched in. It was a huge group effort. Our only motivation was to help this family beautify their property. Each of us would smile at each other as sweat covered our bodies. With the help of all the Good Samaritans, we got the yard landscaped in record time. Melvin, Mareta, and Cameron were so pleased. We gathered in a circle to say a prayer for our fortunes in life. Even though I had been suspended from work for two months without pay, this act of kindness gave me a sense of satisfaction no amount of money could buy.

I heard from Paul's mechanic. More bad news. The motorcycle repair was delayed further. After two weeks, I couldn't wait any longer. Paul gave me a great deal on another bike. I didn't know it at the time, but that bike would be named Andiamo and would carry me around the world for a decade. The Kindness Quest morphed into "The Ride" and what it became.

Dear Paul and Kathy,

The two of you are the cornerstone to "The Ride". Without your kindness and hospitality, it would not have become the love and focus of my life for ten years. Thank you very much for opening your hearts to me.

Sincerely,
Bob

My days with Paul and Kathy on their plantation left me a couple of weeks behind schedule, so I had to focus on "making miles." After the forty-eight-state ride, I didn't want to stop riding. I returned to work but had fallen in love with long-distance motorcycle riding. I had a lust for adventure and travel. I wanted to see if I could ride down through Mexico and farther south to Panama. So I did.

Chanda

Central America

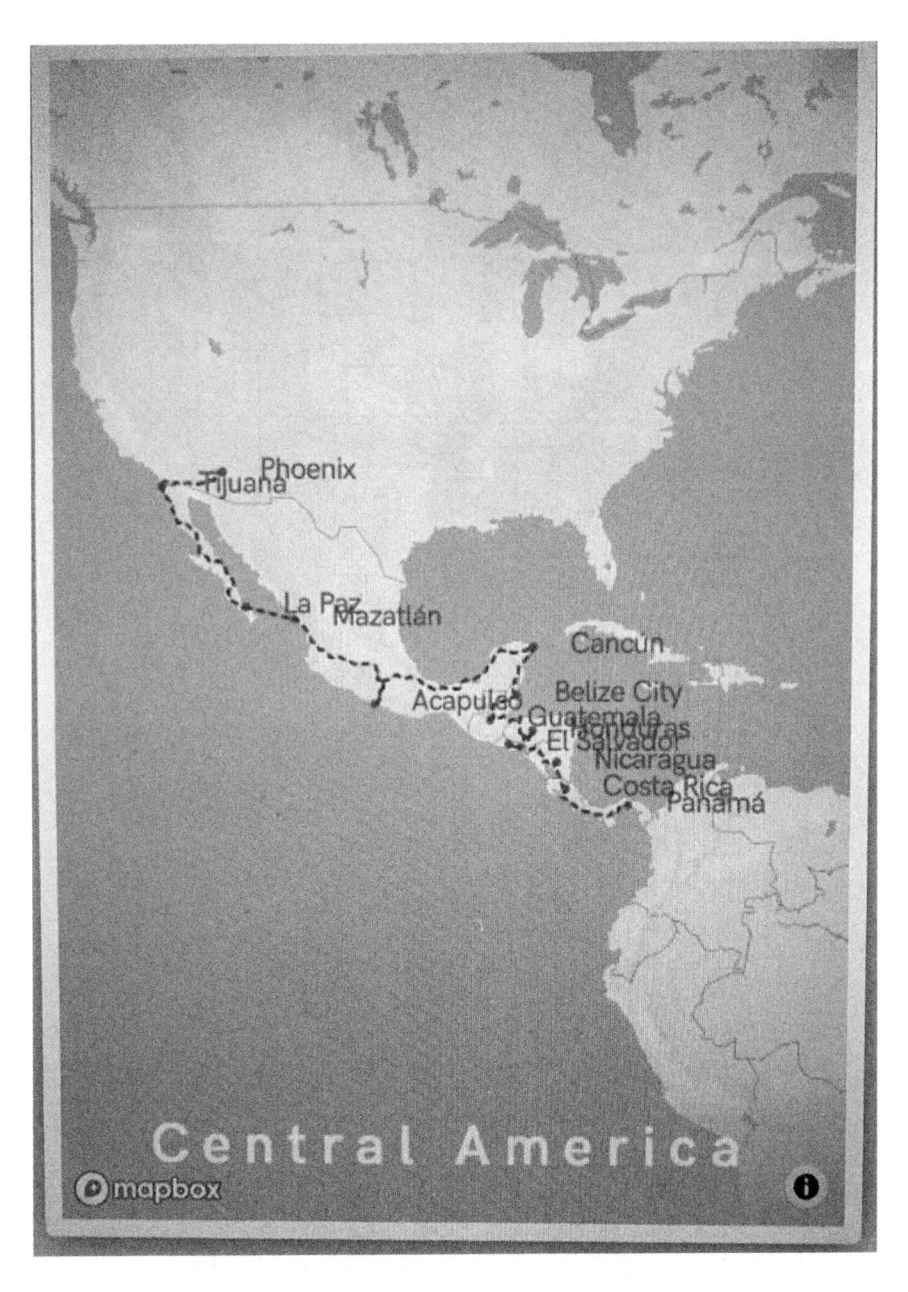

A portion of my route through Central America

Explanation:

Each chapter starts with
"ingredients"
that I use in a
"recipe"
to help illustrate a story.
Kind of like an interactive cookbook

Mexico

2009 (Dates are approximate)

Mileage: 10,000 (Miles are approximate)

Ingredients: one spray bottle, one fan, four ounces lemon juice, twelve ounces warm water

My motorcycle was new, fresh, and clean. My body was bendable and intact. I was a novice at "adventure riding." I soon learned several things can threaten your life as you ride a motorcycle around the world. Riding south out of San Diego and into Mexico, I saw signs warning motorists of *topes* (pronounced to-pez). These aren't your typical "speed bumps." These are obstructions in the road that will rip your undercarriage off if not approached at an angle and a snail's pace.

One scorching day south of Tijuana, I was following an overloaded 1950s flatbed semitruck with ten-foot-high rickety wooden slats containing a mountain of coconuts—massive Mexican bowling-ball-sized coconuts called "cocos." I was tucked in tight behind the wide truck, too close to notice the roadside *TOPE* warning sign. As the truck's rear wheels hit the tope, the rickety slats collapsed, spilling the cocos like bouncing basketballs. One hit my mirror and elbow, twisting me into an uncontrollable skid. Another hit my foot, bruising my toe. I had managed to get my speed down to about ten miles per hour before they hit, which almost certainly saved my life. Like an orbiting spaceship, I made it through the coco galaxy to reenter a normal atmosphere.

> Recipe: Fill the spray bottle with twelve ounces of warm water. Add four ounces of lemon juice. Place your face in front of the fan. Spray the bottle with the fan, blowing the mist on you. Feel

the evaporative cooling effect? Feels refreshing and nice, right? Read on with that refreshing feeling in mind.

Adventure riding runs a wide spectrum of environments and emotions. Temperatures can get extreme. The heat can be unbearable. The next sweltering day, riding the Baja in Mexico, I unzipped my jacket to get a breeze on my red-hot body. I glanced down to reference my tank bag map. My finger traced the route as I rode. While looking down at the map, I experienced a refreshing mist in the air moisturizing me. The cool vapors seemed so invigorating on my face and body. I looked up to see the "cattle truck" in front of me spilling its contents out the back like Niagara Falls. It was my first bovine golden shower, not refreshing at all. I pulled over to use a wet wipe to cleanse myself.

I rode through quaint old towns like Santa Rosalia in Baja California, Mexico, perched on steep mountains running into the Gulf of California. The town has a church designed by Alexandre Gustave Eiffel, the engineer who designed and built the Eiffel Tower in Paris. A mining company shipped the stamped-steel church piece by piece from Europe and assembled it in this charming old town, with its contrasting local architecture. It pleased me to think engineer Eiffel's magnificent works are revered around the world, not just in Paris.

After a seven-hour ride south, I wound up in La Paz, Mexico, to ride onto a car ferry for a twelve-hour trip across the Sea of Cortez to Mazatlan. I secured my motorcycle to the car deck. The ferry chugged as playful dolphins fluked alongside and whales lovingly mated in the warm waters. The sun reflected off the calm blue sea onto my sunburned face. One crew member reeled in a dorado (or mahi-mahi) and barbecued it on deck to share with me and five others.

"Eat as much as you like," the captain of the ferry said.

I doused my slab in salsa that burned my throat. It was delicious and so fresh, probably the best fish I had ever tasted.

I rode off the ferry into Mazatlan, to have my first of many encounters with corrupt police. It was hot, so I rode through town not wearing my helmet.

On the outskirts of town, a cop who was ostensibly directing traffic, but in reality was standing on the shoulder of the road looking for prey, signaled me to stop. "Cabeza," he said and pointed to my helmet.

"*Si, señor*," I said. "I'm loco in el coco."

He laughed and extended his empty open palm. "*Dinero*," he said.

I laughed, smiled, put on my helmet, and zoomed off. Since we had established a jovial, joking relationship, I figured if he had any further issues with me, I could throw out more nonsensical Mexican sayings and act like I was only kidding about zooming off.

I've learned when dealing with foreign police to be friendly and show no signs of fear. I'll discuss throughout the book my many encounters with corrupt cops and how I dealt with them. Rather than corruption or forced bribes, think of it as how they make a living.

The next day another cop flagged me down from the side of the road. "This lane is reserved for *bicicletas*," he declared, meaning bicycles.

I had knowledge of lane usage in Mexico, and I was using the correct lane. I smelled alcohol on the cop's breath, so I used the "crazy gringo technique" with him. I spouted off nonsensical Spanish words like "*hola Coca-Cola, que pasa calabaza, explico Frederico, entiendes Mendez.*" When he demanded money, I suggested, "Let's go to the local cantina, and I'll buy you another beer."

From his guilty demeanor, I thought he must have realized he shouldn't be drinking on the job. In defeat, he waved his arm in the direction I was riding, confirming I was free to go. I headed inland, away from the coast.

The rural roads in Mexico ran through villages where the entire population had gathered around fifty-five-gallon drums converted into barbecues. Riding through each village engulfed me in the same sights, sounds, and smells—grass huts, young and old people sharing their bounties around barbecues. Piercing mariachi music played from home stereo speakers placed outside on plastic chairs. Barbecue smells generated clouds of smoke so thick, visibility vanished.

Upon my exiting one smoke cloud, the road reappeared as a little girl ran out in front of me. I locked up my antilock brakes and twisted off the bike to avoid impact. When I stopped rolling down the pavement, I noticed her flip-flop wedged in my spokes. She had disappeared into the crowd with neither a scratch nor her flip-flop. The music played, the smoke bellowed, and the little girl was gone. Sitting on the pavement, I was worried about her, the poor little girl in a sundress, nowhere to be seen. I held up her flip-flop, wondering how I could confirm she was really okay. No one seemed worried. No one approached me. Nothing seemed to slow the pace of the smoke and mariachi music. I hoisted the motorcycle upright, leaving her flip-flop on an empty chair nearby.

I was nearing Mexico's east coast on the Gulf of Mexico, where there were no towns, just sandy coastline, mangrove forest, and the road. It was mostly sunny riding down the Yucatan Peninsula, headed for Cancun. That day, I saw a massive thunderstorm brewing on the horizon. On my left was a virgin white sandy beach with clear turquoise water, on my right, a dense mangrove jungle, and a hundred miles ahead, centered on the road, a thunderstorm like a giant sequoia growing to heaven. I felt like a pilot contemplating a route around a storm. With only one road, there was no possibility of zigzagging around the beast. I knew hail would sting me in thirty minutes.

I pulled over to batten down the hatches. With no wind or road noise, I heard gunfire coming from the mangrove jungle. A *pop, pop, pop* on my right. Return fire: a *pop, pop, pop* on my left. It was drug cartel season in Mexico, and I didn't have a license to shoot. I did the quickest mount, start, and throttle down the road you've ever seen. Thunderstorm or not, I did not want to get caught in the cartel crossfire.

Thirty minutes later, I penetrated the edge of that storm. Marble-sized raindrops and hail blasted my face shield like gravel and rocks. After fifteen minutes of water torture, I had made it through to the other side, drying in the windblown sunshine, again relieved I had survived.

Cancun was now in sight. As a commercial pilot, I had a lot of Cancun layovers back then and had befriended Alex, the front desk manager at our crew hotel. He had a humble dwelling near the beach with a small garage, where he allowed me to keep my motorcycle while I returned to the States for a month. With the motorcycle secured, I waved goodbye and headed for Cancun International Airport and a flight home.

Andiamo Full Circle

~~~

I did my ride around the world in stages, every other month. My mantra was "one world, one bike." I'd work solid for a month, then have two weeks off to ride to a new destination. I maintained this schedule for ten years and fifty-six parking spots.

People have asked me if I was ever concerned about somebody stealing the motorcycle while I was away. Many of the places where I left the motorcycle were not all that secure. A thief would have needed a key to unlock the steering, but that wouldn't have stopped someone determined enough. A large pickup truck and four guys could have made off with it, key or not. But I didn't waste time worrying about it. I couldn't live my life controlled by fear. Material items can be replaced, so if something had happened to the bike and my gear, I would have considered it a write-off and replaced the items. I was driven by adventure, not fear.

I returned to Cancun one month after I had left my motorcycle in Alex's garage. I ran the gauntlet of tourist and rental car agencies looking for a taxi back to my first parking spot. It was Alex's birthday, and he had friends over to celebrate. I apologized for the intrusion. My bike was intact and exactly where I had left it. I unzipped my carry-on bag and pulled out the attached keychain.

To my shock, I realized I'd forgotten the key to the bike. We pondered the dilemma. Alex produced an old electric drill and dull drill bit. It took an hour to bore out the lock of my left pannier. Once we got inside the side box, my spare key was ready to go. I never forgot my keys again.

Dear Alex,

Thank you for your kind hospitality. I'm sorry I disrupted your birthday celebration. You were so patient and understanding. I hope you are well.

Sincerely,
Robert

The next day, I rode south to the border of Belize.

At the Mexican border town Chetumal, a money changer who spoke perfect English wanted to change my Mexican pesos into Belizean dollars. Favoring ATMs, I rarely did money exchanges, especially at border crossings, but it was late, and this guy seemed nice. He gave me his exchange rate, and I did a quick mental estimate of Mexican pesos into Belizean dollars. What I forgot to include was my US dollars converted to Mexican pesos, then into Belizean dollars. Twenty-five miles into Belize, I redid the math and realized the money changer had gotten the best of my quick math.

Belize

2009

Mileage: 15,000

Ingredients: one can of ice-cold Coke, one pair of dirty saggy shorts, four feet of rope

Sunny and laid-back, Belize is a wonderful country with two main roads, one running north/south and one running east/west. Hard to get lost. I headed for the capital city of Belmopan.

> Recipe: Put on the dirty, saggy shorts. Slip the four-foot piece of rope through the remaining belt loops. Tie the rope in a knot. Take a sip from the ice-cold can of Coke and imagine that is all you had in life.

I was pointed southbound on the north/south road and needed route clarification. On the empty country highway, I pulled up alongside a fellow leading a donkey with a piece of frayed rope. The barefoot man's shorts were soiled and saggy, held up by a piece of the same rope he used to lead the donkey. He was shirtless, shining a toothless smile and holding a can of cold Coke. His blissful aura emanated a pure contentment with his life as he offered me a sip from his can. I declined his generosity and asked which direction to Belmopan. The language barrier prevented much more communication. The man seemed to have everything he desired in life—a smile and a cold can of Coke. I envied his minimalist satisfaction.

An hour later, in Belmopan, I became more vigilant after a man on a street corner snatched my Bob Marley dreadlocks hat from under my cargo net as I rode by. The chaotic traffic prevented me from turning around. On the next corner, a uniformed cop issued me a verbal ticket for riding a motorcycle, though riding one wasn't prohibited. He ordered me to pay a fine at the courthouse. He gave me directions, which I observed until I realized he hadn't recorded my name, plate number, or driver's license. I aborted my plans of paying a fictitious ticket at a courthouse that I couldn't find on the best of days.

Friends of mine were vacationing on Ambergris Caye, an island thirty-five miles offshore from the mainland. We had planned to meet up for scuba diving and hanging out on the beach. I needed a secure place to park my motorcycle for a few days. Then I spotted the distinctive seal of the United States of America hanging from a heavy metal fence protecting a lavish building. It was the US embassy. A guard picked up the phone to ring an embassy representative to help me. With all my international travel, I had never called upon an embassy for help. This was an exceptional opportunity for them to allow parking my motorcycle inside the embassy compound for a few days while I went scuba diving.

Out walked Anthony, a young embassy worker with a boyish face, combed hair, and blue jeans. He explained that post-9/11 procedures prohibited such unique requests. "I've found a chic hotel for you," he said with a young man's squeaky voice. "Follow me to it."

"Okay, man, thanks," I said. "Don't lose me in the traffic congestion."

It was a trendy hotel but not too extravagant. Anthony warned me not to go downtown because it was lawless. I told him about the guy stealing my Bob Marley hat and the corrupt cop.

"Don't go downtown and don't worry about any traffic infraction where they didn't record your information," he said.

I secured my motorcycle at the hotel in a garden shed next to wheelbarrows and lawn mowers.

The next day at the airport, I boarded an eight-passenger Cessna Caravan bound for Ambergris Caye. The pilot flew over the Great Blue Hole, where I had reserved a dive trip with my buddies the next day. A nice landing on a tiny runway, and a taxi to the open-air terminal. Across the street from the tiny Ambergris airport was an agency that rented golf carts and scooters. Since a scooter couldn't handle my gear bag, I rented a golf cart. The island's only roads were packed down by barefoot tourists stumbling

Andiamo Full Circle

from tiki bar to tiki bar. Belizean life is lived at a slower pace. On Ambergris Caye, it was like telling time with a calendar instead of a clock.

I parked my golf cart outside the palm leaf hut hotel room. It had a sand floor and no electricity and no air conditioning, but it did have modern, beachy decorations. It was primitive, but what the heck, I'm a motorcycle rider used to harsh environments.

My buddy Greg, who had invested heavily in Belize real estate, convinced a group of guys to invest with him. Combined, they own a large portion of the tiny island. At happy hour, Greg waited silently at the bar with two cold beers.

His silence broke as he turned his head, blew a big puff of cigar smoke, and yelled, "I can't believe you made it!"

He handed me a beer, and we clinked bottles, followed by a man hug, followed by a joyous reunion with my other buddies, who were deeper into happy hour.

Mike, a shaved-head motorcycle maniac, said, "We had bets on you making it to Belize."

Shocked and amazed, they would not let me pay for a beer. Even though I had ridden long and hard, I felt at home and relaxed surrounded by friends. The energy increased as the night progressed into mayhem. I welcomed my shut eyelids on the pillow in my basic hotel hut.

In the morning, we jumped into a boat headed for the Blue Hole, our dive site. Jose, our dive master, was at the helm. It was a drift dive in the current. We could just let the current push us along with little effort. Preparing our gear was like locker room football players suiting up for a big game. We all had underwater cameras to photograph the countless species of colorful fish. It was a relaxing aquatic experience.

The lengthy boat trip back went quickly. Refreshments were served by Jose as we toasted our day's adventure. The camaraderie of friends filled my heart. Back at the resort, swinging in hammocks, toes in sand, we shared our photos. The best was of Greg's surprised expression with a ten-foot-shark behind him ready to attack. Good thing it was only a docile nurse shark.

Since each segment of my ride was about two weeks, I maintained a strict schedule. In the morning, we said our goodbyes, and I turned to walk away.

"Dude, I want to ride with you someday," Greg said.

"Awesome," I responded. "Let's plan on it somewhere down south."

A quick flight to the mainland to collect my motorcycle, and I was riding again. I needed to end that month's ride in Guatemala, find a place to park my motorcycle for a month, and get home to America to show up to work on time.

Crossing the border into Guatemala was easy. The wooden outpost dictated a certain casual approach to border formalities. Stamp, stamp, and I was in Guatemala.

Guatemala

2009

Mileage: 16,000

Ingredients: one ancient Mayan city, one lake with clear water

On my scale of Central America exotics, Guatemala carries more weight than Mexico and Belize because of their recent history of guerrilla warfare, political strife, and scarcity of common tourists. The people are more indigenous and traditional. The towns are less developed and more isolated. You feel like you're far from home even though you're only two countries away from the United States.

My first destination in Guatemala was Antigua, a Spanish mission town once adopted as the capital of the Kingdom of Guatemala. Designated as a UNESCO World Heritage site, the walled city has cobblestone streets surrounding a central square bordered by covered walkways, shops, and restaurants.

I enrolled in a Spanish immersion class with a friendly young guide named Juan, who walked me around the city speaking only Spanish. Juan identified objects as he asked me questions. At a fruit stand, he said, "*Te gustan las manzanas?*"

"Yes, I like apples," I answered, but in my Spanglish.

Juan taught me in a three-dimensional environment, not a book. It was fun and interactive when the locals laughed at my mispronunciations.

I spent one hour with another young guide named Maria, who taught me bracelet-weaving techniques. I made three bracelets and wore them to remind me I was on vacation.

In this sensational walled city, I stayed at the El Convento Boutique Hotel, a former convent turned into a luxury hotel featuring architecture, design, and works of art, making it a destination in and of itself. Google it for pictures. A traveler can explore the hallways with a lust to wander, content not to leave the hotel property. After a couple days, I was sad to leave Antigua, but I had to ride.

> Recipe: Submerge the ancient city in a lake. Scuba dive on the main street. Swim around the foundations of the city's buildings. Explore the underwater history. Wonder how the inhabitants lived. Now imagine not seeing any of that. I was let down too.

Back on my motorcycle, I traversed the mountain ranges of Guatemala en route to Panajachel on the shores of Lake Atitlàn, reputed to be one of the most beautiful lakes in the world. Surrounded by high, lush mountains, this 1,100-foot-deep lake has been the lifeblood of local Mayan people for centuries. I had planned a dive trip to explore several underwater archeological sites. Conditions for the dive trip were not suitable, so the dive shop canceled it.

"Too much wind," the owner of the shop told me with an apologetic smile. "Too stormy to see anything under the water."

I was bummed out. The dive was my primary reason for visiting the lake. Exploring ancient ruins underwater provides a different perspective compared to merely walking them. Oh well, I rolled with the news, and then rolled out of the city. The bike began to feel like home.

Traveling up the hills from Panajachel, I met Nick, Mike, and Jarod, three former superbike racers riding down from California to Costa Rica. They were on smaller, lighter bikes kitted out for off-road riding. Their light bikes and their superbike skills smoked me in the turns, but on the straightaways, my big BMW caught them like they were on bicycles. As the four of us rode through towns, waving to the cheering residents, I felt like a race winner in a parade; although I knew there was no trophy.

The next day at BMW Guatemala, I met the sales manager, Jose, who was an "adventure rider" himself and could appreciate my situation. He welcomed servicing and storing my bike until I returned a month later.

Andiamo Full Circle

Dear Jose,

Thank you for allowing me to park my motorcycle at your shop. I always enjoy seeing your posts on Facebook and getting updates on your life in Guatemala.

Cheers,
Robert

I returned home for a month.

El Salvador

2010

Mileage: 18,000

Ingredients: one can of sardines, one old school bus, one palette of primary colors paint, one bag of bling

I often traveled standby back then, which meant an unsold seat needed to be available or I didn't go. The day of my return to Guatemala, they had oversold all the flights, so I flew into El Salvador and took the "chicken bus" up to Guatemala to reunite with my motorcycle at BMW Guatemala.

I had a first-class ticket from Houston to San Salvador on Continental Airlines. It arrived early morning. I took a taxi from the airport to the central bus station. Once at the bus station, things came alive, with locals swarming and selling their items. I dodged the commotion and bought a cheap ticket to Guatemala City on the local bus. On the best of days, it's a six-hour trip, excluding transfers.

> Recipe: Pour the paint over the top of the school bus. Cover the entire bus with bling. Place the can of sardines on a seat inside the bus. Imagine yourself a sardine on this wildly decorated old school bus on a hot day with no air conditioning.

I was in the mood for adventure, ready to accept the terms of the quest. I had yet to experience such a journey, but had heard stories of the infamous chicken buses of the region. The first bus was reasonably comfortable, with mostly tourists on board. Once in Guatemala, I transferred to a local chicken bus. These were former school buses splashed with every color of paint available, adorned with shiny bling, with huge cargo carriers on the roofs. The locals traveled to market on the chicken bus with their chickens caged and secured to the racks on top of the buses. Absent air conditioning, the windows were all slid down, allowing a bit of fresh air inside.

I interacted with the locals, who laughed at my Spanglish. They all had a presence of seasoned chicken-bus-users. Rosa, an elderly woman with a big smile, was trying to tell me something I didn't understand. She pointed outside, then to me, and laughed.

One thing became obvious to me: the prized aisle seats were what everyone wanted. Only Rosa and I sat in the window seats. I figured the acclimatized locals didn't desire the cool breeze from the windows, so I enjoyed my window seat like a child. There seemed to be an evaporative cooling effect, which increased as the bus weaved left and right around corners.

On one tight corner, I discovered the source of that evaporative cooling. The chickens on the roof must have drunk a lot of water and not used the toilets at the rest area. At that moment, I offered to trade places with the man in the aisle seat next to me. He and Rosa had a good laugh at my expense. He put his duffel bag in the aisle and sat on it as I skooched over. I had survived another disgusting event.

It was a short walk from the bus station to BMW Guatemala, where I collected my bike. Jose had prepped the bike for my ride south. He made me feel so at home on this journey.

Jose,

Thank you so much for the wonderful service and hospitality. I hope you're well,

Robert

I crossed the border back into El Salvador, getting the feel for an unfamiliar country and traffic traits. Each country has its own unique style of obeying traffic rules. For example, signaling left in Mexico means you're turning left. However, in El Salvador it means it's clear to pass. The learning curve is short, and traffic rules must be understood immediately to avoid catastrophe.

I was following a little Toyota Corolla signaling left, but I couldn't pass the vehicle. There was something large in its trunk bottoming out the suspension. At a stoplight, I got a closer look. It was a donkey, his head, neck, and legs hog-tied and hanging out onto the road, while most of his body was inside the tiny trunk. He looked dead. I stared into his eyes, huge brown spheres lined with thick eyelashes. He blinked. My heart ached, witnessing his mistreatment.

The donkey seemed to say: "Dude, help me outta here. This sucks."

The stoplight changed to green, and there was nothing I could do.

I needed a new image in my mind and new tires. I stopped at a Pirelli tire service facility to see if they could direct me to a motorcycle shop for a tire change. It turned out, a fellow adventure rider owned the shop. His name was Carlos, a prosperous-looking Salvadoran, who offered help. I met Mario, a friend of Carlos, who was out for a ride on his adventure bike. Mario offered to show me to a hip hotel on the beach where I could stay the night.

I followed Mario down the twisty coast road to a hotel built on a cliff. While I checked into the hotel and stowed my bags, Mario ordered up our meals in the restaurant. He knew the local dishes and ordered us their specialties. Over dinner, we chatted about adventure riding.

He told me a story about riding with his friend. "Two years ago while riding around a tight corner, my friend hit and killed a woman who was crossing the street to sell a jocote." Pronounced ho-co-tay, jocote is a local tangy fruit with a creamy-like consistency. "Paramedics took my friend to the hospital, then into custody at the local jail. Laws of the road in El Salvador require the two parties to agree on a settlement immediately, or they detain both parties until an agreement is reached. Since he killed the woman, my friend had to come to an agreement with the woman's family. He was a wealthy individual, and the family knew it. She was a poor farmer. The woman's now-orphaned daughter complicated things. After six months in jail, the family settled on a six-figure sum, causing great financial harm to my friend."

I told Mario about hitting the little girl in Mexico.

"Consider yourself lucky," he said. "The locals could have claimed fake injuries to her and held you for a payout."

I asked about hitting a goat, chicken, or dog.

Mario gave me his advice about what to do if I were to hit either a person or an animal. "Don't stop," he said. "Keep riding. It never ends well for the gringo. The locals will see it as an opportunity for money and will lie, cheat, or steal what they can from a foreigner. The courts will always rule in favor of the local. The foreigner always loses and loses big. The courts receive a kind of commission for their part."

Those words of advice ring in my ears to this day.

The next day, it was pouring rain on the ride back to Carlos's shop. He had agreed to store my bike and change the tires and oil. He suggested washing my riding jacket and pants and not leaving them to mold while I went home to work for a month.

"Great idea, Carlos," I said. "I'll see you next month."

When I returned the following month, Carlos had my bike ready with brand-new tires, fresh oil, and my suit clean and fresh, not moldy like it usually was. To avoid the rancid smell my suit can develop, I now douse my gear in patchouli oil. That's a better smell than moldy motorcycle gear, trust me.

Dear Carlos,

Thank you for taking good care of my bike and for the informative advice on riding through Central America. I hope you are well.

Sincerely,
Robert

Honduras

2010

Mileage: 20,000

Ingredients: one feeling of euphoria, one feeling of animation, one feeling of rapture

As I approached the border from El Salvador into Honduras, a local man in a threadbare T-shirt and frayed jean shorts flagged me down. He looked homeless, and I assumed he would be asking me for spare change. I was wrong. He told me that his name was Guermo, and he offered to help me with the border formalities.

I was skeptical. "Why do I need help?" I asked. "It's just a border."

He gave me a gap-toothed smile. "No, no, señor. This border is not like other borders. This is Honduras."

So I allowed him to help me. He led me from building to building, back and forth, with a stamp-stamp here, and a stamp-stamp there, everywhere a stamp-stamp. It seemed the sole purpose of these procedures was to keep Guermo employed and to keep the gringo confused. One form had three sheets of carbon copies that had to be typed, not printed. Guermo led me to a shack housing a forty-year-old typewriter and a bored typist demanding five cents to type the form in triplicate. After the border formalities were completed, I was allowed to transit Honduras.

> Recipe: Use the feeling of euphoria, mix it with the animation, sprinkle in the rapture, and ingest. Experience endorphin levels higher than any synthetic source. Nothing else is on your mind. Nothing can harm you. The best feeling you've ever had. Total ecstasy.

About ten miles into Honduras, I experienced my first EAR, an acronym I coined for Extreme Adrenaline Rush.

Having successfully completed the difficulties of crossing the border into Honduras, I sped down the highway, with tall grassy hills to my left, blue ocean waves to my right, and glistening sunshine above. My world was perfect. Coldplay's "Beautiful World" came on my iPod. The lyrics hit me like a freight train full of happiness. "We live in a beautiful world." I literally had shivers from this wonderful feeling, an endorphin rush with pure contentment, one where I felt on top of the world, floating on a cloud of joy. I wished everyone could feel that good naturally, without synthetic origins. Truly a natural high.

Only a few hours to transit Honduras and I was at the border of Nicaragua. Honduras will forever be credited for my first EAR. I sincerely hope you can enjoy an EAR of your own.

Nicaragua

2010

Mileage: 20,000

Ingredients: one Baby Ruth bar, one VHS of Caddyshack, one bucket, one locust

As in Honduras, I was met at the border by a young man offering to help with the border formalities crossing into Nicaragua. Leon had short hair, a puffy-cheeked smile, and an intelligent wit that I liked. I told him I didn't need his help, but he wasn't going to take no for an answer. He was tenacious and followed me to each window for the requisite stamps. He added humor and assistance when needed. I liked him more after learning he didn't do drugs. He was a border tout because it was the best job in his little border town in northern Nicaragua.

"Leon, you're my man," I told him.

He then took me to the front of the next line to get my motorcycle title stamped and validated. He saved me about fifteen minutes of waiting in line. With Leon's help, my border crossing was expedited.

Dear Leon,

I hope you are well and have saved your money and worked hard to progress as you see fit.

Sincerely,
Robert

Recipe: Place the bucket over your head, release the locust under the bucket, and agitate. Hear the buzzing? Feel the wings flapping against your face and the bucket? Think how unappealing the experience is.

Fifty miles into Nicaragua, the sun had set. There were no indications of any town or signs of civilization. At that moment, I rode through a locust swarm. The large insects hit my face shield like marbles: *ping, ping, ping*. Eventually, my face shield was completely covered with a splattered mess. This limited my visibility, so I opened it. Bad idea. A locust became lodged between my head and the helmet, buzzing in my cheek and temple, fluttering in my ear. I slammed on the brakes, threw off my helmet, and freed the medium-sized creature.

My patience was gone. I needed a town and a hotel soon. My map wasn't much help, since I didn't know exactly where I was on it. My GPS was a macro version, without small cities displayed.

The first three rules of adventure riding are as follows:

1. Never ride at night.

2. Never turn around to help an apparently stranded local.

3. If you hit a dog, cat, chicken, or anything, don't stop. It never ends well for the gringo.

I was riding in blackness on a desperate road, miles from human habitation through northern Nicaragua, violating rule number one of adventure riding. With no signs of civilization and frustrated by the locust swarm, I saw an object on the side of the road. I shined my high beams and decelerated. As I got closer, I could see a guy apparently working on his motorcycle. I hoped he was another adventure rider. I had spare parts and tools. I could help this guy, and maybe he could direct me to the next town and a hotel.

I turned around, violating rule number two, and approached slowly, directing my headlight on him. He was alone, working on his bike. I stopped near him. Immediately, he shined a huge beam of light in my eyes, blinding me.

Two guys jumped out of the bushes with bright flashlights and shined them in my eyes. They grabbed me, my bike, and my gear. "Money, money, money!" they yelled.

They were hostile and aggressive but couldn't get a grip on my whirling presence. I kicked the shifter into gear, popped the clutch spinning my rear wheel in the gravel. I was out of there in a cloud of dust, thankful to have escaped the encounter. I was desperate for a town and safety.

Twenty-five miles down the road, a few cars appeared in the darkness, indicating possible civilization. Low and behold, before my eyes the unmistakable glow of city lights appeared on the horizon. I didn't care what kind of town it was; I had found home for the night.

The town was Leon, Nicaragua, one of the oldest cities in the Americas, marked with revolutionary successes and bullet holes on buildings from 1979, when students, farmers, and artists overthrew the US-backed Somoza dynasty. Fun fact: Leon has the most educated people in Nicaragua.

Riding into town, I embraced the historic Spanish colonial architecture, which lifted my wilted spirit. Some buildings were restored; some were in great disrepair. Both versions were magnificent. Even the bullet holes throughout the city seemed beautiful after my attempted hijacking.

Going through Leon was like living real history, not like being cooped up in a museum or a textbook. This town was real, and I was living it. The locals were proud of their history. They seemed educated and aware. They were on front porches, calmly sitting in chairs.

My thoughts were a little crazy. *Out of all the front porch people, not everyone wants to mug me for money.*

The townspeople became my friends without words.

I stayed at Hotel La Perla, a former personal residence built in 1858 by a wealthy cotton trader. It had recently been converted into a boutique hotel. I loved the interior courtyards with lush green gardens and the walkways weaving along ponds and streams. My room was small, yet elegant. I had a private pool outside my door. As I walked along covered paths with pillars and arches, I imagined the harsh history this old house had survived.

In the morning, I had settled down from the previous night's drama. I packed my motorcycle and headed for my next destination, Ometepe, an island formed by two perfectly conical volcanoes offshore in Lake Nicaragua, Central America's largest lake. Nicaragua's primary source of freshwater, it is home to a unique kind of freshwater shark. For years, there have been attempts to build the "Grand Canal" connecting the Pacific Ocean with the Atlantic Ocean. Running through Lake Nicaragua and rivaling the Panama Canal, this would have a colossal impact on the region.

I took a rusty old ferry out to the island. Two cars and my motorcycle were the only vehicles on the tiny ferry, which bobbed with the small waves. I met Richard, a nice young man wearing a collection of junk jewelry on his wrist. Richard worked for an American NGO helping local farmers improve their sustainability. He had lived on the island for two years and was finishing up his last few months there.

I rode off the ferry onto the muddy streets and headed for an open-air hotel on the beach that rented hammocks to sleep in. As I rode down the main street, a policeman driving his car in the opposite direction gave me the finger. Then he swerved toward me and rammed into my helmet as it hung off the side of my bike. The impact cracked my face shield. That was bad enough, but it would have been much worse if I hadn't taken quick evasive action. I nearly collided with an applecart but regained control before I made applesauce. I looked in my rearview mirror. He still had his finger extended. I'm not quite sure what his problem was.

I forgot all about the cop as soon as I collapsed in my hammock on the beach. I slept well all night, relaxed by the cool lake breeze and the sound of gentle waves rolling on the beach.

> Recipe: Put the VHS tape of *Caddyshack* into your VCR. Pause it at forty-three minutes, twenty-seven seconds. Take a bite of the Baby Ruth bar and hit play. Watch Carl, the groundskeeper, played by Bill Murray, take a bite of a Baby Ruth as he cleaned the pool. He seemed to enjoy the candy bar. Shocked, Ted Knight's wife fainted. It was a memorable scene from the comedic classic.

On the border into Costa Rica while I waited for my paperwork to be completed, I watched a pig poop in a mud puddle, then turn around and eat it. That's what pigs do. Disgusting. All I could think about was Carl taking a bite of that Baby Ruth. Let's move on to Costa Rica.

Costa Rica

2010 ish

Mileage: 22,000

Ingredients: one showerhead, one pair of foggy sunglasses, one bottle rocket

"*Pura Vida*" is more than a saying in Costa Rica. It translates to "Pure Life" and describes the laid-back pure enjoyment of life Ticos (a nickname for the locals) have. The lush and fertile land gave me the feeling that if I planted a soda can in the ground, it would grow. The fresh, crisp air made breathing worry-free. Unique and colorful wildlife, with red-eyed tree frogs and scarlet macaws, and mountains like green amphitheaters of rain forest with broad-leaved palms made the ride through Costa Rica like riding through heaven's vacation spot.

I was forty miles south of the border, riding on a muddy road in the vast jungle, surrounded by thick greenery and vertical streams, when a great song came on my iPod. It was an EAR moment. I stood up on my foot pegs and accelerated, while euphoric goose bumps covered my skin. I rode no-handed, my arms outstretched like airplane wings, my smile wide as the rain forest. Endorphins coursed through my veins. It was the greatest feeling in the world.

The cement-slab bridge surprised me. Just before the slab of concrete was a deep pothole. My front wheel went down into the pothole, then hit the corner of the cement slab with a deafening crunch. I lost control, my head thrown forward of the handlebars. My hands fought for a grip. My tubeless front tire quickly deflated, and I swerved to the side of the road. The rim was badly damaged. Instead of being round, it was now like a Pac-Man-shaped semicircle.

Deep in the rain forest, I had only myself to depend on. I removed the front wheel. The rim needed to be pounded round. I carry tire irons to separate the tire from the rim. Unfortunately I don't carry a hammer, so I searched the ground for a heavy rock to use. I found a jagged rock and pounded until my hands bled. The problem with tubeless rims is they need to be perfectly round to seat the tire and hold air. I carry an emergency inner tube for this exact situation. I inserted the inner tube, connected my Aerostich mini air compressor, and inflated the tire. That emergency fix worked for six thousand miles until my next tire change later in Colombia.

Fix in place, it started to rain, like rain forest rain.

Recipe: Put on the pair of foggy sunglasses. Turn on the showerhead full blast into your face. Can you see anything? Nothing is visible. It's somewhat painful on your face too.

I had four days left on that month's ride. Then I had to return to the US for work. The rain had not let up for a week. My entire life was wet. My forty-eight-page passport, although kept in a waterproof pocket in my riding jacket, was so wet the stamps bled off the pages, creating blank pages. Unfortunately, my entry stamp into Costa Rica had disappeared.

As I rode into the darkness, my glasses became worthless, blinding me. Thick radiation fog above the road made the road all but vanish from my sight. I followed a truck, tucked in tight behind him, and used his lights to identify the road, twisting and turning through the dense rain forest. The rain was so heavy, it passed through me like a personal river. I had to urinate but didn't want to lose my "follow-me truck." Emotions wrecked, I drained my bladder in my riding pants. A slight temperature difference is all I felt.

My savior follow-me truck eventually went a different way and became another thankful memory. The tropical storm had washed parts of the road away.

It was then a florescent-vested, hard-hat-wearing roadman flagged me to a stop. "Road closed," he said as raindrops dripped from his eyelashes.

Behind him was a powerful rushing river cascading over the portion of roadway I needed to reach my destination. I hoisted my motorcycle onto it's center-stand to discuss the predicament with the roadman.

Water dripped off his nose. "We should have the trees and debris cleared from the road in a couple hours," he said. Pura Vida!

Instead, the rain intensified, the river raged, and *crash, bang, crumble*, the roadway washed away before our eyes. It was the jugular vein of roadways. I was dead until the road became passable.

With no reasonable alternative, I joined the three-man road crew to help them clear the road and construct a makeshift bridge across the raging river. We were deep in the rain forest. The only tools available were shovels, axes, and a small chainsaw. The buzz of the chainsaw, the rush of the rapids, and the scrapes of the shovels combined to create an orchestra of desperation.

The four of us worked well into the night. They had a tarp held up by tree branches for shelter from the rain. We huddled around a small fire in an attempt to dry ourselves. I set up my camp stove and made spaghetti. My new friends shared their rice and beans with me. I shared my spaghetti with them. It was the most enjoyable terrible situation I had been in.

They slept in their maintenance truck bench seat, and I slept in my camp chair under the tarp, with my head propped against my motorcycle.

The tarp was of only limited benefit, and by dawn I was drenched. I awoke to howler monkeys vocalizing their presence and marking their territory. They are the loudest monkeys in the world, and their howls can resonate for three miles. These were natural sounds of the rain forest. Another natural sound is rushing water. Our raging roadway river had reached its crescendo. This was our opportunity to clear the road. The idea was to build a bridge for our tires to cross the collapsed portion.

Buzz, scrape, hoist—music to my ears. These were the sounds we heard as we placed the last tree to form our makeshift bridge. I was first to attempt the crossing. It seemed secure but slippery from all the rain. On my right was a sheer drop into the depths of the rain forest. Extreme concentration was required. Slow and steady won this race. Voila, I had made it across. My Costa Rican compatriots' truck made it across, too, but it was so heavy that in the process it destroyed the tree bridge. We gave the pinky-thumb wave and yelled "Pura Vida!" The entire experience internalized my belief that I could make it through anything.

My destination was San Jose, where I rented a self-storage unit for my motorcycle. A few short blocks from my flight crew hotel, it was perfect. I would bid Costa Rica layovers, then go out and explore the country while being paid. I decorated my cinder-block refuge like a college dorm room, taping an Imperial beer towel on the wall and a map of the region next to it. My riding gear was spread out like a college kid's dirty laundry. I had signed a six-month lease for Unit #1. It had electricity and one light bulb and felt like home away from home. I rode the entire country, returning several times per month on paid work layovers. It was a sensational setup.

A special place I visited several times in Costa Rica was Tabacon Thermal Resort & Spa. It was a three-hour ride from the storage unit in San Jose. On long flight layovers, I could spend the night at the luxury resort. Arenal Volcano is the source of thermal activity for Tabacon. It erupts continuously, emitting lava and belching smoke. The volcano heats the water that flows through the resort. There are natural private pools created by small rivers with different temperatures. I hiked farther into the rain forest upriver and found more romantic private pools for adults only. Along one natural river with a private pool densely covered by drooping palm trees, there was a tiki hut bar that served tropical drinks. I sipped a cold piña colada in the private pool while looking up at Arenal Volcano continuously rumbling, smoking, erupting. One way to experience one of nature's great powers. At night, it's magnificent.

> Recipe: Put the bottle rocket in a bottle. Light the fuse. Run. Watch the bottle rocket shoot toward the sky, trailing a line of sparks (tracer). It ends with a sparkly report (explosion). Gorgeous pyrotechnics, right?

I want you to feel my experience. Imagine yourself soaking in a naturally formed hot tub. Sipping a cold drink. Looking up at an erupting volcano as the sun sets. The best is a dark night. The rumble of the volcano is all you can hear. The lava flow is all you can see. It looks like an inverted bottle rocket. Think about a bottle rocket. It shoots up into the sky in a straight, fiery-red line, like a tracer, then explodes into a ball of shooting sparks. Invert this spectacle. This is the only way I can describe the beautiful phenomenon. The molten lava spills out the top of the volcano within a lava trough, flowing down in a straight, fiery line. When this fiery line of red-hot lava hits an obstruction, it explodes into a ball of shooting sparks. You ooh and aah at this spectacular display. It's my most favorite natural manifestation.

I was getting familiar with Costa Rica. The problem with staying too long in one country is that temporary importation permits for vehicles expire. In Costa Rica, they're valid for six months, which meant that after six months, my motorcycle had to exit the country and simply reenter on a new six-month temporary importation permit. In the back of my mind, I was scared to leave the comforts of Costa Rica and my "mini bodega" (storage Unit #1).

At the end of my first six-month TIP, I rode north, crossed the border into Nicaragua and came back into Costa Rica with a new TIP and six more months' validity. Nicaragua was familiar to me. I had been in and out of the country several times.

Six months later, when my second Costa Rican temporary importation permit was about to expire, I made a border run south into Panama. I had two reasons for this. One was to renew my permit and buy me more time. Second, if Panama was too dangerous or problematic, I could return to "comfy Costa Rica" and ride north back to United States. At this point, I hadn't thought about riding around the world. That seemed way out of my league, with too many obstacles preventing me.

I spent the night at an all-inclusive resort in Panama. It had plenty of kids and families diving into the buffet, which had neatly carved watermelons, cantaloupes, and other fruits. I likened the waiter's conversation to a timeshare sales pitch. An evening dip in the massive pool, with alcoves to escape the pandemonium, felt great. It was a nice resort, but a place I was unlikely to return to.

The next morning, I crossed back into Costa Rica. I found a nice, shady spot under a tree to escape the intense sun at the border immigration area.

In an attempt to outfox the system, I asked a border tout with chalky black hair and skeletal arms, "Can you get me more than a six-month TIP?"

Of course he said, "Si, señor."

Like a green gringo tourist, I saw no reason to be suspicious of this tattered tank-top-wearing solicitor. For two hours, I saw him run from building to building, giving me the impression he was working on my paperwork. He eventually returned with an official-looking document written in Spanish. It had very nice stamps and signatures.

"I had to pull some strings, but I got it done for you," he swore. "You can't tell anyone that I did this for you because I could get in trouble."

"Thank you so much," I said. "This really helps me out. Now I can stay in Costa Rica longer and continue to explore your beautiful country."

"You're very welcome. Now remember, you can't tell anyone I did this for you." He professed the document was legal and allowed me one year's validity for my motorcycle in Costa Rica. The cost was 39,000 colones, about $70.

Back at my hotel in San Jose, I had my buddy at the front desk translate the lengthy document. In summary, it stated the following:

> *This document holds no weight, and a naive tourist was just swindled out of 70 USD. Live and learn, gringo.*

That night I nursed my wounded ego with fellow flight crew members. It was always nice to spend time with friends, have a beer, and talk about Costa Rican adventures at happy hour in the crew hotel. A few evenings stand out. A shout out to Orville, Greg, Chris, Diane, Terry, Burt, Eric, Shawn, Shane, Kirk, Dave, and all the other working crew members I've enjoyed the splendors of Costa Rica layovers with. Cheers to all of you.

A few months later, I headed south to cross into Panama for real this time.

Panama

2010

Mileage: 27,000

Ingredients: five payolas, five twenty-dollar bills, one big bully

The border into Panama was familiar this time across. I knew the correct procedures, the correct windows to get the correct stamps on the correct documents. I felt like a well-seasoned traveler. If a border tout approached me with misinformation, I would smile and wink, then go about my business of temporarily importing my motorcycle and myself into Panama. I had no need for anyone but myself and the guy with the correct stamp.

> Recipe: Have the one big bully demand you pay him one twenty-dollar bill. Repeat four more times within a twelve-hour period. How do you feel toward the bully? What is your reaction to being a target?

I was southbound and speeding when a cop walked into the middle of the road with his arms crossed, signaling me to stop. As I decelerated, he moved farther into my path, demonstrating his dominant authority over me. If I hadn't braked harder, I would have hit him head on. Where I had stopped wasn't good enough on the empty country road. He made me back up the motorcycle four feet. I usually plan my parking to avoid the efforts required to pull the seven-hundred-pound motorcycle backward. He relished my struggles and aggressively motioned me off my bike. I complied with his every demand and cooperated fully. As I stood at attention, from his throat he expectorated sputum onto my riding boots. My fury redlined. It was a vial act worthy of my retaliation; however, I did not give him the satisfaction of exerting more authority with his weapon.

Andiamo Full Circle

He held out his hand and demanded my passport. That was his mistake. Local cops will ask for a driver's license first. They don't handle immigration issues. They handle driving issues.

I reached into my right chest pocket, where I kept a fake passport. My real passport was in my left chest pocket. I had learned about schemes corrupt cops play. This exchange was a dramatic theatrical game he played with me.

He scribbled something in his notepad. "You need to go twenty-five miles back into the last town and pay a fine to the judge."

"What did I do wrong?" I asked.

"You were speeding," he said. However, he had no speed-detection equipment other than his keen eyesight. He put my passport into his pocket with an exaggerated gesture, then gave me lengthy instructions on how to pay the fine back at the courthouse. Once I had paid the fine, my passport would be returned.

"Okay, great," I said. "I'll go back and pay the judge."

He stopped me. "Wait a minute, it's twenty-five miles back into town and very hard to find."

"No worries," I assured him. "I have GPS."

He reiterated that he had my passport and I wouldn't get it back until I paid the fine. He then gave me the option of paying him a hundred dollars directly.

"I'll go pay the judge," I said calmly.

"If you pay the judge, it will be two hundred dollars," he said.

"I'll pay the judge," I reiterated.

"Okay, fifty US dollars."

I maintained my cool and declined his offer to pay him directly.

"How much?" he asked.

"Zero," I said. "I'll pay at the courthouse."

He explained again how difficult that would be.

The fake passport has some value to me. I didn't want to backtrack twenty-five miles, so I relaxed my stance. When he dropped his price to twenty dollars, I grabbed a five-dollar bill from my pocket and said, "That's it."

Hastily, he snatched the five, threw my passport at me, and waved his arm in the direction I was headed.

Moral of the story: carry several versions of identification, extra cash, and remain calm. You'll get through it.

That cop stop was the first of five that day in Panama. Yes, I was stopped *five times* in one day. I had paid these corrupt cops throughout all Central American countries, but I felt I had to take a moral stand. These "*propinas*," as they called them (tips), had to have a baseline value. Any amount above this baseline value, I considered a loss. Any amount below the baseline value, I considered a win and the cost of doing business. I set my personal baseline value at twenty US dollars—not too much, not too little. This is how police officers in many countries around the world supplement their living. It made me appreciate the *United States of America*. I remained upset for a while as I continued southbound on the longest road network in the world.

The Pan-American Highway is a road network measuring nineteen thousand miles. It starts in Prudhoe Bay, Alaska, and ends in Ushuaia, Argentina. The only interrupted portion is the Darien Gap, swampland that separates Panama and Colombia. My first goal was to cross it. I hadn't seriously considered riding around the world yet. It was still day by day and see what happens. I didn't know what lay beyond Colombia. To cross the Darien Gap meant another continent, South America. I wanted to see what it was like and whether I could ride it.

Just before the Darien Gap was the Panama Canal, an engineering wonder. A beautiful trench dug in 1914 and forty-eight miles long, it shaves off eight thousand miles from the alternate route around Cape Horn. The charge to use the canal can reach $300,000 plus for the big ships. The smallest amount ever paid was in 1928 when Richard Halliburton paid thirty-six cents to swim the length of the canal.

In Panama City, I found a cargo airline called Girag Cargo. I rode to their offices and arranged my motorcycle to be flown across the Darien Gap into Bogota, Colombia. The cost was $800, cash only. I hadn't yet increased my ATM withdrawal limit, so it took several transactions to get $800 cash. Veronica, the cash-taking woman at Girag, requested I disassemble the front end and disconnect the battery. Then the men palletized my bike and threw it in the back of an old Boeing 737. Three days later, I could collect it at the Bogota airport cargo facility.

I had three days to myself, so I grabbed a taxi over to the Panama City airport passenger terminal, where I stared at the departures board. They had flights going everywhere. Where should I go? I wondered. Okay, there was a flight to Cartagena, Colombia, leaving in an hour. I bought a ticket, cleared the informal security procedures, boarded a regional jet, and bang, I was on my way to a beautiful historic Colombian city on their north coast.

South America

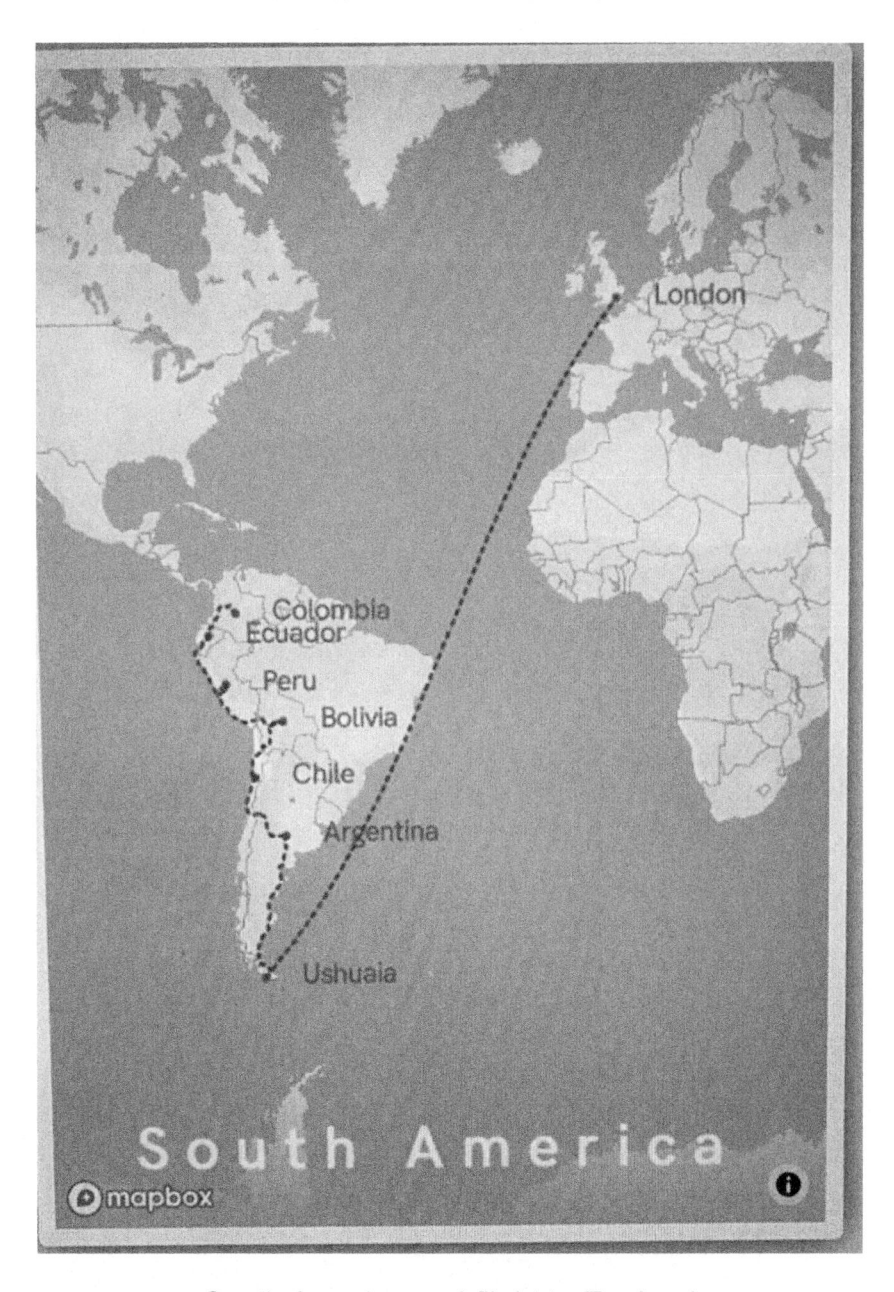

South America and flight to England

Colombia

2011

Mileage: 28,000

Ingredients: one coffee mug; one warm, foamy beer

Colombia has a questionable reputation due to the FARC guerrilla movement, Pablo Escobar, the drug cartel, extreme poverty, and kidnappings for ransom. I was warned by everyone not to go there. These warnings had been given to me since leaving the United States. It seems like every country fears its neighbor. They all issue warnings against attempted visits to their neighbors. The United States says don't go to Mexico. Mexico says don't go to Guatemala. Guatemala says don't go to El Salvador, and so on. I'm used to these warnings, but it was Colombia where I learned the most feared places are usually the most pleasant and enjoyable, except North Korea.

    I booked a room in Cartagena, Colombia, at Casa San Agustin, an elegant boutique hotel consisting of three former residences joined together to form one unique luxurious experience. Of typical Spanish colonial design with courtyards and covered walkways, it had whitewashed walls with original frescoes and pottery three hundred years old. Massive solid-wood beams supported the ceilings. I loved all the stone columns and arches. It's located within the old walled city, not far from the center square.

> Recipe: Pour the warm beer into the coffee mug so it's mostly foam. Sip it like a latte. Pretend no one suspects you're drinking a beer.

    It was election time in Colombia and illegal to serve alcohol anywhere in the city. This didn't stop the waiters from serving beer in teacups and coffee cups to fool inspectors. At my table, I sipped from my teacup as if at an afternoon luncheon. Men would lean down and quietly ask me if I wanted some "white Colombian coffee," wink-wink. These men all had the same general appearance of temporary affluence with shallow wealth. Eventually I connected the dots. They were sales associates working for the cartel.

Still on guard for any attempts to kidnap me, I booked a flight to Bogota. While waiting at the Bogota cargo terminal for my motorcycle to arrive, I witnessed strange activities. Small rundown trucks with tarps covering their cargo would discreetly back into a separate loading dock, where they unloaded identical cans of brand-name paint. Each rundown truck would unload and rush away. Over and over, this happened. The receiving agent on the loading dock would stack them onto a pallet. When it was full, an empty pallet was brought over. This didn't make sense. Why would independent small trucks be used to transport identical cans of fresh paint apparently manufactured at a large paint plant? I asked the humble loadmaster what was going on.

"The paint is bound for America," he replied. "Please don't ask anything else."

I was skeptical. A large paint plant would use a more efficient means of delivery, such as large semitrucks. During my surveillance, I saw the US embassy nearby. It had direct access and oversight of this unusual activity. Why would the US embassy be across the street from the airport cargo facility? My conspiracy theory was confirmed after a security guard escorted me from the area, nervous that I had seen something I wasn't supposed to. He demanded I delete any pictures I had taken.

Safely back at the loading dock where I was meant to stay, I watched for the one special pallet that eventually arrived carrying my precious motorcycle. It arrived in perfect condition and on time. I unloaded, unwrapped and reconnected everything, and was on my way to BMW Bogota for service on the bike.

Bogota is a beautiful town in the shade of steep mountains. BMW Bogota was the best dealership I had seen thus far. Actually, comparing all

BMW shops I've been to in the past eleven years, I'd say it's the best in the world.

A receptionist greeted me at the entrance. "Welcome, Mr. Dolven. May I get you a cup of cappuccino?" She showed me the professional facility with free Wi-Fi, free food, private showers, and clean restrooms.

My service adviser, Marco, was so cool. He was an adventure rider and loved hearing my stories about riding Central America. He recommended I visit Salar de Uyuni in Bolivia, which I will describe in the chapter on Bolivia. I left the bike in good hands for a month. This changed my attitude about Colombia. I had gone from fearing it to falling in love with it. BMW even paid for my taxi to the airport.

I returned a month later. Marco had read through all the previous service orders from the Central American countries. The receipts were in Spanish, which I couldn't read.

"BMW Guatemala over torqued one of your head bolts and put on a non-BMW-approved fix," Marco told me.

One of his mechanics installed the BMW-approved fix. I appreciate the dealer networks sharing service history performed on my motorcycle. Marco had made a custom map for me to navigate the steep mountains of Colombia en route to Ecuador.

Dear Marco,

Thank you for taking care of my motorcycle. You were right. Salar de Uyuni was sensational. I hope you're well.

Robert

The mountains in Colombia are terraced and steep. They appear impossible to climb, yet the local farmers are cultivating crops in traditional Incan style. The steep land is cheaper to own for the peasant farmers.

On the beautifully paved and marked roads, I noticed a number of road bicyclists, indicating that people had taken care of their basic needs and could focus on exercise. This was a good general sign. Another good sign was the presence of women and children. These facts gave me insight into locales, whether to be on guard or relaxed.

Goodbye, Colombia. Thank you for a safe experience and for easing my concerns about your country.

Ecuador, here I come.

Ecuador

2011

Mileage: 30,000

Ingredients: one spell of vertigo, one dozen roses, one blender, one apple

In Quito, Ecuador, I kept my motorcycle at the Swissotel. When I returned, the battery was dead. The grand hotel had a flower shop in the basement to prepare fresh flowers for the hotel public areas. The flower shop lady allowed me to roll my motorcycle into her shop so I could plug in my battery charger. My motorcycle partially blocked her work space, but she was okay with it. She just kept on cutting flowers. The floor was covered with fragrant clippings, giving my motorcycle a pleasant scent.

> Recipe: Activate the spell of dizzy vertigo. Try to balance yourself on one foot. It's difficult.

With my battery charged, I rode to the equator. It was my first time to witness the effects of the earth's rotation while standing on the equator. I visited a museum with all sorts of demonstrations showing theories about our world.

My science guide pointed to a large white line running east-west. "That's the equator," he said.

The two smaller parallel lines on either side indicated the Northern Hemisphere and Southern Hemisphere. I stood one-legged on all three lines. Balance was easy north or south of the equator. However, standing directly on the equator, I struggled to stay upright, feeling a sense of vertigo. Simply put, the earth's rotation gives us balance inputs absent on the equator itself.

Another demonstration showed the Coriolis effect on water rotation down a drain. The scientist had a plugged kitchen sink filled with water. He walked across the equator to the Northern Hemisphere and pulled the plug. Water drained down the sink in a counterclockwise funnel. He walked south of the equator and pulled the plug. The water drained clockwise in the Southern Hemisphere. He stood directly on the equator, and the water drained directly down without rotation. I made a Facebook video conducting a controlled experiment demonstrating this. Another cool thing was an equatorial sundial, a vertical apparatus different from other sundials, that shadowed the time on a wall instead of the ground.

> Recipe: Set the apple in direct sunlight. Let sit for two weeks.
> Shriveled and wrinkled, it takes on the form of a tiny head.

On an undeveloped road shortly after crossing the equator, I spotted a sign on the side of the road that stated, *HEADHUNTERS*. It had an arrow pointing to a group of small primitive huts. These people were, indeed, indigenous headhunters.

You may be wondering if I was worried that they might decide to add a gringo head to their collection, but in fact, I felt safe interacting with the tribe. It didn't worry me. They were eager to expose me to their culture.

Each tribe member wore Western-style clothes that clearly had been acquired through charitable donations from the United States, their adaptations to modern living evidenced by a television playing a Spanish soap opera. Old wrinkled men and women gathered around a TV, silently transfixed by the poor-quality production.

One man approached me wearing a University of Montana sweatshirt. "Would you like a tour of our community?" he asked. He smiled. "I didn't actually attend the university. This was a gift from my wife."

I was immediately at ease. "Yes," I said. "I would like to learn about this practice of head-shrinking."

I followed a tribesman into a rudimentary laboratory lined with shelves housing what looked like shriveled apples encased in glass. I examined the applelike heads close up. Each had tiny, shrunken eyes, noses, mouths, and ears, with a faded black patina. The human heads, layered in dust, were eerie and peaceful.

Shrinking heads is a ritual common to the Jivaroan people of Ecuador. The practice celebrates the deceased by preserving their face. To do this, postmortem, they make an incision up the back of the neck and one completely around the neck. The shaman peels the face off, places it on a wooden ball, sutures it closed, and leaves it in the sun to bake. Progressively smaller balls are used over the months. When ready, the head is put in a glass box, sealed shut, and placed on a shelf where relatives can make face-to-face visits. Oh yeah, this tribe also hunts with blowguns and poison darts. I welcomed exiting the experience on my motorcycle.

It took fifty miles to regain my appetite. I stopped at a cute cafe in an adobe building. On the menu was the most delicious food item in Ecuador, *maiz tostado*, made from corn called *cancha*. It's like popcorn that pops on the inside and tastes like the "old maids" of US popcorn or like Corn Nuts. The treat accompanied ceviche. Scrumptious. I was back on the road to recovery.

It was September 2010. The week after I rode through Quito, a presidential coup shut down businesses, causing riots and widespread looting. The rioters were the police and military protesting for reinstatement of certain bonus programs paid to them. The president took refuge in a hospital. A helicopter was sent to evacuate the president, but protesters kept throwing debris on the landing pad, preventing a safe landing. Chaos ensued.

Recipe: Place the dozen roses in a blender. Mix in sugar. Blend for fifteen minutes. Place in freezer overnight. Taste it. It tastes like roses.

I rolled into Cotopaxi and the sensational Hacienda San Agustin de Callo. This is a private and exclusive boutique hotel with huge rocks chiseled into fences and walls supporting beamed ceilings. The most unusual thing about the hotel was that, after the five-course dinner, they presented me rose-petal sorbet (made from real rose petals) served in a music box.

When I opened the box, a song played while I savored the flavorful sorbet. My mom collects music boxes and would have loved the place.

It was time to ride across the border into Peru and sew their flag on the back of my jacket. When my jacket had no more space, I sewed future flags to straps attached to my jacket.

Peru

2011

Mileage: 31,000

Ingredients: one power outlet, one Wrigley's tinfoil gum wrapper

The Pacific Coast route of Peru is composed of steep, rocky cliffs with occasional uninhabited bays limiting access to the water. I had never witnessed barren, untouched coastline like it. I rode many miles, winding along the ocean, with no signs of life other than the waves crashing onto the jagged rocks, high and vertical. All the dirt and sand had blown away centuries ago, leaving only larger rocks. It was my own windblown raw slice of seclusion.

I spotted a tree branch stuck into the ground with a weathered rag tied to the top. It was like a primitive billboard. I hadn't seen this much development the entire day. I thought it must identify civilization of some kind. I followed the dirt route down to water's edge. The branch was the advertisement for a small oceanside village. The sun was setting over the ocean, and I was ready for the three Bs: a beer, a bite, and a bed. I rode slowly down the path to the beach, where hammocks were strung pole to pole in a commercial way. Palapa umbrellas with small tables indicated food could possibly be available, although absent neon Coca-Cola signs. Actually, there were no signs at all.

A dark-skinned man emerged from a grass hut and approached me.

I pointed to the hammocks and asked, "*Alquiler?*"

"Si," he answered. The dark-skinned man turned and walked back into his hut. The check-in procedures were rather informal in this isolated village.

My kickstand needed a solid foundation to avoid sinking in the sand. I positioned a flat rock beneath it, but the weight of my bike and gear cracked the rock. The dark-skinned man returned with a piece of two-by-four in one hand and a plate of fresh ceviche in the other. He presented both to me like a chancellor presents a diploma to a graduate. The two-by-four worked perfectly, supporting my bike. The ceviche was no ordinary ceviche. It was a Peruvian specialty fresh from the ocean. My taste buds were skyrocketed into outer space. Pretty much the best mixture of fresh fish, citrus, spices, and cilantro I had ever tasted.

Meanwhile, back in the hammock, I was lulled to sleep by the calm waves sneaking up onshore, churning the pebbles round. I was at ease with the kind man. However, I maintained awareness of my surroundings. At night, I tied my gear to the hammock so anyone trying to steal it would wake me like an alarm.

I got an early start that morning and headed south to Lima, Peru. The outskirts were a collection of terribly decrepit dwellings made from corrugated tin and baling wire. Inside the city limits, things changed into manicured bushes and trimmed trees. Miraflores was my destination, an affluent district in Lima high on the cliff overlooking the ocean.

That was the last day of the month's ride. It was getting late, and I was tired. I needed a hotel and a place to keep the motorcycle for a month. I kicked my side stand down onto a beautiful tiled driveway in front of the Belmond Miraflores Park Hotel. The valet guy gave me a look of approval, having assessed my efforts riding from the United States. As I shuffled through the opulent lobby, well-dressed guests hid their aversion to my dirty, weather-beaten appearance.

The front desk woman greeted me without judgment.

I had two questions. "Do you have a room for tonight?"

"Si, señor."

"Can I leave my motorcycle here for a month?"

"Si, señor. Give your keys to the valet."

Within an outside valet parking area, Carlos, my valet buddy, and I secured my cover over the bike. I was a bit leery about leaving the bike partially exposed in harsh, salty air for a month.

I checked the loads and listed myself on a flight home the next morning.

~ ~ ~

Back at work, discomforts and inconveniences were less significant. This adventuresome lifestyle was changing the way I approached the world. A person in need was no longer a disruption to my day. It was a fellow human, mutually dependent for survival. Perhaps I had been in need and received help from locals so many times, I wanted to even the score. Perhaps I had a newfound empathy for humankind. Perhaps I had become more accepting of adversity. My horizons were rapidly expanding, and it felt great.

~ ~ ~

The next month, my Continental Airlines red-eye flight from Houston to Lima arrived early morning as the city was coming to life. People swept their front porches and hosed down their driveways. My taxi driver parked in front of the Belmond Miraflores Park Hotel. Carlos, the valet, opened my taxi door. I stood up and gave him a big hug.

"*Como estas*, Señor Dolven?"

"*Muy bien, y tu*, Carlos?"

It was so nice to see a friend.

"*Moto* very good!" he said.

Music to my ears that warmed my heart. "*Gracias*, Carlos."

My elation plummeted when the front desk manager said, "*No tengo habitacion.*"

She had no available rooms. Traveling standby, I can't make reservations.

"All I have is the presidential suite, and that's four thousand dollars per night," she added.

I had been flying all night. My motorcycle was parked there. There were no other hotels nearby. I was inclined to stay. "Please check again for a cheaper available room," I said.

She recalculated and offered me the presidential suite for $400 if I could be out by nine the next morning. Faced with this one option and a slight desire to live like a king for one night, I agreed to be out by nine.

The bellman wheeled my gear on a trolly up the elevator to my suite on the top floor and gave me a tour. Through the front door of the suite were floor-to-ceiling windows overlooking the city and the ocean. The suite had a huge patio with a private pool. In the living room were fresh flowers and tables with local art pieces. The massive bedroom had a king-sized bed and a TV that rose from a hidden cabinet. The bathroom had huge dual sinks, a private sauna, and a very private hot tub on a triangular deck with only the roofs of low-rise buildings in view.

I felt like a king and wanted to share this extravagance with someone. I was accustomed to camping on the beach in a hammock without a shower or electricity and had done so only the month prior. Not every person's ideal vacation itinerary. I have the desire to experience everything: good, bad, and ugly. Five-star resort one night, followed by sleeping on the beach. I'm okay with both. It builds character and appreciation for life.

That evening, I met Rusty. We were each having a beer at happy hour, both gazing out over the Pacific Ocean far below. I told him how "rusty" my motorcycle was after a month of being parked outside in the salty air. We chatted and drank a few beers. Rusty was a lieutenant in the British navy. His ship was docked up the coast a few miles at the military port. He invited me to take a tour the next morning.

"I need to be out of my presidential suite before nine," I told him, "so that should work perfectly."

He gave me entry procedures for the secured port area and told me where he would meet me in the morning.

I slept well in the king-sized bed. Then a short ride up the coast to the port, and I was greeted by Rusty. He escorted me up the gangplank to the ship like a foreign dignitary on a tour of a floating display of power and superiority. United States and Britain being closely aligned, I felt welcomed and intrigued by the sophisticated systems on the state-of-the-art warship. It carried helicopters recently used on humanitarian missions to save civilian lives from an earthquake.

Rusty showed me everything. The ship was only a few years old, and I could tell. It had a new-car smell, unlike older musty and rusty ships. A multitude of computer screens filled the bridge. It looked like Mission Control at NASA. The captain's quarters were cramped, the seamen quarters were like putting fifty men in a shoebox. The galley was the size of a small bedroom where the chef could cook for month-long tours. The personal tour was a great honor for me.

In every room we entered, the other sailors would snap to attention and salute Rusty. Even men relaxing on their bunks would jump up and stand at attention until Rusty returned their salute. He clearly had the respect of his fellow shipmates.

Dear Rusty,

Thank you for your service and allegiance. It was a great honor to learn about your fine ship on a personal tour.

Sincerely,
Robert

I was surprised how well my motorcycle was running. The thing is bulletproof. It felt good riding in the ocean air.

Down the Pacific Coast of Peru and inland a bit, I survived the ride through the Nazca Desert, famous for the Nazca Lines. These are massive geoglyphs (lines formed with elements of the surface either placed or dug). The lines form shapes best seen from an airplane. I had no time to waste. I hiked up an observation tower to where I could see lines curved and straight, forming images of animals and geometric patterns. If stretched out in a straight line, the combined length would extend eight hundred miles. The lines originated around 100 BC, and their purpose has been debated. The leading theories are they were astronomical maps, indicators of sacred routes between religious sites, or my personal theory: welcome signs for people above.

Riding south, I coasted into Cusco, Peru, circled the center square, and found a hotel. My intended destination was Machu Picchu. Cusco is the gateway to Machu Picchu.

Cusco could be a destination in itself, but Machu Picchu captures the tourist's interest. It's a shame because Cusco was the capital of the Incas. It has the most amazing "Great Square" surrounded by several palaces built by former rulers. Each ruler tried to outdo the former. Progressively, the palaces became more intricate and sophisticated. I found a historic hotel on the "Great Square," drank a beer on the patio, and planned my trip to Machu Picchu the next day.

There are several options for getting to Machu Picchu. With time constraints, I chose the "old man" option: a first-class train. Hiking the Inca Trail and camping would have been my first choice, but I traveled every other month for two weeks, then went back to work. I didn't have enough time to hike it. A friend of mine described my travel life as "served up in tray-table-sized portions." I agreed. I got a small taste of a big world. I'd love to do everything and see everything, but life is short.

Machu Picchu had been on my world travel itinerary for years. I had heard stories of its mystical beauty. Arriving there in person was spectacular. I was living my dream. I entered the ancient Inca citadel as clouds drifted over pointed, grass-covered peaks. I strolled the walkways and imagined Incan women carrying vegetables back to carved stone dwellings to prepare meals for their family or perhaps the emperor Pachacuti, who resided there in the mid-1400s. The location is stunning, but very remote at an altitude of 7,900 feet, protected by nearly vertical mountains. They had terraced gardens and a nice irrigation system watering the small crops.

I theorized why the Incas vanished from there. Used for only a century, then abandoned during the Spanish conquest, Machu Picchu disappeared off the radar until 1911, when American historian Hiram Bingham rekindled the world's attention and planned to build a Starbucks there. (Just kidding about the Starbucks.)

I spent the night in Aguas Calientes, a town near the base of Machu Picchu. It featured locals selling Incan treasures and had a river running through town. I ate guinea pig for the first time. It tasted like chicken but had tiny bones that disrupted my chewing.

The first-class train back to Cusco was enjoyable, especially because they offered an open bar. I shared a table with a likable married couple. We really hit it off, sharing travel stories and adventures. We laughed and drank until the wife thought her husband and I had had enough to drink, so she poured our drinks into the vase of flowers.

In an act of defiance, I raised the vase and professed, "Nothing can stop me" as I guzzled. The next morning I decided to direct my ambitions more selectively.

After miles and miles of road construction, I made the steep descent into Puno, Peru, on the shores of Lake Titicaca. It's the highest navigable lake in the world. Arriving in a town looking for a hotel had become second nature to me. I spotted a huge white building on a point stretching out into the lake. Sure enough, it was Hotel Libertador, a beautiful five-star hotel and resort on the shores of Lake Titicaca.

I crossed my fingers as I approached the front desk. I needed a place to stay the night and a place to park my motorcycle for a month.

The front desk woman seemed receptive. She had a room. However, she said, "We can't allow your motorcycle to be kept for a month."

I heard papers being shuffled in the back office. I asked to speak with the manager.

Juan emerged from the back room with an enthusiastic "*Buenos dias.*" He had a dark Spanish look with thick eyebrows and a kind face. Short and round completed his appearance.

I explained my situation.

He shook my hand. "I am a motorcycle rider and want to do a long-distance ride someday," he said. "Of course we can keep your bike."

I followed him down the loading dock entrance into a huge basement hallway.

"Park here," he said.

It was a little corner surrounded by electrical components and sewer pipes. Some of the pipes were wrapped with insulated tape, but still radiated heat.

"Great. Thank you, Juan. I need to get a couple hours sleep then to the airport to fly back to the States. I'll see you in a month."

~~~

A month later, I returned to Hotel Libertador to find Juan had sectioned off the corner where my motorcycle was parked with caution tape and traffic cones. He was so helpful and accommodating. Over the years, I would return to each parking location with new gear and dispense with the old gear. I always found a person who appreciated my old gear. I had brought a new helmet, and Juan was a rider. I presented him with my old helmet outfitted for music. It fit him perfectly and was in better condition than his current helmet. My old helmet had the blood, sweat, and tears of two continents. I was delighted it would continue providing safety for another rider.

> Recipe: (*Warning:* don't actually do this recipe.) Fold the tinfoil gum wrapper into a U shape. Insert into the power outlet. Notice the smoke, flames, and possibly worse. This recipe is for illustration purposes only. Do not do this!

Most foreign countries use 220-volt electricity, whereas the United States uses 110 volts. This means if you plug your 110-volt American battery charger into a 220-volt outlet, smoke will fill the room and flames will follow. That's why I carry a convertor to reduce the voltage. Unfortunately, I had fried my convertor the month prior and forgot to bring a new one. Juan and I decided to test my battery charger without the convertor to see what would happen—a hasty, foolish decision resulting in smoke, then flames. I gave the fried battery charger, unplugged and hot, to the maintenance guy, who said he could fix it. Thank goodness the warm pipes next to my motorcycle had kept the battery at a charge level able to eventually crank my engine.

I arranged an afternoon boat trip on the lake to visit the Uros people, who live on floating reeds on the lake. It's extraordinary how they use the reeds for food, shelter, and boats. I toured their reed-built huts and interacted with some of the 1,200 total residents of the sixty-two floating islands.

The history of the Uru people is a bit tragic. The Incas tried to force the Uros into slavery, so they fled the mainland to seek refuge on the marsh islands and adapted their lives, sustained by reeds. They have massive boats made of reeds, with dragon heads adorned with ribbons and flags. They parade them on special occasions. The main island has a tower to watch for invaders. They keep a stock of fish from the lake, ibis birds for their eggs, and cats to catch rats. They make a living selling handicrafts, so I purchased a couple of their handwoven hats. It was wonderful to see how they turned adversity into livelihood.

The next morning, veering left around Lake Titicaca, I crossed into Bolivia. This border crossing was *unusual* and *usual* at the same time. It was *unusual* that I left my GoPro helmet cam filming during a *usual* border scam.

Bolivia

2011

Mileage: 33,000

Ingredients: one thousand-foot-tall Christmas tree, one strand of tinsel, one ventilator, one wheelbarrow, one two-hundred-pound bag of salt

On the Bolivian border, my GoPro helmet cam recorded a scheme called "the faux guard." The scam involves a legitimate guard and an accomplice. The real guard follows procedures and handles your real paperwork, while his accomplice serves no official capacity other than separating you from your money. The real guard allows his accomplice to use official uniform articles to portray authority. The faux guard will step in at an appropriate time to apply pressure and confusion in an attempt to rattle the tourist into offering a bribe to expedite the border crossing. I filmed this exchange as it happened to me.

The real guard was totally legitimate and fully uniformed, while the faux guard only wore an official hat. A civilian black Members Only jacket from the '80s gave it away. He implied I had several immigration violations. Officer "Legit" recognized I was not fooled even though Mr. Faux applied more pressure for money. He raised his voice, with threats of detainment. In the end, Mr. Faux laid down his hat and held his hand out in desperation. I would have been sympathetic if he hadn't tried to scam me and I don't know how many other tourists.

I headed for La Paz, Bolivia, the highest capital city in the world. I noticed the effects of high altitude at twelve thousand feet above sea level. More breathing was required during physical exercise. It left me lightheaded.

I entered La Paz on top of a mountain ridge. From this vista, I had an unobstructed panoramic view of the city below. It looked like a rolling valley covered with multicolored Lego pieces. The Lego pieces were actually dwellings clumped next to and on top of each other. It was an amazing landscape. From the top of the mountain, I felt like a giant, like I could extend my arm out over the city and feel its texture.

> Recipe: Place the thousand-foot Christmas tree upright. Rotate the strand of tinsel around the tree, top to bottom. Imagine the tinsel strand is a road. Imagine yourself in a tiny vehicle on that road. Look out the window of your tiny vehicle and imagine how far the relative drop is. The pit of your stomach rises to your throat.

I went in search of *El Camino de la Muerte*, the Road of the Dead, a forty-mile route that once claimed three hundred lives in one year. The mountains in the Amazon forest are covered with vegetation. From afar, the road resembles a strand of tinsel wrapped around a Christmas tree. I needed to see if it was scarier than it appeared in my research.

Late in the day, I descended deeper into the Amazon forest. Lost, I asked what few humans I came across where the epic road was. The local people were peasants wearing rags, mostly living off the land from what they could gather from the forest or shoot with their bow and arrows. They had no idea where the Road of the Dead was because it was their normal road they used to transit the Amazon forest.

I knew the rules. Drive on the left side while on this trail of terror. The reason? Drivers can poke their head out the window to get their wheels as close to the edge of the thousand-foot cliff as possible to allow opposite-direction vehicles room to pass.

Nighttime arrived. Frustrated and tired, I saw the headlights of an oncoming car coming down the mountain. I planned to stop the driver and ask where the Road of the Dead was. In the darkness, his headlights shone directly in my face. He didn't slow. Closer and closer we converged. He wasn't moving over. He was on my side of the road, the "right" side. On a collision course, he was going to ram me head on. I had two options: one, move over to the left and face riding off the sheer cliff, or two, swerve right and descend into a deep culvert. Making a split-second decision slowed by controlled fear, I elected to swerve right and take the motorcycle into the culvert. As my front wheel rolled into the culvert, my body activated a hypo injection of adrenaline. With the burst of exaggerated strength, I extended my right leg to catch my bike, and before we hit the rocks, I stopped the bike's inertia, which resulted in a detached bicep. I yelled Spanish profanities at the driver as he passed without stopping.

He yelled, "*Lado izquierdo.*"

I translated it to mean, "You're a fool for being lost and not realizing you're on the world's deadliest road." Actually, it means "left side" in Spanish.

Paralyzed by fear, I collected myself and continued.

Eventually I found a cluster of structures. I slept in a hot and humid screened hut the locals called a place to sleep. I snapped a picture of my dangling bicep, a saggy and swollen black-and-blue blob. Doctors later said they could operate, but I could leave it dangle in my arm to avoid further complications.

I woke up to the sounds of the Amazon rain forest totally not refreshed. A local man drew me a map back to the Road of the Dead. I rode slow and steady on the Road of the Dead, which was emblazoned with crosses and memorials honoring persons killed using it. The road was narrow, with a vertical rock wall rising a thousand feet above and below.

I remember one rock. Yes, I remember one particular rock among millions of other rocks. Let's call this one rock Harold. Harold was in the middle of the road. Riding at a reasonable speed, I saw Harold in my path. If I swerved left, I would hit the cliff wall. If I swerved right, I'd ride off the cliff and fall a thousand feet into the Amazon forest. Neither choice was optimal. I chose to hit Harold head on. He launched me off the seat and spun the bike sideways. I regained my balance, to survive my encounter with Harold the rock. My motorcycle and I emerged unscathed without a scratch. We had survived the world's deadliest road, and that gave me confidence. I've thought about Harold many times since then, hoping he has lived without turmoil.

Recipe: Activate the ventilator with 100 percent oxygen. Enjoy effortless breathing. Dial the oxygen level to minus 30 percent. Exert yourself physically. Try to breathe in the thin air. How do you feel? Dizzy, short of breath? Continue until you have a feeling of euphoria. This is called hypoxia and can kill you in extreme situations.

Bolivia is a land of extremes: extreme natural resources, extreme poverty, extreme altitude, and extreme remote areas.

I rode by an overturned produce truck. Mountain people appeared from nowhere to steal the dumped produce. They were like vultures descending on roadkill, picking the best bits. I felt terrible, riding at an altitude of fifteen thousand feet, exhausted and light-headed. I stopped for something to eat at a roadside shack. It was an unpainted cinder-block box with a tin roof. Inside the shack were a few Bolivian truck drivers eating steaming-hot soup.

When the waiter approached me, I pointed to the soup and said; "one."

It was boiling-hot soup with vegetables and whole chicken feet in it. Cold and hungry, I slobbered it down. I would have eaten anything. I considered asking to sleep on the floor of the noisy cafe shack, but there was no quiet spot to sleep, so I exited.

Deeper and deeper I rode into desolation. I was stopped by a cop. My headlight illuminated the insignia on the side of his police car, which had a picture of a coca leaf that made me think the police were going to protect and serve coca production instead of people.

He asked the usual questions to determine my sobriety and then told me to go to jail.

"Why?" I asked.

He only repeated, "Go to jail."

I again asked why.

"Señor, it is the only place you will be safe." He gave me directions to the next town.

The jail was the only building in the high-altitude town. I reluctantly entered the small structure.

Behind a large wooden desk was El Comandante. "Sit down," he said.

I wasn't sure if I was in trouble or not. He was thick and intimidating. I had a flashback of the "Blue Chair Stare" of an intimidating old chief pilot I'd once known. He offered me a filthy cup of coca tea. The people there drink coca tea and chew coca leaves to combat the effects of high altitude, hunger, and fatigue. It's like drinking five cups of strong coffee. I declined his offer for tea. I needed sleep. We chatted as best we could using my Spanglish. He was similar to me in age and asked a lot of questions. I politely asked where I should sleep.

He rose from his desk and took me to a jail cell. When he forced open the door to my cell, it emitted a long screech, sending shivers through my body. The single light bulb didn't have a switch, only two exposed wires. I had to connect the two bare ends, completing a circuit, to turn the light on. This was nothing like you'd envision a jail cell to be. Disgusting filth stained the walls. The bed was a rusty steel grate.

"This is your toilet," he said, pointing to a five-gallon bucket stained from previous prisoners. He slammed the door as he exited.

I was left to worry and wonder if he would open my door without ransom in the morning. There was no heat in the frigid cell. I laid on the steel grate fully dressed, riding gear boots and all. I tried but couldn't sleep a wink, disturbed by the moans of another prisoner. The extreme altitude gave me a severe headache. I struggled to breathe. I was exhausted. However, I couldn't even relax. Unquestionably, the worst night's sleep I've ever had. The positive side is, without the pain, the pleasure wouldn't be as appreciated.

In the morning, my headache was so severe, five ibuprofen couldn't relieve the pain. On days like that, I had to bite the bullet and press on. There was no turning back. Each time, I managed to get back on the bike and continue the ride. With self-analysis, I admired my dedication to success.

I rode through Potosi, Bolivia, famous for a silver mine. Indigenous people and slaves from Africa were used by the Spanish invaders to extract vast amounts of silver. The Spanish sent the silver back to Spain, making the Spanish Empire the richest in the world at the time.

Legend has it, the hazards at the mine reduced mortality to days and perhaps hours. For good luck, miners would light a cigarette and leave it burning before they entered the mine, hoping to finish the cigarette at the end of their shift. The country is "mineral rich, people poor."

About 7 percent of the roads in Bolivia are paved. The rest are dirt tracks. While I was in search of Salar de Uyuni, the world's largest salt flat, my fuel was running low. I hadn't seen a town for hours on the dusty, desolate roads. On vapors, I rolled into a town which supposedly sold gas, according to reports from locals. I knocked on a tall metal gate.

One side swung open, and a fella walked out with a white plastic gas can. "Ten liters," he said.

"I need thirty liters."

He refilled his ten-liter gas can approximately three times, and I was making dust clouds down the road. Ignorantly, I arrived in the town of Uyuni. I searched for more gas and a place to spend the night.

A guy riding a Kawasaki KLR 650 pulled up alongside me. "A-low mate, I'm Ben," he said. Ben was tall, with thick curly hair and hands worn and callused from working in the mines of Australia, I would later learn. He was going to save my life several times over the next four days. "Where ya headed, mate?"

"The salt flats," I said.

"Let's go together. It's far too dangerous to go it alone."

I wondered if Ben was lonely or if the salt flats were that dangerous. I followed him to his hotel and checked into my own room.

After Ben and I had bought provisions to last four days or so, we went over the route plan and drank beer until bedtime. Our meager supplies weighed the bikes down but were essential for survival, with no opportunity to resupply. I had six liters of water, pasta, tuna fish, salami, cheese, bread, and four bottles of red wine. Ben had less and planned to survive on cigarettes mostly.

> Recipe: Empty the two-hundred-pound bag of salt into the wheelbarrow. Use the shovel to spread the salt into a six-foot square. Lie down in the salt. Make a salt angel. Feel the grit. Smack your lips and taste the salt dust. Multiply the salt square a million

times. Now you have an idea of what it's like being on Salar de Uyuni.

In the morning, our wheels splashed onto the world's largest salt flats, completely flat and completely white. Hundreds of miles on the horizon, blue sky faded into the white plane, obliterating depth perception. Absent depth perception, objects known to be small appeared large and vice versa. It was an opportunity for epic Instagram photos. I took a photo that depicted our motorcycles in my hands.

We rode thirty miles out to a hotel made entirely of salt. The hotel was dingy but uniquely carved from salt blocks, with salt floors, walls, and a corrugated plastic roof. The furniture was even carved from salt blocks that left white powder stains on my pants.

Our next destination was Tunupa Volcano, which has a collection of three-thousand-year-old mummies. There were no roads on the salt flats, nothing to indicate direction other than the needle on my compass, similar to an airplane. I was headed northwest, so I rode a compass heading of 315 degrees, keeping the needle centered like a VOR approach using an RMI. Since there were no roads, there were no police. Speed was our discretion. Riding 150 miles per hour no-handed on the Bolivian salt flats is something to try! It was much like flying an airplane. I wished all my pilot buddies could experience it. I was in my element.

Near Tunupa Volcano was an oasis town with people celebrating on the dirt street. They were partying and dancing.

The leader waved me over and offered me alcohol from his home-distilled supply and cocaine from his personal stash. He had a mound of the white powder. "Amigo, it will make you strong and protect you from the sun."

I declined.

He offered me an unusual compressed ball. "Eat it," he said.

I curiously touched it to my tongue and removed it. My tongue instantly went numb. I struggled to pronounce words. It felt like a dentist had injected Novocain. By the way, the president of Bolivia started his career as a coca farmer. No wonder Bolivia produces 45 percent of the world's cocaine.

Ben and I looked for a place to spend the night. We found another outcrop from the salt for protection from the illegal traffickers crossing the salt flats at night into Chile. If you camp in the middle with nothing around you, they can't see you, and some campers have been run over in their tents.

After two days camping on the salt flats, we headed inland to find Arbol de Piedra, made famous by a BMW motorcycle poster advertising my model 2004 BMW 1150GS. To get there was no easy task. We needed to ride the salt flats, then fifty miles of deep, rutted tracks made by four-wheel drive vehicles. Once there, we saw the most unusually shaped rock. It looked like a bonsai tree made from stone, hence the name "stone tree." It was formed over millions of years from the harsh winds and erosion. We snapped a few photos and rode on.

Next on our route was Laguna Verde and its striking shades of green. To think a lake could become green as a go light stunned me. It changes colors, depending on the winds and minerals being stirred up.

Then we were on to the pink flamingos of Laguna Colorada. We decided to camp on the shores of the lake, in the remains of a burned-out shack. We were at fourteen thousand feet, surrounded by the high Andes Mountains. On the airplane I fly, passenger oxygen masks automatically drop at fourteen thousand feet if an emergency occurs, making Laguna Colorada a high-altitude lake, and I felt the effects. My head ached, and I was short of breath. The temperatures were dropping. I had a minus-thirty-degree sleeping bag and was fine. However, Ben had a thin zero-degree bag and froze. We woke to a thin layer of ice covering the lake and the pink flamingos walking on top of it. The glassy ice reflected the mountains and pink flamingos, amplifying the sight.

We packed our gear and turned the keys to start our bikes, with no response. Both our bike batteries were dead from the freeze. We disconnected Ben's battery and walked it up into the sunshine to try and thaw it a bit. After an hour, he reinstalled it. Slow crank, but not enough to ignite the engine. We pushed his bike up the hill to try a bump start. At the top, the physical exertion at fourteen thousand feet exhausted us. A short rest and push, push, push. Pop the clutch. No dice. We sat there for a few more hours trying everything we could think of. About that time, a guy in a four-wheel drive vehicle drove up. I carry jumper cables, so he jump-started my bike. Then I jump-started Ben's bike, and we were off to the next destination in the Bolivian Altiplano.

My motorcycle is fuel-injected, which compensates for high altitudes. Ben's smaller bike was carbureted and not performing well. Finally, his motorcycle conked out and wouldn't start. His battery went dead. We were on a rocky portion of deeply rutted trails. I didn't need a kickstand. I just leaned my bike against the rut. Ben had his gas tank off and bike torn apart in no time. Being closer to the sun was intense. I could feel my skin burn. I tied my Costa Rica Imperial beer towel to my bike. The wind blew it perfectly horizontal, creating a sunshade. I lay under it while Ben needed no assistance.

After doing a quick carb clean, Ben had his bike back together. We used my tow rope to pull him on his bike to attempt another bump start. That can be a tricky procedure, especially in that environment. He hung on to the tow rope while I accelerated. Once we had enough momentum, he let go and popped the clutch. His bike sprang back to life.

Back in business, we headed for the national park. I was running 80 percent road, 20 percent dirt tires on my big heavy bike. Absolutely the wrong tires. I had no traction. The ruts would swallow me. It was so hard to balance the weight and stay in the deep ruts. Zip zap, left and right, I went tumbling. I couldn't upright my bike and gear solo, so Ben turned around and rode back to help lift my bike. Upright again, we were off to the races. One hundred yards later, zip zap, left and right, and I was down. Ben rode back again to help me lift the bike. Once upright, we were off. Zip zap, left and right, and again I went down. Multiply this ten more times to understand my weariness riding Bolivia.

I carried an emergency locator transmitter in the event I needed emergency evacuation. This device uses satellites from anywhere in the world to request immediate extraction to safety. The service advertised an average worldwide response time for evacuation of less than eleven minutes. The transmitter has three buttons: green as a check-in option, yellow, as an "I'm okay, but in a situation" option, and red for *immediate evacuation* only. Under my policy, the cost to push the red button is $10,000. Remaining expenses are covered up to $1,000,000. After going down ten or fifteen times, I experienced an extreme headache, dehydration, and complete exhaustion. I could not continue. I had reached the end of my physical strength. I had hit the wall. Bolivia broke me.

Unbeknownst to Ben as he viewed me in his rearview mirror, I had reached my limit. Ben would need to carry on without me. I was going to push the red button. This means authorities immediately initiate search-and-rescue operations. I would be evacuated via helicopter, while my bike and gear would stay in the middle of nowhere to rot into oblivion. My finger was close to the red button.

When I was growing up, my mother always told me I could do anything. Popeye used spinach to get his physical strength. I used my mother's positive words of encouragement for my mental strength. At the top of my voice, I proclaimed, "I will make it through this. Yes, it's hard right now, but eventually, I will complete the remaining miles and make it to my destination. If I give up, I will never be able to complete anything again."

I did not press the red button. If I had, I would have failed and felt terrible the rest of my life. And yes, I went down several more times that day. And yes, Ben turned around every time, rode back, and helped me lift my bike. Multiply my thanks by infinity, take it to the depths of forever, and you will have merely a glimpse of my gratitude for Mom and Ben. Without them, I may have pressed the red button or been the next mummy on the Bolivian Altiplano.

Four days off-road without resupply was a challenge. That night at the national park, we were able to purchase food, water, and get a cold beer. Of course, I bought Ben's beer and meal. He saved my life. We made numerous toasts to a victorious celebration. I felt strong, borderline invincible, similar to after I had completed my one and only full marathon. It was a great feeling of achievement. I had survived the Bolivian Altiplano.

The deep-rutted dirt was my nemesis. Ben would say, "You're gonna kiss the *bitchman*."

I didn't know what he meant.

"In Stralia, they call asphalt bitumen," he explained.

The border into Chile is where we hit asphalt, and *yes, I kissed the bitchman.*

Back on paved roads, we made good time. Ben's bike was better off-road. Mine was better on-road. So to make up for lost time, we decided to say goodbye and schedule a rendezvous New Year's Eve at the campground in Ushuaia, Argentina, the end of the road. We waved goodbye, and that was it.

I exited Bolivia and entered Chile.

Chile

2011

Mileage: 35,000

Ingredients: one key to your vehicle, one magician

Northern Chile is untouched moonscape, a perfect place to erect unusual monuments. With only shallow, barren mountains, a "gigantic hand" eclipsed the sun, sixty kilometers south of Antofagasta, Chile. The palm had tall, thick fingers reaching from the sand, lusting toward heaven to be saved from the harsh conditions of the desert. At the base, my head pinned back looking up, I could see the detail of the fingernails carved into the concrete. The *Hand of the Desert* was built by Chilean sculptor Mario Irarrazabal in 1992, who included wrinkles at the knuckles. It's thirty-six feet tall, made from concrete over an iron frame, To photograph my motorcycle and me with the giant hand made me feel like a real adventure rider.

I reached Santiago, Chile, a few days ahead of schedule and left the bike at BMW Santiago for service. It was a small shop with no storage space, except outside. I feared the bike would be covered in rust upon my return and headed home with my fingers crossed.

> Recipe: Drive your vehicle to a remote location. Give your key to the magician. Have him make it disappear. How do you feel about the magician and being stranded without your key?

Concerned because BMW Santiago wasn't returning my emails, I had no choice but to fly to Chile and hope the bike was good to go. I walked in the front door of the shop and was greeted by Fernando, a casual surfer dude.

"Did you get my emails?" I asked.

"Hey, yeah, man," he said. "I just didn't want to give you the bad news."

"What bad news?"

"Oh man, the guy lost your key, man. We're waiting on the replacement. It should possibly, who knows, be here today."

The key is not a normal key. Only original BMW keys work and are shipped from Germany. I was irritated, with no alternative other than to wait for the replacement.

The next day, Fernando received my replacement key. The End.

With my shiny new key, I raced to the Santiago airport worried I would be late. My buddy Greg, whom I had last seen in Belize, had expressed interest in renting a bike and riding with me to the "End of the World," Ushuaia, Argentina. We planned a nine-day ride from Santiago, Chile, to Ushuaia, Argentina, down to the tip of South America. He was due to land in ten minutes. My GPS estimated time of arrival was twenty minutes. I split the lanes and filtered between cars to the front of the intersection stoplight. The light turned green, and I was alone, with all the cars in my dust. I made it to the terminal, where I stopped in a no-stopping zone. Then I saw a familiar face.

Habitually happy Greg strutted out of the terminal wearing a smile and a small carry-on bag, since I had loaned him my extra gear.

"How long have you been waiting?" I asked.

"Dude, I didn't wait at all," Greg said. "I just walked out."

As if we were two swell chums, he hopped on the back of my bike, and we headed for his motorcycle rental agency.

Greg's can-do attitude was infectious. Any obstacle, big or small, he tackled head on with success. With his rented bike, helmet, borrowed riding suit, and bike formalities for crossing international borders complete, we were off.

Our first destination was a town described in my tourist book as not worth stopping for, except to take a picture with "the bull," a solid bronze bull ready to charge. Greg and I felt juvenile and decided a photo near the hindquarters of the huge anatomically correct statue had to be taken. Laughing hysterically, I snapped a photo of Greg looking envious.

Greg had heard stories of me sleeping in unforeseen locations. His objective: to sleep in an exotic place, one he could tell about to starry-eyed listeners when he returned home.

That night, riding into a remote village in southern Chile, we were forced to a halt. Our gas tanks were nearly empty, and the only gas station was sold out. There was no gas for hundreds of miles. An angry crowd gathered, yelling things in Spanish and shaking their fists at the gas station attendants.

The attendants pleaded with the mob. "The petrol truck will deliver tomorrow."

With little gas in our tanks, we searched for a place to sleep. Circling the streets, we found the angry mob had formed around the only hotel in town, which displayed a *No Vacancy* sign. We rode slowly to conserve our gas. In front of a trucking depot near some bushes, like a miracle, I spotted a small structure. Doorless, primitive, and unoccupied, it was a five-by-ten-foot roadside prayer room adorned with crosses and depictions of a divine deity. We parked our bikes. I bumped my forehead on the entryway. Inside were candles burning, incense smoldering, and colorful paintings of Christ.

"Does this accomplish your objective of sleeping in a unique place?" I asked Greg.

"Perfectly."

Noticing no objectors, we arranged our gear within the miracle. I carried two sleeping bags and mats. We spread the sleep systems on what little floor space there was. Greg's feet were at my head and mine at his. The tile floor was cold to the touch, but our mats provided insulation. Sleeping in unique locations demonstrates one's ability to adapt. With the right headspace, sleeping is easy, but if you have worries on your mind, sleep is not what you'll get. With earplugs and the right headspace, it was a great night's sleep.

The hiss of air brakes woke us in the morning. The petrol truck arrived as the sun rose. We quickly packed our gear to get a good place in line before they ran out of gas again.

The angry mob formed a line, waiting to fill up. Wheel to wheel, we inched forward as each driver filled their tank, some with extra gas cans.

Ten vehicles in front of us, nine, eight, seven. We were sixth in line when the pumping ceased.

"*Lamento que nos quedemos sin 80 octanos solo tenemos prima,*" the gas station attendant yelled to the crowd.

"What did he just say?" I asked an angry Chilean next to me.

"He is sorry, but they are out of 80 octane gas and only have premium."

My breathing resumed. I only use premium. With five cars in front of us, hopefully there was enough premium remaining. I felt like a winning game-show contestant when our turn came. We filled our tanks to the brim. Relieved, we left the town with 320 miles in our tanks.

Headed for the Perito Moreno Glacier in the Los Glaciares National Park in southwest Santa Cruz Province, Argentina, we met a group of riders on an expensive guided group tour. Among the riders was a retired woman named Kathy. She was from Willmar, Minnesota, where my father was born. Her husband had had an accident three days prior and was airlifted home. Kathy continued on the ride without him. She handled her big BMW like an expert and was a pleasure to talk with. At age sixty-five, Kathy had the look of an aged schoolteacher, with years of disciplining students chiseling wrinkles into her face.

In El Calafate, Argentina, we drank beer and swapped riding stories with Kathy and a few folks from her group.

The next day, Kathy led the way to Perito Moreno Glacier, leaning her bike low in the turns. We had to push our abilities to keep up. In the parking area for the world's fastest-moving glacier, we secured our gear for the kilometer hike to view the ice close up.

On the viewing platform, I pulled my beanie cap over my ears to escape the cold emanating from the 121-square-mile ice flow. The sunlight between the crevasses tinted the ice shades of blue. I could see the ice creep down the mountain as it regenerated itself, calving throughout the day. The ice field is the world's third-largest reserve of freshwater. Ice bridges are created by flowing water below. The money shot is to video an ice bridge collapsing, causing a tidal wave in the frigid mineral-green water.

Hurried by our itinerary, Greg and I said goodbye to Kathy. As we turned and walked away, we heard a thundering crash. The bridge had collapsed, and a massive wave was headed in our direction like a tsunami. We could only stare in amazement as the wave thundered toward us but then began to dissipate before we even had time to think about running.

~~~

The media was reporting demonstrations by the Chilean people, protesting a 25 percent price increase in heating oil. We watched news reports of people putting tires across roads and lighting them on fire, closing the roads in protest of the heating oil price increases. Greg and I had adventure in mind. We decided to ride down to Punta Arenas, Chile, and join in the protests like rebel revolutionaries.

We put our beers on the table and high-fived each other, saying in unison, "Power to the people."

It seemed like a good idea at the time. Picture two gringos raising their fists, chanting whatever the group was chanting, looking side to side confirming group acceptance, dumbfounded by the quest. Ah, to be so young and naive.

The protests ended the next day. Adventure had been stolen from us, although our lives were spared. Disappointed by our good fortune, we hung a left and ascended the mountain pass to Bariloche, Argentina.

Bariloche is the Lake Tahoe of Argentina, with world-class ski areas, beautiful timber lodges, and a crystal-clear lake glistening beneath the mountain peaks. The thing to do in town is take a picture with the adorable Saint Bernards equipped with rescue whiskey barrels around their necks. Puppies and adult dogs pose with you. The thing to eat is garlic French fries. These are piping-hot French fries covered with garlic butter and salt. Wash them down with a locally harvested steak.

Pressed for time to reach our goal of going to the End of the World, Ushuaia, Argentina, and having loose plans to meet Ben, who had saved my life in Bolivia, we left the beautiful alpine village.

We struggled southbound, riding *Ruta Tres* (National Route 3), known for its infamous wind. I found reviews stating, "Watch out for the wind," "blown over by the wind," and "worst wind ever." I surmised it would be windy.

South of Comodoro Rivadavia, Argentina, the wind was fierce on that thin portion of earth, separating the warm Pacific air from the cold Atlantic air. On the rough asphalt road, we leaned ourselves at 45-degree angles into a direct crosswind. My neck muscles grew fatigued after five hours of fighting, one hand gripping my handlebars, the other hand holding my head upright as it was blown off my shoulders. We battled the ferocious wind for two days nonstop.

News reports announced eighty-mile-per-hour winds. I falsely rationalized that was during a storm, not a normal Tuesday afternoon. I confirmed the windspeed when the road turned left. Suddenly the only thing I heard was my engine revving at 4,500 rpms. I felt no headwind, crosswind, or tail wind. It was then I stood up on the foot pegs and truly rode with the wind. I looked down at my speedometer. It indicated eighty miles per hour. I was one with the wind, leveling the land like a cyclone. I have not feared riding in wind since.

The wind had died down to relaxing and calm when we crossed the Straits of Magellan on a ferry. In and out of Argentina and Chile several times, we were in range of Ushuaia, Argentina, the End of the World, confirmed by a sign. A photo with this sign is another adventure-rider achievement. It marks the end of the Pan-American Highway, which starts in Prudhoe Bay, Alaska, 17,848 kilometers north, and ends at the sign where Greg and I took our "bucket list" photo.

The next land mass is Antarctica. I eventually did make it to Antarctica, on an expedition without the motorcycle. I made a video about the trip and posted it on my Facebook page.

Greg was able to secure return of his rented motorcycle and a flight home in short order. We said our goodbyes and promised to exchange our photos.

Dear Greg,
I appreciate the enthusiasm you exhibit whenever we are together. Our ride was no exception. You make the best of adverse situations which makes hanging out with you so positive and enjoyable.
Thanks again for your contribution to The Ride!
Sincerely, Bob

Argentina

2011

Mileage: 37,000

Ingredients: one cigarette, one ceiling fan, one six-foot ladder

I did not start this ride with the goal of riding around the world. My first goal was only to cross the Darien Gap between Panama and Colombia. The next goal was to cross the Straits of Magellan. The goal after that was to ride to the End of the World, Ushuaia, Tierra del Fuego, Argentina. Ushuaia is the farthest point south on the Pan-American Highway and marks the end of the ride from Alaska.

Those goals achieved and not wanting to battle Ruta Tres northbound, I decided to fly the bike to England and see if I could ride there. I thought I could just abandon the bike if it didn't work out for some reason.

I needed a place to store the bike in Ushuaia for a month while I worked on shipment. Walking the streets of the quaint village, I stopped at a travel agency.

Ruben, the owner, greeted me. "Buenos dias, señor."

"Buenos dias," I responded.

His accommodating approach allowed me to pop the question. "Can I keep my motorcycle at your house?"

His answer? "Si, señor." He had a nice house on the hills of Ushuaia. The bike fit perfectly in his empty garage.

The next day, I headed for the airport and back home for a month.

~~~

Unfortunately, the week I had scheduled for my vacation and return to collect my bike from Ruben's garage, his wife was flown up to Buenos Aires for emergency surgery. He wasn't comfortable leaving his garage keys with neighbors, so I had to reschedule another return for the following month. I traveled standby back then. My return coincided with Easter weekend, and all flights from Buenos Aires to Ushuaia were completely sold out. I again rearranged my return.

I had to get the motorcycle from Ushuaia to England. I worked with Victoria, a tourist information specialist in Ushuaia. We searched for a means of transport to England and eventually found a trucking company to deliver my motorcycle to Buenos Aires, then prepare it for a flight on a British Airways 777 to London.

I arrived in Buenos Aires as the truck unloaded my bike. I rode to Dakar Motos. As I pulled into their garage, Javier and Sandra, the owners, both pointed to my rear shock, which had burst and leaked all its oil onto their floor.

Javier grabbed a towel. "No problemo, amigo."

They prepared and packed the bike for the RoRo (roll on, roll off) $1,900 flight to England.

Javier gave me a few papers and said, "Collect your bike in England next month."

With a heartfelt thank-you, I turned and walked out of his shop, trusting it would all work out.

> Recipe: Position the ladder under the ceiling fan. Put the cigarette in your mouth. Climb the ladder with your head tilted back so the cigarette is progressively closer and closer to the fan. As the distance narrows, feel the fan blades rotate inches from your face. Allow one blade to slice the cigarette out of your mouth. Scary, huh?

I toured Buenos Aires with my niece, who was on a college study abroad program. Taylor gave me the "locals only" tour of Buenos Aires, starting with La Boca, a barrio made famous by seceding from Argentina in 1882. Later it became a refuge for the poor, and now a tourist destination because of their multicolored buildings. We ate lunch at an outdoor cafe that had entertainment. Then I became part of the entertainment when I was hailed up onstage. The gaucho (Argentine cowboy) placed a cigarette in my mouth. He had a set of *boleadoras* (three balls on a rope, used in Argentina to capture running cattle). By this time, my heart was hammering, but I decided I had to go through with whatever was going to happen next. I didn't want to be embarrassed in front of my niece.

The gaucho was blindfolded. He started swinging the bolas round and round, with huge rotations, inching closer to my mouth with the cigarette burning. I stood completely still. Closer and closer he swung, until he sliced the cigarette out of my mouth. As the crowd cheered, I thanked him for not redesigning my face.

Taylor and I were strolling the streets of La Boca when a little gypsy kid squirted water in my face. I knew the distraction game. My hand reflexed to my wallet as the other gypsy pickpocket kid was reaching for it. They were half my size, so I shrugged it off. Careful out there. It's a petty crime but can be a huge inconvenience.

Time for the Superclasico, an annual football match (soccer), first played in 1913 between Buenos Aires rivals: Boca Juniors versus River Plate. Student tickets were priced at twenty dollars and were considered outrageous. The stadium held forty-nine thousand screaming fanatics. It was a madhouse squeezed together in the student section. I bought Taylor and her friends beers, but the glasses were spilled by the elbows of cheering fans. When Boca scored a goal, the students jumped up and down in unison, causing the triple-tiered stadium to flex. My adult mind considered the danger.

After the game, our exit was locked, trapping the rambunctious students and me in the upper-deck section to allow lower decks to exit the stadium first. I was the only adult in a gigantic group of screaming college-aged Argentines. It was fun because I want to try everything at least once, but I'll never do Superclasico again.

That night we attended a tango show at El Viejo Almacen, the best tango show in Buenos Aires, providing a terrific display of costumes and the art of tango in a traditional setting since 1969. I loved watching the graceful, long-legged women being swung and spun effortlessly by suave men. The clothes were elegant and tailored to accentuate the dancers' bodies. The show was a progression of styles through the years, starting with the '30s fedora hats and zoot suits and ending with current styles with muted tones and skintight pants. My favorite was the '80s period with multicolored one-piece jumpsuits and belts cinched at the waists.

After the show, we took a taxi to my favorite place in Buenos Aires, a vacant warehouse, where Monday nights only, the most amazing percussion group drums out hypnotic rhythms called La Bomba de Tiempo. We danced and drank to the beat of their drums. They're teenaged kids enjoying themselves like teenagers do. It's a BA must, a show worthy of extending your vacation for.

Time to make my way to England and see if my motorcycle had arrived.

United Kingdom

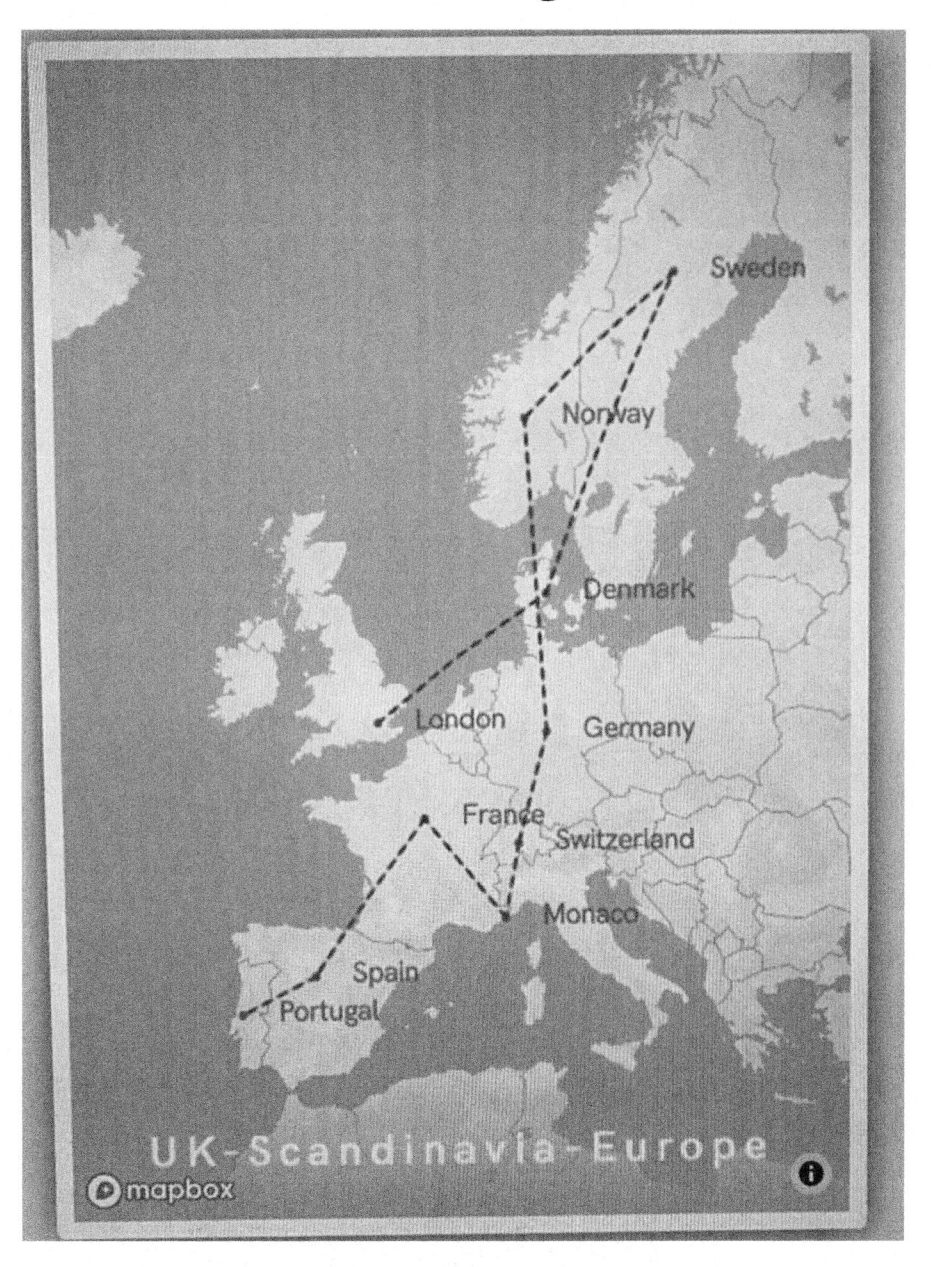

A rough look at my route

England

2011

Mileage: 40,000

Ingredients: one diorama of a World War II battlefield filled with Nazi memorabilia

I bought a ticket on British Airways to London Heathrow. The delayed flight arrived too late to collect my bike from James Cargo, the receiving agent. I had to wait until morning. Steve, my contact, offered to let me stay at his house.

Steve loves American-made Harley-Davidsons and fits the part. His wife, Ellie, is a housewife who enjoys her job. They gave me a tour of Windsor Castle, which I hadn't visited since my study abroad semester in 1985. We ate at a local pub, delicious fish and chips wrapped in newspaper and soaked in malt vinegar, of course.

> Recipe: Observe the diorama filled with Nazi memorabilia. In your mind, wonder which side the creator sides with.

Later that night, Steve offered me a tour of his attic. He pulled the hinged ladder down from the ceiling. We climbed the rungs into a bunker-like crawl space, where he had an impressive display of World War II memorabilia, mostly German army items: uniforms, helmets, swords, guns, bayonets, camo netting, shovels, even a record player playing vintage war music that started automatically when we entered the bunker. I felt like a Nazi soldier stationed in Germany, questioning the purpose of our efforts.

I slept well in Steve's spare bedroom, and in the morning, he drove me to the warehouse, where I was reunited with my motorcycle. We then had to go to the customs house for some signatures, then back to the warehouse. When the formalities were completed, the bike fired right up. I thanked Steve, popped the clutch, and I was on my way down the A3.

The rear shock had blown out back in Buenos Aires at the sending agent's garage. I had arranged the service to be done at Vines of Guildford BMW south of London. With a broken rear shock, I felt like I was riding a pogo stick. Just the spring was left. *Boing, boing, boing,* I bounced down the A3.

I was greeted in the usual fashion at this BMW shop.

"Hello, Mr. Dolven. May I get you a cappuccino?" Except in England, they offered tea.

I explained the services I needed. They were glad to complete the work while I returned to the United States.

A first-class seat on an American Airlines 767 and I was home.

Back at work in the States, all I could think about was returning to my motorcycle for more adventure. I thought, since my motorcycle was in England, I could head north and visit my relatives in Norway. I researched the entry procedures for each country and scheduled a first-class ferry ticket from Harwich, England, to Esbjerg, Denmark, where I could ride the rest of the way to Norway.

~ ~ ~

The next month, I returned to England to find my bike repaired and ready to go. On my way to the port, I stopped at Harlaxton College, a castle north of London converted into a college, where I had spent a semester on a study abroad program in 1985. To pay for this wonderful experience, I used my life savings of $4,500. My grandmother matched my $4,500 for the tuition. There I became friends with students from all over the world and learned so much from them. It was like living a history lesson. I learned about the Israeli conflict from two roommates, one from Israel and one from Palestine. They both told stories of personal bloodshed over the ancient dispute. In our castle-college, they were friends, but back in their homelands, they'd be arch enemies, ready to slice each other's throat.

The semester sparked my lust for travel. On weekends, we traveled the

UK and Europe. We had events like the medieval ball, when we dressed in period costumes and had a feast at a forty-foot-long table in the "great hall." The castle is an amazing display of art in the form of architecture. Google Harlaxton College to see pictures. Riding my motorcycle to Harlaxton gave me a feeling of going full circle. I had evolved from poor college kid to adult able to pay my own way.

I arrived at the port of Harwich, England, to find my ferry was a cruise ship that you could drive your vehicle onto. My stateroom suite had two beds and a private bathroom with shower. I ordered lamb and potatoes in the formal dining room. I had a feeling of content wanderlust. My desire to travel was being fulfilled. Sleeping in my stateroom on the overnight ferry, I dreamt of Denmark.

Scandinavia

Denmark

2011

Mileage: 41,000

Ingredients: one Scales of Justice, one conscience, fifty dollars

The next morning, the ferry arrived in Denmark. Ferry disembarkation procedures are always interesting. I had to squeeze myself between road-grime-covered semitrucks to gain access to my motorcycle on the lower vehicle deck, breathing diesel exhaust until my turn to ride off the ferry. The decks are always covered with slippery oil spills from cars and trucks.

Once in Denmark, I felt like a world traveler exploring a new country. Venturing down the Danish roads, I was amazed by the change in architecture and modern lifestyles.

> Recipe: Put the fifty dollars on one side of the Scales of Justice and your conscience on the other. Which side weighs more? Which is more important to you?

I pulled into a gas station. Back in Latin America, you pay before you pump your gas. I was accustomed to that procedure. In Denmark, you pay after you pump your gas. I had filled my tank, secured my gear, and cleaned my mirrors. I hopped on the bike and headed for Sweden. Twenty-five miles down the road, my heart sank. I had forgotten to pay for my gas. I did a U-turn and headed back to the gas station. A couple of one-way roads and I was lost. Searching for the station took forty-five minutes, but I eventually found it. The attendant thanked me for my honesty as I handed him the equivalent of fifty dollars in Danish kroner. Cleared conscience, I set out eastbound.

In Denmark, the infrastructure has an artistic look with a modern engineering flare. It was hard to watch the road and admire the magnificent country. The Oresund Bridge connects Denmark to Sweden and is an engineering marvel. It started with a 2.5-mile tunnel underwater, then up onto an island and over a 5-mile bridge. After I crossed the bridge, I was in Sweden.

Sweden

2011

Mileage: 41,000

Ingredients: one tray of strawberries, one growling tummy, one napkin

Sweden has the most polite drivers in the world. There are signs suggesting, not requiring, moving over to allow merging traffic to join the motorway. Politely put, one sign read MAY WE RECOMMEND THE LEFT LANE TO ALLOW SPACE FOR MERGING VEHICLES. That was the kindest way to say, "Move the heck over."

> Recipe: After not eating all day, position the tray of strawberries in front of your eyes. Feel the hunger in your growling tummy. Use the napkin to wipe your watering mouth. Now throw the strawberries away. How does the deprivation feel?

Starved, I stopped at a farmer's roadside stand. He was selling luscious-looking strawberries, each freshly grown and cared for. These strawberries were tiny, a rich red, and appeared bursting with flavor, unlike the huge, pinkish, watered-down ones at Costco. My mouth watered. I had no Swedish kronor, and the farmer would not take any other currency. I was denied even a sample. This was my most disappointing strawberry-buying experience I've ever had.

When I reentered the motorway, other vehicles moved over, allowing me room to merge with the considerate drivers. All I could think about was the strawberries. I needed local currency so I could satisfy my hungry taste buds.

I rode up the E6 to Gothenburg, Sweden. I found an ATM to withdraw some Swedish kronor. I hunted for the same type strawberries, but to no avail. I can't remember what I eventually ate, but it wasn't as good as the strawberries would have been.

I said goodbye to Sven and hello to Ole. In other words, I left Sweden and entered Norway.

Norway

2011

Mileage: 42,000

Ingredients: one willow shoot, one ancestral connection, one dark room

Norway was the most captivating country I had ever seen—the deep fjords filled with frigid clear water, the blue-eyed people, and a countryside of farms. The most unusual feature was the grass growing on the farmhouse roofs. These sod roofs were made with thick roof boards, covered with layers of birch bark, and topped with sod. Reasons given were insulation, ascetics, and sustainability, and besides that, cattle could graze on the roofs. The log cabin structures looked cozy and romantic. I pictured my ancestors hunting and gathering food for the family and sharing meals on hand-built furniture with kerosene lamps lighting the room.

I have second cousins living in Oslo, Norway, and that's where I was headed. They have lived on the same acre of hilled land for seventy-five years. Three homes occupy the gorgeous setting. Kari, the mother, lives in the main house. Her two daughters, Marianne and Kathrine, each have homes with their families in corners of the property. Kari, a ninety-year-old woman spry as a forty-year-old, cleared a sweet spot in her garage for my motorcycle parking.

> Recipe: Take a willow shoot from Norway. Plant it in Minnesota. Take a shoot from that tree back to Norway. Plant it. Take a shoot from that tree and plant it back in Minnesota. Take a willow shoot from that one and plant it up in northern Minnesota. This is what happened in my family.

My favorite story about my Norwegian heritage is about a willow shoot crossing the Atlantic Ocean back and forth between the family farm in Norway and the United States.

Ole Dolven, my great-great-grandfather, was part of the "Great Migration" from Norway to the United States between 1880 and 1930. He left the Dolven farm in Norway with several relatives bound for a new life in the United States. The Dolven group of relatives was aboard the doomed SS *Atlantic* when tragedy struck. Another steamship crashed head on into the *Atlantic*'s midsection. The *Atlantic* sank, claiming precious human lives and an American Express strongbox full of gold. Ole Dolven was the only survivor from the Dolven group. He settled in Morris, Minnesota, and started a Lutheran church. He had a son, A. O. Dolven.

In 1897, A. O. Dolven, my great-grandfather, offered his nephew, Gustav, the opportunity to leave the Dolven farm in Norway and come to the United States to live and work in Minnesota. Gustav was just thirteen years old when he traveled to America alone. He arrived with a homemade trunk filled with his belongings and some gifts for his hosts: bed-sized lambskin robes, a large brick of cheese, and a willow shoot from a tree on the Dolven farm in Norway. Gustav planted the willow shoot next to the family church. It grew rapidly and became a tree. Beal Dolven, my grandfather, used to sit in the shade of the willow tree with his brothers, picking four-leaf clovers in the summer months.

In 1940, the Germans dropped a bomb on the Dolven farm in Norway, destroying the two-hundred-year-old log cabin and the original willow tree.

In 1992, my great-uncle, Rev. Oswald Dolven, visited the old church where in 1897, Gustav had planted the willow shoot. Ninety-five years old, with a four-foot-diameter trunk, the tree was thriving. Reverend Dolven carried a shoot from the Minnesota tree back to Norway and planted it on the family farm where the original tree had been destroyed during World War II.

In 2014, my sister, Barb, visited Norway and the family farm. She brought a shoot from the Norway tree back to the United States and planted it in her backyard. It has grown tall and thick.

In 2020, I cut off a shoot from her tree and planted it in Grand Marais,

Minnesota, where I spent thirty days working on the first draft of this book.

> Recipe: Visit the place where your family tree was originally planted. Feel the ancestral connection with the people of your origin. It feels like home.

I grew up in Minnesota and feel it's my real home. Minnesotans and midwesterners are generally hardy, down-to-earth, honest, hardworking, and usually of Scandinavian descent. In Norway, I had a connection with the people. Their blue eyes attracted mine like windows into our souls. Our conversations were calm and sincere. I had never felt this bond in any other country. I felt at home among Norwegians.

The number of waterfalls per capita allows each person to have a dozen or so private waterfalls. For that reason, hydroelectric power is popular. The fabulous fjords can be defaced with huge turbines and aerial cables for the power plants. The government is in the process of burying these mechanisms in tunnels. It's an expensive process and an expensive country to live in.

> Recipe: Spend thirty minutes in a dark room. Allow your night vision to adjust. Now spin in a circle and stop. Is your balance thrown off? Do it again. This time turn the light on, then off. How is your balance?

Norwegians are great at building tunnels. I rode through the Laerdal Tunnel, the world's longest car tunnel at fifteen miles in length. It was a narrow two-lane road with jagged walls that periodically protruded out into my lane. I feared my handlebar grip might get caught and throw me off-balance, tumbling me into the dark road. After a few miles of darkness, my eyes adjusted somewhat. Then the lights of an oncoming car ruined my night vision. That was a dangerous state of affairs. I was completely blinded for two seconds every time a car approached. I would have a feeling of vertigo, not knowing which way was up or down. It was one of the most dangerous riding situations I've encountered. About seven miles into the tunnel, I decided to stop every time an oncoming car approached me. I made it through to Oslo.

Then I got on a cruise ship ferry bound for Germany. They actually called it a "mini cruise." The route took me through the Drobak Narrows, where the Oscarsborg Fortress defends this narrow channel to Oslo. The fortress has tunnels equipped with underwater torpedoes. In 1940, a Nazi heavy cruiser headed for Oslo was sunk by the underwater torpedoes installed at the fortress. I hoped there wasn't going to be any friendly fire as my ferry sailed past the fortress to Germany.

Europe

Germany

2011

Mileage: 44,000

Ingredients: two napkin rings, two toilet paper tubes, two paper towel tubes, two Christmas wrapping paper tubes

At 1:00 p.m. the next day, the ferry docked in Kiel, Germany. I disembarked and headed for Hamburg. I wanted to reunite with Mr. Heinz, the owner of Prinz & Koenig, the bar I frequented on acceptance flights of brand-new Airbus A319 and A318 aircraft in Hamburg, Germany. I was so fortunate and grateful to be selected by Captain Wes for the acceptance flight and delivery of the second Airbus A318 N802FR to be flown commercially. The Airbus executives treated us pilots like royalty, with formal dinners and activities after work each day. Often at Prinz & Koenig, we ate steaks grilled on hot stones, and drank strong German beer. One such night, Mr. Heinz let me guest bartend. It was so much fun trying to figure out what the German guests ordered, then serving them my translated rendering.

That evening, I parked out in front of Prinz & Koenig to find the bar had closed. My link to Hamburg had been severed. I headed for the autobahn, southbound to the Rhine River Valley.

> Recipe: Hold the two napkin rings up to your eyes. Look through them like a pair of binoculars. Your field of vision is pretty wide, right? Now look through the toilet paper tubes. Your field of vision is reduced, right? Now look through the paper towel tubes. You only have one inch of visual acuity. Now look through the Christmas paper tubes. It would be hard to do much with so little vision.

The German motorway, or autobahn, has an advisory speed of 130 kilometers per hour (80 miles per hour) called "*Richtgeschwindigkeit.*" There are fewer and fewer "unrestricted speed zones" as years go by. Driving on the autobahn in the unrestricted areas seems to be a professional sport and for serious drivers only. At fuel stops, it's not unusual to see Mercedes, BMW, and Audi drivers wearing driving gloves, driving shoes, and other race-worthy pieces.

I was putzing down the German autobahn at 150 miles per hour, passing semitrucks drafting off each other. The trucks were tucked tightly together like railroad cars, avoiding the head wind, cruising at speeds above 100 miles per hour. It's a demonstration of cooperation and fuel savings. Passing them, I felt huge gusts of wind. Riding at 150 miles per hour reduced my peripheral vision, like looking through a Christmas wrapping paper tube. The faster I rode, the more focused I became, until all I could see was a small dot of vision in front of me. Here's a calibrated scale: 75 miles per hour equals a napkin ring, 100 miles per hour equals a toilet paper tube, 125 miles per hour equals a paper towel tube, and 150 miles per hour equals a Christmas wrapping paper tube.

Buffeting and bobbing, revving and raging at 150 miles per hour, I was being passed by Lamborghinis, Ferraris, and other super cars like I was standing still. I was unable to reference my rearview mirrors often enough, and these cars were flashes of paint, brushed by in an instant. It scared the pants off me.

Suddenly, a red warning light illuminated on my instrument panel, and I pulled off the autobahn.

Safely at a rest area, I plugged in my GS-911 diagnostic tool. The fault code indicated that a component of my ABS system was inoperative. Not comfortable riding at those speeds with a potentially failed braking system, I calculated a new route to the Rhine River Valley.

At my new reduced speed, my peripheral vision widened. I now noticed the terraced vineyards, the lazy river, and the green mountains forming the Rhine River Valley. I explored the area for a few days on the named routes: Castle Road, highlighting castle tours; Romantic Road, highlighting romantic tourist towns. I camped on the banks of the Rhine River, sipping local wine and admiring the beautiful Bavarian architecture.

One night I stayed in the honeymoon suite at a hotel near Rheinfels Castle. The suite had an arched entryway leading into a sitting area with grand throne-like velvet chairs. The tables beside the chairs were made from antique wood with wrought-iron lamps atop. The oversized king bed emanated royalty with a thick satin bedspread and fringe dangling to the hardwood floors.

Rheinfels castle was built in 1245 as a fortress for tax collectors. The ruler, Count Diether V of Katzenelnbogen, would collect taxes from anyone traveling up or down the river. The castle was still in good repair at the time. The windows were hazy lead glass fired centuries ago and cleaned to a foggy finish. The hallways were narrow and low, giving me the feeling humans had evolved larger and taller since the castle was built.

After a tour of the castle, I enjoyed a five-course meal at the hotel's quaint restaurant. Tables were positioned in a way to allow each party a romantic experience. A massive natural fireplace provided a smoky smell that penetrated the wood floors and ceiling while the mantle displayed medieval antiques of interesting purpose.

I also enjoyed a bottle of local wine, then went looking for the *baño*. That's Spanish for toilet. Spanish is widely spoken in the United States, while German is widely spoken in Germany. Directed down four flights of wooden stairs to the quiet basement, I faced two doors with words indicating gender. I wasn't familiar with the German word for male toilet. I had my legs crossed while I contemplated my uncomfortable dilemma. I wished they used pictures. I could usually decipher them correctly. I racked my brain, thinking of derivatives of male and female. Suddenly a barrel-chested, lederhosen-wearing German man barged through the left door with deliberate affirmation. I was saved.

Next stop, Switzerland.

Switzerland

2011

Mileage: 48,000

Ingredients: one ruler, one pair of manicure scissors

Recipe: Locate a lawn. Can be yours or a neighbor's. Hold the ruler up to each blade of grass. Use the manicure scissors to cut each blade exactly 2.5 inches. When completed, step back and admire your precision. Welcome to Switzerland.

I left Germany and entered Switzerland. Switzerland is small, but it packs an exquisite punch, with its manicured lawns looking like carpet. Everywhere I looked, the grass was exactly 2.5 inches long, as though someone had taken a huge lawn mower and mowed the entire country. I rode through little Swiss villages with their timber and stucco alpine buildings like I was in a fairy tale.

The mountain roads energized my blood. I leaned left and right, never on the crown of my tires, up the Swiss Alps to Interlaken, Switzerland. I looked forward to seeing the garden clock made from fragrant flowers. The clock hadn't changed a bit since I had last seen it in the '80s. I felt the pride of the people who maintain the aromatized timepiece.

Near the clock, there was a gas station, where I paid nineteen dollars per gallon. After that, I felt poor. I was tempted to buy one of the wonderful cuckoo clocks Switzerland is famous for. Unfortunately, I didn't have the money or the space to carry much else.

From Interlaken, I took a local train to Grindelwald, where I boarded a "cogwheel train." This is a train capable of climbing the steep tracks to the "Top of Europe." There is a third rail in the middle, for a sprocket-type drive system. They serve wine in custom wine glasses that have a tilted base so the wine doesn't spill when the train climbs at a forty-five-degree incline.

Once at Jungfraujoch, I walked through the glacier—actual tunnels bored through the thick glacier ice. It was amazing to slide along ice floors made smooth by a mini Zamboni-type machine. The floors, walls, and ceilings were ice. I slid up to an ice bar to have a shot of peppermint schnapps. The observation deck overlooked the surrounding snowy, jagged Swiss Alps, providing a dramatic view, a must-see when in Switzerland.

I left Interlaken for Zermatt to get a good look at the Matterhorn. Whenever I think of the Matterhorn, I think of a family road trip my mom took us on to Disneyland. We sang, "It's a small world after all," over and over as my mom pointed out the Matterhorn at the amusement park. At nine years old, I fantasized about one day visiting the actual Matterhorn. Viewing the Matterhorn in person was going full circle: a childhood fantasy lived out.

Crossing the border from Switzerland to northern Italy was as easy as going from Minnesota to Wisconsin, except for when I tried to pay for gas using Swiss francs.

"Ah, you're in Italy," the gas station attendant said. "We use euros."

I felt foolish not knowing what country I was in.

I rode northern and southern Italy. To keep continuity of the countries as chapters, I'll write about Italy later when I reenter in the south.

Monaco

2011

Mileage: 49,000

Ingredients: one Ken doll, one Barbie doll, one GI Joe doll

Monaco is the second smallest country in the world, after Vatican City, but it's also one of the wealthiest. I felt so out of place with the supermodel couples dressed in tuxedos and evening gowns and driving Rolls-Royces, when I hadn't showered or shaved for a few days while camping in the mountains. A short distance and I was riding the Cote d'Azur (French Riviera), familiar to me. I slowed the pace to take in the atmosphere.

> Recipe: Lay Ken and Barbie on a pile of money. Leave the GI Joe doll in the rain, then drag him in a mud puddle. Have GI Joe observe Ken and Barbie rolling around in their pile of money. How do you think GI Joe feels? You're right. Dirty, but with a full heart, content with his life. He knows Ken and Barbie have struggles of their own. He is thankful for what he has.

Monaco is a destination for the rich and famous, perched on a steep portion of coastline between Italy and France. Through the years, wealthy individuals have kept their fortunes there for convenient banking laws and favorable taxes. The well-kept modern buildings and manicured landscapes attract discerning tourists. The shops are all high-end designer shops with impeccably dressed staff ready to turn their nose up to unworthy customers. Riding on the clean, well-maintained streets made me feel dirty and afraid to soil the pristine pavement.

On to France.

France

2011

Mileage: 49,000

Ingredients: one yellow jersey, one podium, one baguette, six slices of cheese, six bags of olives, six slices of salami, six picnic blankets

The Cote d'Azur has been one of my favorite places in the world since I first visited in 1985. I've returned many times over the years, using the trains for transport.

Recipe: Put the baguette, cheese, olives, salami, and blankets in a bag. Get on a train and enjoy watching France roll by. Eat the simple, delicious foods, watching the landscape change.

Here is my favorite four-day itinerary, one I've done many times:

Depart Chicago at 7:00 a.m. Arrive Paris 10:25 a.m. Walk to the Paris Metro station at the airport. Take the Paris RER train to Notre Dame. Walk across the river to the Latin Quarter. Buy a gyro. Walk over the "love-lock" bridge, up the Champs-Elysees to the Arc de Triomphe, down the hill to the Eiffel Tower, then to Les Aubrais-Orleans train station. Board the Trenhotel to Barcelona 8:05 p.m. Private cabin and five-course meal on the train.

Wake up in Barcelona at noon. Tour Barcelona for the day, then board the night train to Rome. Leave in the afternoon and watch the sun set over the Mediterranean sea while sipping French wine along the French Riviera. Book a six-person couchette and reserve the top bunks (hopefully with friend). The top bunks are best, trust me. Listen to music. Bring wine, cheese, bread, olives, salami, and water.

Arrive Rome. Walk straight to Bici & Baci scooter rental. Rent a Vespa. Tour the big sites in Rome. (My record is one hour, fifty minutes.) Hop a night train back to Paris and get a flight home.

This is my favorite way to spend four days. But I digress. Back to touring France.

Recipe: Each jersey has meaning in the Tour de France bicycle race. White – best rookie, polka dot – best in the mountains, green – best sprinter, yellow – overall leader. Put on the yellow jersey. Stand on top of the podium. Tell the world your deepest, darkest secrets. Pause to think about this…

I love France. If you don't want to ride a motorcycle around the country, try a bicycle. Buy a Eurail train pass. Ride the bike, and hop on the train for longer distances. I used to do that each year to watch the Tour de France. I saw Lance Armstrong win each year. These were some of my best vacations: prepping my body and bike for the trip, then riding along with the tour from town to town. It's the best way to see France and a great way to get exercise. Be sure to see the medieval walled cities and stay in French châteaus and mountain chalets. I love it. I digress further.

BMW Nice on the French Riviera is no compromise to the standards at BMW shops. However, money was what this particular dealership was most interested in, evidenced by their high-income, middle-aged clientele and the prices they charged. To help me save a bit of money, the service manager discreetly offered to keep my motorcycle in his garage, for a fee. I needed service, as the red warning light had been illuminated since Germany. I gave them a list of things I needed repaired, hopped into a taxi to the airport, and was on my way home for a month.

~ ~ ~

Each time I was back in the States, I communicated via email with the service shops. BMW Nice was not answering my emails. I had a French friend call them directly. They said it would cost 2,500 euros ($3,374) to fix the ABS system causing the red warning light. I declined their offer and decided braking safely was less important than spending $3,374. (Wait for the chapter on Turkey to find out how this was eventually taken care of.)

Arriving in Paris is always a pleasant feeling for me. I took the night train from Paris to Nice. The next morning, I walked into the shop, paid for what service they had performed, and rode outta there, headed for Spain.

A side note:

I'm often asked, "What has been your favorite country so far?"

My unbiased answer invariably is the United States of America. Other countries may have better flavors, i.e., India. Other countries may have better coastline, i.e., France. But based on all facets of a country, the USA has the best in more categories than any other country in the world. I've explored a good part of the earth. It was in France that I came to the conclusion that anyone who doesn't feel fortunate to be an American citizen should travel to other countries. They don't need to be Third-World countries. Visit First-World countries. Compare the political systems, police departments, legal systems, monetary systems, military, road quality, infrastructure, tolerance, food, people, geographic beauty, amount of poverty. The list continues.

It won't take long to realize that of all the world's countries, the United States of America is the best. America has the finest quality of life for the majority of its population. We are protected, free, and provided with more all-around benefits than any other country. Even though it's not perfect, we should still honor and respect what it means to be an American. I am proud to be an American. Raise the flag!

Spain

2011

Mileage: 50,000

Ingredients: one naive soldier, one gypsy girl, one bullfighter, one CD of the opera Carmen

I had no idea where to keep the motorcycle at the end of most rides, but I knew where I was going to keep it in Barcelona, Spain. My friend Jessica and her family hosted an exchange student from Spain named Gerardo. I asked her to contact him to see if I could keep my motorcycle at his house. He was happy to oblige. For once I was headed for a destination knowing I had a parking spot. A beautiful ride down the Mediterranean coast of Spain, and I was at Gerardo's place in Barcelona.

Gerardo is a hardworking, fit young man. Maria, his girlfriend, is a career woman climbing the corporate ladder. They greeted me at the door of their apartment building. Like old friends, we did the European double-cheek kiss.

I stowed my gear in their apartment and parked my bike in their underground garage. The happy couple gave me the insiders' tour of Barcelona. You may pronounce it Barth-a-Lona. The reasons for this are numerous. I believe the myth: a former Spanish king had a lisp, and out of respect, the people joined in on the pronunciation.

Our first stop was the Basilica de la Sagrada Familia, (the unfinished Gaudi church) and the highlight of the tour for me. It was designed by Antoni Gaudi, who is incorrectly credited for the term *gaudy*, describing flashy dress. Mr. Gaudi was born after the term gaudy, actually a derivative of a French word, was already in use. The church has ornaments intricately carved, creating shadows and light and giving it a Gothic feeling. There are no flat surfaces. Every inch of wall, floor, and ceiling have detailed shapes

Andiamo Full Circle

and crevasses of ornate carved stone. The steeples are multilayered fingers reaching for the sky. The elaborate detail of this church remains unfinished to this day due to the intricate design, a huge fire, lack of financing, and the death of its creator.

After seeing the church, we walked through the open fish market, had tapas with some of their friends, and strolled the streets, seeing an abundance of the caganer. This is a figurine depicting a man sitting on a toilet. The Catalan culture has used these figurines in nativity scenes since the 1800s, and they're very popular to this day.

It was a great evening, made better when we went to an old-fashioned gin-and-tonic cocktail bar. I'm not sure why, but it was the best gin and tonic I had ever tasted. They used Hendrick's Gin, and I believe that was the secret.

Gerardo drove me to the airport the next day.

"I'll see you in a month," I told him.

The day I was supposed to return to Barcelona, I had a house closing. I requested the earliest signing at 8:30 a.m. My flight was scheduled to leave at 10:30. Shaunie at Magnus Title knew my predicament, so she had the papers faxed to her office. As each of the thirty-five pages came off the fax machine, I would sign, and she would position the next page under the pen in my hand. Page after page. It was teamwork. Once everything was signed, her assistant, Troy, drove me to the airport. After I had cleared TSA screening, I realized I still had the down-payment check in my pocket. I called Shaunie, who called Troy. He circled back to the airport and met me on the curb. I gave him the check, ran back through security, and I was off to New York and on to Barcelona. That may be a record: Close on a house and board a flight within two hours.

Gerardo took great care of my motorcycle and gear. My bike started on the first push of the starter. He and Maria were so kind and generous. We said our goodbyes, and off I went.

Dear Gerardo and Maria,

Thank you very much for your hospitality and generosity. I hope all is well with you.

Sincerely,
Robert

Recipe: Listen to *Carmen*, the opera. Try to feel the music flow with the story. The story is of a naive soldier who abandons his wife and his military service to be with a fiery gypsy girl, Carmen. She leaves him for a bullfighter. Jealous, the soldier kills her. To appreciate opera, read the story beforehand, then listen to the music and let it tell you the audio version.

The next night, I camped in Seville, Spain, the city of *Carmen*, my favorite opera. Many tourist attractions around Seville are made famous by the opera. While I was searching for the statue of a toreador, a bullfighter, a massive arm extended from a jalopy caught my attention.

He drove beside me into oncoming traffic and yelled, "Pull over!"

I didn't know what to expect from the large Spaniard man as I pulled to the side of the road.

His shadow turned his white Fiat gray. In broken English, he told me he rides a BMW. "You come my house," he said.

This could have been an abduction attempt or an earnest invitation to dinner.

"*Me llamo* Rafael," he said.

"*Me llamo* Roberto," I replied. "*Mucho gusto.*"

With belief in humankind, I followed him to his apartment. Still skeptical, I chose a parking space that would allow an easy exit in case I needed a quick escape. We climbed two flights of stairs to his door and entered. Inside, a woman dropped a knife in a surprised way. Rafael introduced me to his wife, Catalina, who was still shaking from our abrupt entry.

They spoke in Spanish, while I scanned the rooms for signs of ill intent. On the wall was a poster of a vintage Vespa scooter that eased my apprehensions. Obviously, Rafael had an appreciation for two-wheeled vehicles. I'm a former Vespa aficionado/dealer and still love the reliable machines.

Catalina had settled down enough to ask if I was hungry. I was famished. She prepared a large tray of tapas with locally grown olives, cheeses, and cured meats that had flavor unlike the usual. The three of us relaxed and munched on the tapas, bonding over our common love of motorcycles. Catalina had ridden on the back of Rafael's BMW touring Europe. The Honda clock on the wall read two in the morning when I thanked them for their conversation and hospitality.

I rode back to my campground. This totally random interaction with locals is one wonderful thing about travel. I cherish the moments when I'm so far away from home and strangers take me into their homes to share our common interests and find we are all in this world enjoying life together.

Seville, Spain, is a short ride along the southern coast to Portugal, which was my destination for that month's ride.

Portugal

2011

Mileage: 51,000

Ingredients: one friendship, one family

One of my good friends, Louie, grew up in Portugal. His parents still live in a small village, Sao Bras, north of Faro, Portugal. His family owns half the town, so I asked if I could park my motorcycle in one of their spare barns. Delighted to help me and to allow me an opportunity to experience the places and people he had talked about so often, he contacted his parents that night. They had a perfect spot for my motorcycle on the family farm. I was elated to have a reliable place to park again.

> Recipe: Take the friendship and combine it with family. Feel the bond of both. It's a feeling of pure contentment.

At this point, I hadn't yet made the decision to ride around the entire world and was considering what I would do with the bike if I decided I'd gone far enough. Logistics of shipping internationally could be difficult, especially since I didn't speak the language or reside in the country. I felt comfortable knowing, if worst came to worst, I could give my motorcycle to one of Louie's relatives. This option was like a safety net and the perfect parking situation—the path of least resistance.

I rode along the south coast of Portugal on a brand-new motorway at 115 miles per hour. There were speed cameras installed every mile or two. England was the last time my motorcycle had passed formal customs, so I hoped the Portuguese police wouldn't be able to locate me for a speeding ticket.

I had a calm, peaceful feeling knowing I was headed for my good friend's hometown and a sanctuary for my motorcycle. He had described the beauty of the area several times, but being there was like a dream come true. The sweeping hills running into the Atlantic Ocean and the sandy beaches provide great vacation spots. They made me dream of summer days that Louie had spent with his family growing up there.

I stopped in Faro to reprogram my GPS for the smaller village of Sao Bras. At that moment, my GPS died. It was an old unit and had been showing signs of a slow death. The GPS is a mission-critical item. Without it, I'm lost. With only a paper map, I asked person after person how to get to Sao Bras. Each one I asked for directions looked at me questioningly, since I had only two Portuguese words committed to memory: *hello* and *thank you*. At the time, I had an early beta version of a language translation app. Unfortunately I needed Wi-Fi to operate it.

Roadside, I approached a man wearing a driving cap and tweed jacket. "Hello," I said in Portuguese, then pointed to my map. "Thank you, Sao Bras."

The man looked at me like I was crazy, like I was thanking him for creating the town or something. He shook his head, muttered something I didn't understand, then walked away. I felt so ignorant, but I had to find my buddy's hometown and my much-anticipated parking spot.

A driver of a large road-service vehicle said he was headed up there and I could follow him. Twisting and turning up the mountain roads, I followed the large truck on a small road, his tires hitting the dirt around tight corners. I had a hard time keeping up with him. Finally, we slowed, entering the quaint little village. I stopped in front of a mobile pizza place serving pizzas out of a truck. I had a vague description of where to meet Louie's parents, so I circled the town round and round until I found the shop owned by his uncle. His mom, Cecilia, came running out with a smile and a welcome hug. She greeted me with warm interest and was very much like my mom: enthusiastic, energetic, and very social. While we chatted about the ride, Antonio, Louie's dad, came out and gave me a calm handshake.

That night, Cecilia served us the most delicious cheeses, olives, salamis, and their homemade wine, very strong and tasty. She enticed me with more wine and more wine, while she had maybe two glasses and Antonio drank water. After a few bottles and incriminating stories about my buddy, we dialed his number. Chatting with him back in America, we laughed about embarrassing stories he would have never told me personally. I didn't realize at the time my long-distance charges would amount to $1,800.

The next morning, I followed Antonio and Cecilia to the family farm, where they grew olives and grapes. Antonio raced his BMW car farther up the mountain, almost on two wheels around corners, skidding to a stop in front of a beautiful mountain farm.

It was the best parking spot yet, tucked safely in a huge barn, covered and comfy. Next to my motorcycle was a rusty and dusty kids' Raleigh Chopper bicycle from the '70s, possibly Louie's. I thought it would be fun to bring that old bicycle back to the States and restore it for Louie's upcoming birthday. Unfortunately, Cecilia said it was his brother's bike, not his.

I hung on for dear life riding back down the mountain with Antonio and Cecilia. The roads were narrow, with stone fences on either side, allowing no overshoot. I feared the beautiful BMW would scrape against the stones. Antonio had lived in this village his whole life, so he was very familiar with the roads. In Europe, driving is more a sport than just transportation.

Again, he skidded to a stop, this time in front of his brother's restaurant, built in 1903. They had horse-drawn carriages and distilled their own spirits. Cecilia told me that when Louie was in diapers, he would crawl to the spout of the still like a hamster sucking on a water bottle.

The family farm was the perfect base station for an out-and-back trip to Morocco. All the relatives warned me against going to Morocco because of the apparent civil unrest. I had never been to Morocco and had a great curiosity about the country. I've always been warned not to travel to bordering countries, yet after visiting, I've always had pleasant experiences. So I planned my trip to Morocco.

Time to return to the States. The flight from Faro to Lisbon was $350, while the train was $27.50. I enjoyed the train and saw the countryside of Portugal. Then I got a first-class ticket from Lisbon to Newark, New Jersey. It was so much nicer than coach.

A month of work, then back to Portugal.

~ ~ ~

This month's ride would be an "out and back." I'd ride a loop around Morocco, then back to the family farm in Portugal. My buddy Randy expressed interest in touring Morocco with me, so we planned the trip. He would rent a bike from a rental agency in Malaga, Spain. We would meet at the coast town of Tarifa, Spain, then take a ferry across the Strait of Gibraltar into Tangier, Morocco, and ride for two weeks, touring the historic country.

Africa

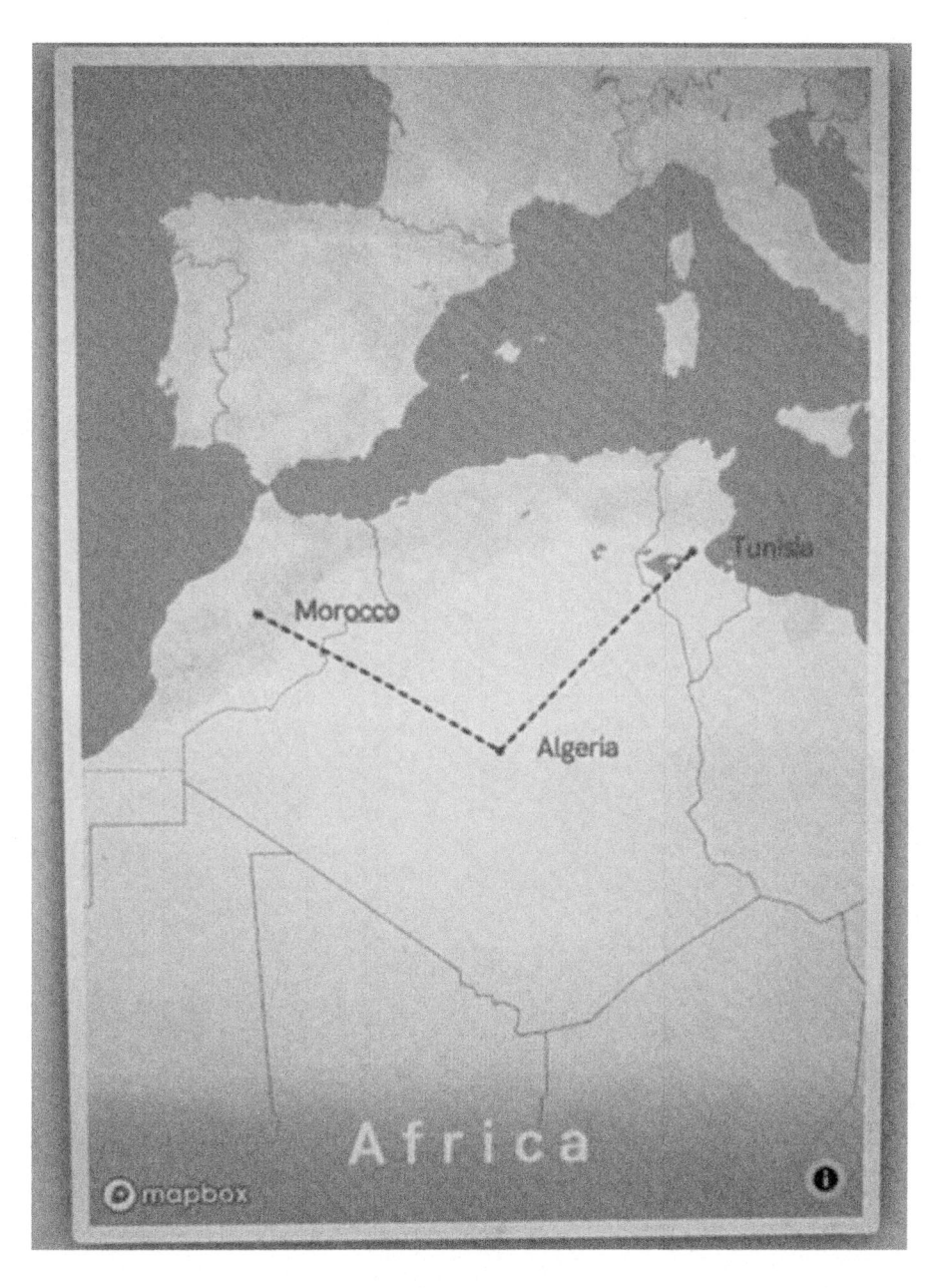

North Africa

Morocco

2012

Mileage: 52,000

Ingredients: one beach towel, one compass

Randy and I met in southern Spain as planned. We parked our bikes in front of the ferry ticket office and bought two tickets to Tangier, Morocco, for $87.27 each, including our bikes. It was a two-hour trip from Europe to Africa.

In 1777, the year after the United States of America was born, Morocco was the first country in the world to recognize its sovereignty and is therefore referred to as "our first friend." I knew this fact and could use it if a situation needed to be defused. It gave me another arrow in my quiver.

> Recipe: Go to your favorite place on Earth. Take a compass reading. If the compass reads ninety degrees, recalibrate the compass to read north. That becomes your personal north, meaning your needle will always point to your favorite place. Anytime you want to show commitment to your favorite place, use the compass to determine the direction to it. From anywhere in the world, lay the beach towel oriented toward your favorite place. It is consolatory to focus your attention in this way.

Morocco is a Muslim country. The route from Spain to Morocco is due south. The rugs in the ship's prayer room were all pointed to the left. I pondered that, then realized, when Muslims pray, they face Mecca. They must have a good sense of direction, or they carry a Qibla compass recalibrated and modified to always point toward Mecca.

The seas were rough, making disembarkation challenging. It's always difficult riding from a moving surface to stationary land. The gangways are always slippery and covered with obstacles. Each time was a test of balance and coordination. Safely on land and stopped at the customs and immigration office, we went through the procedures.

I took Randy's and my motorcycle title for approval with customs. Next was passport control. The real immigration official, wearing a complete uniform, looked me over and stamped my passport. Meanwhile, Randy was subjected to the "faux guard scam" I had filmed back in Bolivia. The official guard had followed protocol with me. The faux guard, wearing only a baseball cap stating *POLICE*, was trying to pressure Randy into a panic and a bribe.

I learned later that the real guards will allow the faux guards to use articles of their uniform to portray a credible impersonation of a guard in exchange for a cut of the proceeds extorted from the victim.

Good thing Randy was a seasoned traveler. We blazed out of there on our way to an ATM to get Moroccan money. Part of the fun of travel is to see and use foreign currencies. The first two ATMs were out of service. Third time was a charm. We each had a pocketful of Moroccan dirhams.

Three hours down the west coast of Morocco, we were chased down by Unnis, a friendly local. He was very excited that two American motorcyclists were riding through his town. He told us his girlfriend was from Tempe, Arizona, near my home. "Follow me," he said.

We followed him to his house, where we felt like celebrities with all the questions he and his buddies were asking.

"Where are you from?" they asked. "Where are you going? How do you like Morocco?"

Unnis lived in a beautiful home of typical Muslim style. We walked into a room used for Ramadan feasts. Its walls were designed with geometric etchings like those in a mosque, and there was crown molding carved from stone with intricate details. It was truly a fabulous residence. Unnis served us mint tea, cakes, and offered to help us find a place to spend the night since my GPS was malfunctioning.

Randy and I followed Unnis to three different hotels. Each time, I would tell Randy, "You watch the bikes. We'll go check on a room."

Randy felt unappreciated by this menial task. His vindication came the following month, when he and I were scheduled for a flight simulator test called a "check ride." Halfway through the check ride, we walked out of the simulator for a bathroom break.

Randy said to me, "You wait here and watch the simulator."

I almost fell down the stairs laughing.

We rode down the A1 motorway, past police every mile or so. We termed them "toy soldiers" because every one of them wore a white belt and shoulder sash, making them look like *Nutcracker* soldiers. We bypassed Casablanca, learning that the real Rick's Cafe was on a Hollywood movie set rather than in Casablanca itself. In Casablanca, there is apparently a Rick's Cafe made to look like the one from the Humphrey Bogart movie. We kept riding south, experiencing this unusual country.

Cautiously, we entered the Medina of Marrakesh, surrounded by chaos and mayhem. Jugglers, sword-swallowers, snake charmers, belly dancers, and barbecues flooded the main square, paved in cobblestones. Darling horse-drawn carriages carried tourists touring the ancient city. The carriages and horses were elaborately decorated. When a speeding car pulled out in front of a trotting horse, the horse slammed on his horse-legged brakes and skidded his hooves over the slippery cobblestones for five feet. The tourists were thrown forward in the carriage. I found that to be an unusual sight.

There were lots of vendors selling pretty much anything. We stopped and chatted with one particular vender selling homeopathic spices and medicines. In his blue robe and blue turban, he was dressed as a "Blue Man" Tuareg nomadic tribesman. I had read stories about the Tuareg culture and its people crossing the Sahara Desert saving lives, so we hit it off.

Randy bought a chunk of sandalwood and a chisel for incense burning. I bought a concoction of ground-up crystals mixed with black seed, used to clear sinuses. Kind of like a Vicks inhaler, except a thousand times stronger, leaving some afterglow.

A side note: I carried this unusual blend for about eight years until New Zealand customs found it in my motorcycle jacket and immediately confiscated it. The next month, I purchased more on Amazon.

While we were chatting with the Blue Man tribesman, a nicely dressed man wearing a pink shirt and pink tie came up to talk to us. He was a doctor on his honeymoon in Morocco. He lived in Arizona, and his father was an imam at a local mosque near my home. I had knowledge of this Arizona mosque and his father. As it turned out, a few months prior to this meeting, my friend Davey and I had been concerned about reports of the Arab Spring and what it meant to the United States. I called a local Arizona mosque to schedule a meeting to get some questions answered. It was the mosque where the doctor's father was the imam. We met with the imam and members of the mosque for a lengthy discussion. It's always nice to resolve concerns amicably. However, our opinions differed.

"I've met your dad," I said to the newlywed doctor.

"No way!" he said, shocked. "I can't believe you're from Arizona and have met my father. My father loves his members and demonstrates brotherhood to all the men. He leaves the women to themselves."

"I've heard rumors of gender differences and the unfair treatment of females in your religion," I told him.

"We believe this is how the prophet Muhammad wanted it," he explained.

I didn't want to argue with him, so I politely exited the conversation. But this random encounter cleansed my concerns. We're all in this world together. Let's enjoy each day and wish happiness for all humans. It's a small world, after all.

That night, Randy and I had dinner at a fifth-floor terrace restaurant overlooking the Medina. We were next to a corner watchtower equipped with a huge loudspeaker. In Muslim countries, they have the call to prayer five times a day. It's like Christian churches ringing their bells, but instead of ringing bells, a man chants or prays out loud and his voice is broadcast throughout the city over loudspeakers. My left ear was inches from the loudspeaker. At that exact moment came the call to prayer. The chanting voice pierced my eardrum and rattled my head, causing prolonged pain.

After dinner, back down in the Medina, Randy wanted a picture with a snake charmer. We approached one who had a cobra with a huge hood. The charmer lifted the snake to place it around Randy's neck.

Randy quickly dodged the snake charmer. "Not me," he said. "Put it around Bobby's neck."

Great friend that Randy is, huh?

The Marrakesh spice market was a cornucopia of colors, with spices displayed on large plates, tapered into perfect conical peaks. I fought the urge to touch the cones. Everyone took such pride in each display. I wondered if a strong wind would blow the spices into a dust cloud. To avoid offending someone, I didn't take any pictures of this remarkable exhibit.

After a short ride on a hot road, we toured Atlas Studios, the location of movies such as *Gladiator, Black Hawk Down, The Jewel of the Nile*, and *Body of Lies*. It had an entire Kasbah with alleyways and passageways. It was a colossal movie set but decaying from exposure to the harsh desert sun. We strolled the alleys Russell Crowe ran through in *Gladiator*. It was interesting to see the facades in person but disappointing to realize the movie was fiction. Our real motorcycles were parked next to the fake Land Rover used in *Jewel of the Nile*. Nonfiction hit me square in the face with the harsh reality of the road.

The sun snuck over the peaks as we rode deeper into the Atlas Mountains to Todra Gorge, a sheer-cliff slot canyon, with walls a thousand feet high dwarfing us.

Randy and I needed a place to spend the night. At that moment, a little fella came buzzing and bouncing out of the sandy desert on a beat-up motorbike, his unbuttoned shirt blowing behind him. Bare feet pricked by his foot pegs and hair washed back on his helmetless head, he waved us to stop.

Alarmed by the urgency of his request, we stopped. He said he wanted to recommend a hotel. It was fairly easy to know his job: find tourists in the small town around sunset and direct them to a hotel in return for a small commission from the hotel owner.

We followed him to the best hotel in Merzouga, Morocco. The town was a collection of mud-brick buildings built from resources natural to the area. It looked like someone had piled the sand into functional structures. The walls camouflaged with the same dirt as the streets, it appeared blended in monochromatic style.

Our motorbike fella led us to an adobe hotel absent a front door to keep the sand out. Our boots ground the sand floor at the wooden slab front desk. The clerk gave motorbike-man a few coins and us two rooms. The town Merzouga is famous for Erg Chebbi, one of Morocco's tallest sand dunes. It's what you would imagine the Sahara Desert to look like, with mountains of sand blown smooth and sharp drifts and shaded valleys, best seen in the morning sun. We scheduled a sunrise camel ride into the desert and set our alarms for 6:00 a.m.

As we exited the doorless entrance, our eyes adjusted to the sunrise to see three tall-legged camels hissing at us.

Our guide, Ali, an Arab man wrapped in a thawb and with a keffiyeh protecting his mouth and nose from blowing sand, yelled, "Climb to blanket!"

Our individual camels were so well trained they knelt on command to allow Randy and me to climb atop their humps and position ourselves on dusty blanket saddles high above the sand for our ride into the vast sand dunes of the Sahara Desert.

The low sun cast long shadows in the brisk morning, giving the illusion the camels had disproportionately long toothpick legs. In all directions, we saw sun-painted shades of orange-brown dunes, some rounded, others jagged. Whether large or small, I imagined skiing down them. I snapped a photo of Randy making an adorable "snow angel" in the sand, which I could use as blackmail.

The next day, we set out on a five-hour ride to Fez for a tour of the historic city. During a gas stop, we saw a woman whipping a cow. The cow was hobbled, unable to walk properly. The woman whipped the cow for not walking. If there hadn't been a language barrier, I would have suggested removing the hobble so the cow could walk. I felt sorry for the cow. Other countries don't have the same compassion for animals as the United States. It can be upsetting at times. Cooling down, we got on our bikes and rode the final hundred miles to Fez.

Our five-star hotel was glamorous, and we were dirty. Morning came quickly. The gates of Fez were grand displays of ancient architecture as we insignificantly entered them. We felt like commoners, strolling the cobblestone streets lined with trendy boutiques. We could smell the tanneries from blocks away. The tanneries are one of the biggest attractions in Fez. Chouara Tannery is the largest and oldest. Built in the eleventh century, it uses the same methods of softening the hides as it did then. Large stone vessels are filled with colored dyes mixed with cow urine, pigeon feces, quicklime, salt, and water. The hides are soaked in the vessels for a couple days, then transferred to wooden caldrons, where they're tumbled for a couple more days to soften the hides. We felt the brittle hides drying in the sun. The whole process hasn't changed since inception and is totally manual, no machines. The horrendous smell pierced my nose with an invisible yellow haze.

We searched the town for a cafe to have a beer. Muslims are nondrinkers. Like Colombia during an election, we were served beer in paper cups. Hashish and kief, concentrated cannabis, was offered by most every person we came in contact with, creating a conundrum. Even tour guides at historic sites solicited us.

Our last city in Morocco until the ferry back to Spain was Chefchaouen, a predominantly Jewish refugee town. After Spain asked Jewish people to leave, some fled to Chefchaouen in northern Morocco. The short story is this: it's a mountain town painted blue, because blue is the color of the Jews. Jews were indigo traders and liked to paint buildings blue to advertise the beauty and to match the sky. The blue walls of buildings curved into the blue pathways in a smooth fashion. It was fun to wander the town and browse the many shops selling local handicrafts. Narrow staircases led us to hidden shops and cafes, making it easy to get lost. We had dinner at our hotel in the main square of Chefchaouen.

When the owner waited on us, he warned me against visiting Algeria, my next country. "The military government there is not safe," he said. He showed us his rifle he used in a civil war in Morocco and warned us not to talk to anyone in town. It was the start of the Arab Spring, and he was paranoid.

I wasn't sure why he was so paranoid. Currently a Jewish town, Chefchaouen has changed ruling religions many times, and perhaps he feared that it was going to happen again.

"*Shukraan,*" I said, thanking him.

He corrected me. "We speak Hebrew here. It's *toda*."

The next morning, Randy was headed back to Spain, and I was headed to Portugal. We waved goodbye to each other, riding on the freeway at fifty miles per hour. As we diverged, I had a sad feeling. I knew I'd miss our laughs and joking around. He was a great traveler and open for new adventures. I looked forward to him joining me again.

Dear Randy,

Thank you for the laughs and camaraderie. You are a true friend. I look forward to riding with you again.

Sincerely,
Little Bobby

I rode four hours back to the family farm in Portugal and the welcoming warmth of my Portuguese *familia*. They were surprised I survived Morocco and called me crazy for wanting to tour Algeria next.

All the uncles and cousins said, "Morocco is okay, but Algeria is not!"

I had to see for myself.

Algeria

2012

Mileage: 54,000

Ingredients: one teaspoon ipecac syrup, one glass of water, one bucket

The 1,600-kilometer land border between Morocco and Algeria has been closed since 1994 due to deadly attacks and political disputes. To cross into Algeria from Morocco, I needed a ferry back to Spain, then a different ferry to Algeria. Unfortunately, that's the only way I could do it.

On the ferry from Almeria, Spain, to Ghazaouet, Algeria, I met a thirty-year-old Algerian man traveling with his wife and daughter. He helped me with the entry procedures into Algeria. He was so kind to invite me for dinner, but our plans went afoul with the chaos of disembarkation. I rode out of the port customs area into the slums of Ghazaouet looking for him. I was afraid to stop in the mess of poverty, the impoverished dirt streets lined with decrepit shacks with shredded awnings dangling from roofs, barred windows, and groups of electrical cables running pole to wilting pole.

I needed some Algerian dinars, but there were no signs of a bank or ATM among the dusty businesses selling knockoff Nikes and carnival stuffed animals. On the outskirts, I referenced my paper map to see how far to the next town. Usually I can plug the nearest ATM into my GPS. However, Algeria is paranoid of spies mapping out their country's oil reserves, military establishments, and anything else Google Maps would provide. They're frozen in decades-old battles between their neighbors and countrymen, oblivious to modern internet capabilities.

It was hard to determine how far the next town was. I folded my map and put it back in the clear sleeve of my tank bag.

Forty-five miles into Algeria with no money and no GPS, I stopped roadside. I was unsure how to get out of this quandary. I had no money, no GPS, no food, and no idea how to fill my gas tank. Across the road, an Arab man with robe and keffiyeh waved frantically. I tried to ignore him, but he approached and grabbed me. He escorted me to an outdoor table on the porch of a convenience store. The table was full of Algerian Arab men sitting in plastic chairs. Algeria was under French rule until July 5, 1962, and the default language is French.

I introduced myself, struggling with my Franglish, worse than my Spanglish. *Bonjour* to all and a smile broke the ice. Soon I was showing them videos of an annual party my friends and I hold in the Arizona desert, called "Desert Party." The video was of me blowing up a state fair stuffed animal with my cannon.

They laughed and passed my phone around the table. Eventually, the conversation turned to careers.

"I'm an airline pilot," I told them.

Largg, the man in charge, said, "I'm a fighter pilot in the Algerian Air Force."

He showed me pictures of him flying his Russian MiG-29, and we struck a common bond of devotion to our craft.

I spent an hour with the men. They shared bread, water, and smiles with me. My apprehension dwindled with every act of kindness they offered. I felt relaxed in the company of my perceived enemies, turned friends. My lesson learned was don't prejudge anyone or anything. Your prejudice can be opposite to actuality.

It was time for me to go. Largg owned the convenience store and gas station. He led me to the gas pumps and filled my tank.

"I have no money!" I told him.

"It's a gift, brother," he said.

I had a pair of white Oakley sunglasses that I gave him. He put them on and smiled like an Arab man wearing a new pair of hip Oakley shades. Interestingly, gas in Algeria in 2012 was seventy-two cents a gallon. Now in 2020, it's thirty-two cents a gallon.

"Where is an ATM?" I asked.

Largg and his buddies got in their cars, and as if in a parade lineup, I followed the three cars to a bank in town. Unfortunately, the ATM wasn't international. I thanked Largg and his buddies and set out for Algiers.

Dear Largg,

Thank you for coaxing me to your kindness. You are a caring man. I hope your life is filled with happiness and content.

Sincerely,
Robert

The kindness and friendship Largg showed me proved there are good people all over the world. I had left the security of my Portuguese family for the feared and questionable land of Algeria. Faced with difficulty, I was shown generosity and fellowship from these Algerian Arab men. But my euphoric feeling was about to die.

Recipe: Place the bucket in front of you. Have the glass of water ready. Swallow the teaspoon of ipecac syrup. Chase it with water. Moments later, you will fill the bucket with the worst feeling in the world.

As I entered the city limits of Oran, I saw a huge statue of the world. I love maps and globes. Rounding the traffic circle, I snapped a picture of the world statue with my waterproof camera that hung around my neck. Next, I needed local currency.

I sniffed out a bank to withdraw some Algerian dinars. As I parked my motorcycle in front of the bank, two police cars and one armored vehicle trapped me. Policemen jumped out, yelling at me. Shocked and unsure what I had done wrong, I pleaded for an explanation. A crowd of spectators had gathered.

I yelled desperately to the crowd in English, "Please, anyone, help me! Tell me why they're arresting me."

No response from the bystanders.

My Franglish is limited, so I switched to Spanglish. "Why have the police stopped me?" I asked one man. "Is it my Algerian visa? Is it my international insurance?"

"They think you're a spy," he said.

The two police officers tried pushing me into the armored vehicle. The bars on the windows looked impenetrable. I objected to this with physical force, shaking their hands and arms loose. If I'm separated from my motorcycle and gear, I die. My motorcycle is my lifeblood. My subconscious hung from the lamppost above, glad to be separate from my fear. They insisted I be taken to the station for questioning. Since the crowd of bystanders presented an obvious security risk to my motorcycle and gear, the officers agreed to a convoy to the station, squeezing me with their bumpers.

Two officers on either side escorted me into the police station, down a hallway, and into the office of the commandant. I sat in front of a beautiful grand desk flanked by flags. In walked a powerful short man, adorned in braided gold ropes, colorful shoulder boards, and with a chestful of medals Muammar Gaddafi would have envied. He introduced himself as head of some kind of national security department.

His broken English was hard to understand. Clearly, he wanted to demonstrate his knowledge of my native language as he struggled to speak. "I have reviewed your background and visa documents. I have questions about your visit to my country."

"I'm here as a tourist curious about your country's rich history, and I'm willing to cooperate fully," I responded.

"Give me your camera," he demanded, making sure the sunlight glared off his chestful of medals. He hastily turned the camera on. "This camera records GPS coordinates, yes?"

"Yes, sir, but it doesn't provide navigation, so it's not like a normal GPS."

"That wasn't my question!" he exclaimed.

I thought this to be unusual, knowing Algeria was a conservative Muslim country, I tried to remember what pictures were in my camera. Then I realized I had snapped a photo of roadside prostitutes soliciting truckers in Spain, who flipped me off. This could be some kind of Algerian pornography violation. But how could they know this? How could they know what pictures I had taken? My camera has GPS. I concluded that somehow, they had hacked into it.

Scrolling through my pictures, the commandant exclaimed, "Yes, that's it! Take him away."

Two officers rushed me to another building. They placed me in a small cell with four metal chairs and slammed the door.

Minutes later, a muscle-bound black-T-shirt-wearing guy barged into my cell, accompanied by two nerdy guys carrying laptops. The black-T-shirt guy sat in the steel chair opposite me. To begin the interrogation, he calmly lit a cigarette and blew the smoke in my face.

"This is a required interrogation," he said. He motioned one laptop guy to show me a website they had found.

The website was for the Kindness Quest I had done in 2009. I admitted it was mine.

Then he showed me another website that featured my father, who was a navy pilot. "This is you, military?" He pointed to the screen with his muscles flexed.

"No, that's my father," I said.

He showed another website of my uncle, who was also a navy pilot. I have the same name as my uncle.

Mr. Black T-shirt said, "This is you, navy pilot?" as the vein in his bicep created a shadow.

"No, it's my uncle."

He reconfirmed I was in fact a pilot.

"I'm a commercial pilot, not a military pilot," I clarified.

The three men stormed out of the cell.

Ten minutes later, the door swung open again. After a few hours of Mr. Black T-shirt blowing smoke in my face while questioning me, I was terrified.

"You are a pilot, correct?" he asked me several times. "Why are you in my country? What is your purpose traveling the world? Why do you have no family with you? Why don't you have children? Are you Muslim? Why are you not Muslim?"

I got thirsty, but they said no food or water until I answered all their questions. I was told a toilet would be available after the required information was obtained from me.

We had a language and communication barrier. I requested contact with the United States embassy.

"I don't know what you mean," he said.

"I would like to call my embassy."

Again he denied me, violating international law.

My anxiety increased. "I would like to leave," I said.

"This is not pus-e-bull," Mr. Black T-shirt said.

I had never been detained and held against my will. I was frantic with fear. We seemed to be at a stalemate as they left my cell.

Alone, I turned on my new satellite communications device. The new emergency locator allowed me to type a message on my phone, then send it via satellite. I stuck my arm through the bars of my cell window for unobstructed sky to acquire a satellite signal. Unfortunately, my phone battery died before it could connect with the emergency device. My heart was beating like a machine gun firing. Sweat beaded on my forehead. My palms became so hot and clammy, they pruned up.

I'm used to emergency procedures, and I formulated my "escape plan." I had sewn a left sleeve pocket on my riding jacket, where I keep a non-lethal tactical pen. This disguised weapon was equipped with a handcuff key, a fire starter, a whistle, a glass breaker, and a sharp, pointed end called a "DNA Catcher" that can be used to stab someone. My plan was that during a toilet break, I would fake left but go right, wielding my tactical pen, ready to disable any objectors to my escape. I would run down the hallway to my motorcycle on the street, key ready, and zoom off, riding a tight twisty route through town, losing anyone attempting to follow me. That was my emergency procedure I would use if needed.

Prior to a big game, athletes can become so nervous they vomit. I had never been that nervous, except for that day in the Algerian jail cell. The nerves in my knotted belly rolled slowly north to my throat, touching my tonsils like a steamroller. I realized what was going to happen. I was going to vomit. I slapped myself across the face and tried to listen to my inner voice. *You'll get through this. Get hold of yourself. Calm down. Breathe.* I had endured Bolivia. I could endure this.

At that moment Mr. Black T-shirt burst through my cell door. His demeanor was more amicable. He explained the reason for my detention. They found on my camera a picture of a military establishment, including GPS coordinates.

"I didn't do this."

He produced my camera and the picture I had snapped of the world statue. Behind the statue was a military base. Pro tip: don't photograph Algerian military bases.

He deleted my picture and handed me postcards of the city to replace the deleted picture. "You're free to go," he said.

I had a weird feeling of gratitude toward Mr. Black T-shirt. I believe it was the "Stockholm syndrome," when a victim feels gratitude toward a captor when released. I was on the bike and outta there in an instant.

It wasn't until late that night that I could relax. That day had been a swing of emotions, going from the warmth and kindness of Largg to being detained and accused of being a spy. Each experience on this world tour taught me something. This one taught me to always remain calm, and when things are at a breaking point, press on to overcome the adversity.

The next day on the north coast of Algeria, with great views of the Mediterranean Sea, the highway ended. On a detour, I skidded off the road and slid down a ditch. Unable to get my motorcycle back onto the road, I hiked a kilometer to the highway for help. Two Algerian men walked the kilometer back to where my bike was down in the ditch. It took all three of us to upright my bike and push it up onto the gravel road. I thanked the two and offered them money.

They refused compensation. "Enjoy Algeria brother," they said.

For me, Algeria was a roller coaster of emotions—pleasant, painful, pleasant. Back on the main road, I made good time.

That night, I saw two veiled Arab women in my hotel lobby, each with their right-hand fingers removed from the palm, leaving only the thumb. It's a common penalty for theft in the Arab world. This was a shocking example of the harsh reality of justice in some countries. The United States justice system has its faults, but I'd rather have our system than any other around the world.

Tunisia

2012

Mileage: 55,000

Ingredients: four ounces ketchup, four arm slings, four head bandages, four pair of crutches, one large tray of bite-sized treats, one clock

I rode ten hard hours from Jijel, Algeria, to Bizerte, Tunisia. The eastern part of Algeria is more lush and prettier. I climbed on top of a mountain and looked over the border into Algeria. I was glad to have made it out virtually unharmed. I found a five-star hotel in Bizerte.

In my room's bathroom mirror, I photographed bleeding saddle sores on my bum once again. The pain made me question why I had this burning desire to ride my motorcycle around the world. I had survived near-death experiences, followed by extreme pleasure. I never took for granted my exposure to danger around every corner could change my fortune instantly. My travel experience covered the spectrum of emotions. I learned to deal with the ups and downs. I felt stronger knowing things always turn around and get better. If I were to identify the point I first learned to make lemonade out of lemons, it would be as a boy growing up and being told by my mother to make the best of everything. She always saw the bright side of things, the silver lining in every cloud.

In the beginning, if I had known how difficult this ride around the world would be, I have to admit I wouldn't have been strong enough, smart enough, nor rich enough to complete the endeavor. The obstacles I overcame along the way gave me strength and confidence to endure the pain and savor the pleasures. With the lessons my mom taught me ringing in my ears, I had persevered and knew I would complete this journey.

Recipe: You and three friends wrap your heads with bandages.

Spray one ounce of ketchup on each. The four of you put your arms in slings. Use the crutches to move yourselves around a hotel lobby. Imagine another hotel guest sees the four of you. What kind of review do you think that hotel guest would write on Trip Advisor?

It's a one-hour ride from Bizerte to the capital city, Tunis. I scouted out the airport, then a place to keep my motorcycle for a month. The first hotel I tried was broken down and nasty. The second was not a hotel at all. The third was out of business. I was riding sixty-five miles per hour near the airport when out of the corner of my eye, I spotted a sign: *Hotel Cesar*. I did a U-turn and went down the wrong way on a one-way street. I parked in front of the hotel next to a beautiful Porsche Cayenne, a rare vehicle in Tunisia. I walked down the hallway to the front desk. Sweaty and dirty, I asked for a room.

Without checking, the front desk guy quickly said no.

Sensing his hasty response, I figured I was not the caliber guest they catered to. Dejected, I turned and walked back down the hallway to the front door.

A nice-looking man dressed in a European tailored suit and carrying a briefcase approached me as I exited the front doors. We greeted each other.

"Do they have rooms?" he asked me.

"I was told they had no rooms," I said, "perhaps because of my scruffy appearance."

"No," he said. "It's because Europeans are complaining about the recent guests."

Assessing the situation, I asked the fine gentleman, "Is that your Porsche parked out front?"

"Yes."

"Do you have something to do with the management of this hotel?" I asked.

"Yes, I own it," he said. "My name is Kaifer."

He went on to explain the current situation in Tunisia and why I was denied a room. The Arab Spring was fading by mid-2012. The ousting of

Muammar Gaddafi in Libya and control of that country was the current local conflict. The wounded Libyan freedom fighters came to Tunis for medical care, since Libya had virtually none. The interim Libyan government agreed to pay Kaifer $700 per refugee per month, so he housed four fighters per room, making it extremely profitable. The lobby area became filled with young men on crutches, their bandaged heads bleeding and their arms in slings, making it appear more like a hospital emergency room rather than a three-star hotel lobby. For this reason, European guests would write bad reviews on Trip Advisor. Kaifer therefore instructed his front desk staff to deny any European guests.

"Do the fighters hold animosity toward me, being an American?" I asked. "It could have been a US bomb that injured them."

"They're fighting for the same interests as the United States," he said.

About that time, I popped the question to Kaifer. "Can I park my motorcycle here for a month?"

"No," he said, "but you can park it at my private residence."

We then set off for his home. I followed the shiny Porsche to an affluent Tunis suburb. The guard at Kaifer's residential compound opened the gates, and we entered. Kaifer signaled me to ride farther past the pool area down to the servants' quarters. What a sensational setup! I embraced the warm welcome and hospitality.

Kaifer invited me in for a bite to eat. His home was very Muslim, with gathering rooms for events as you walked in. There were several sitting areas with long couches and pillows used for Ramadan celebrations. He had a huge hammam, a large steam room typical of North Africa. Throughout history, public hammams were the only place commoners could bathe and scrub, since private bathrooms in a house were considered a luxury.

Kaifer's brother, Sala, was impeccably dressed in a shiny royal-blue slim-fitting dress shirt with flat front slim-fitting dress pants with a wide leather belt, and pointy-toed brown leather shoes. He wore an expensive Raymond Weil watch and had meticulously trimmed hair. The three of us sat down to a spread of fruits, vegetables, meats, and sweets fit for an entire army. The servants were in the kitchen. If we needed anything, Kaifer would clap his hands twice and a servant would rush out for instructions.

The servants each wore puffy harem pants, with puffy-sleeved shirts tucked into a sash belt that made me think they were actors in an Arabian movie.

Sala also owned a chain of hotels, mostly in London. We discussed the importance of attention to detail, especially smells when you enter a hotel lobby. Sala and I debated the United States's participation in Libya and other world events. That night, Sala took me out for dinner to one of his restaurants. We debated the entire night, interrupted only by introductions to his friends, who said hello.

After a night of dining in Tunis's best restaurant, Sala drove me back to Kaifer's hotel, where he arranged a large comfortable suite for me to spend the night. He instructed the staff to attend to my every need. I felt unworthy of such VIP treatment.

With my motorcycle parked securely in Kaifer's guarded walled compound, I felt confident leaving it for a month.

~ ~ ~

Recipe: At sunrise, place the large tray of bite-sized treats and the clock on a dining room table. Sit at the table, staring at the tray. Don't eat anything the entire day. Feel your hunger biting inside. Imagine people less fortunate than you and their hunger. Feel compassion for them. Use the clock to count down the minutes until sunset. At sunset, take a bite of a treat. Appreciate the taste, texture, and satisfaction it provides.

Upon my return to Tunisia, my bike was exactly where I had left it and in perfect condition. Kaifer had a huge tray of ornate bite-sized delicacies with several types of fresh juices prepared and ready. Kaifer, his wife, kids, and sister were there. None of them ate any of the delicious treats because it was Ramadan, when Muslims fast sunrise to sunset for thirty days.

Ramadan is also a time for encouraging the rich to give to the poor. Kaifer had accommodations for poor people coming to his compound in need during Ramadan. A small door on the large gate allowed the entry of one person, who could receive gifts Kaifer gave them. I related this to Christian tithing. All religions have good ideas. I'd like to take the best of all those ideas and create my own religion. I will do that someday when I'm ruler of the ROB, Republic of Bob.

The next night, I stayed at the Africa Jade four-star hotel. Calm waves meandered on the hotel's beach. What I found unusual was that Muslim women went into the water, covered head to toe with their hijab. It must be very difficult to swim, perhaps like swimming in a bed of seaweed tangling your limbs.

I packed for the ferry trip to Sicily.

Europe

Sicily

2012

Mileage: 56,000

Ingredients: one oven, one oven mitt

On the ferry from Tunisia to Palermo, Sicily, I booked a presidential suite and slept well. I woke up to the public address system announcing our arrival at Palermo. The customs and immigration procedures were conducted on board the ferry, mainly because a lot of illegal immigrants choose this ferry route for easy entry to Europe. With hundreds of tightly squeezed people waiting to disembark, it took three hours for the one official to process all the passports. Eventually, I was allowed entry with my motorcycle.

> Recipe: Preheat the oven to 150 degrees. Reach into the oven without the oven mitt on. Put the oven mitt on and reach into the oven. Which can you tolerate? The oven mitt protects and insulates.

Sicily was experiencing a heat wave. Why would an adventure rider choose to wear a thick, heavy jacket when the outside air temperature was 110 degrees Fahrenheit? I tested this theory of riding with and without my big insulated adventure-riding jacket. The heavy and vented jacket is protection from road abrasions, and it provides insulation. I rode the entire day wearing only a thin Under Armour long-sleeved shirt. At the end of the day, I had heat stroke. It felt like a trillion heated needles pricking my body. I couldn't cool off. Moral of the story: wear the big and bulky riding jacket. Think of it as an oven mitt.

Sicily is small and historic, with ornate architecture built with pride by craftsmen of yesteryear. Each building, be it business or residence, held great design details that are uncommon in present architecture. This increased my appreciation of the historic buildings of Sicily.

Short ride through Sicily, then onto a ferry to Italy.

Eastern Europe

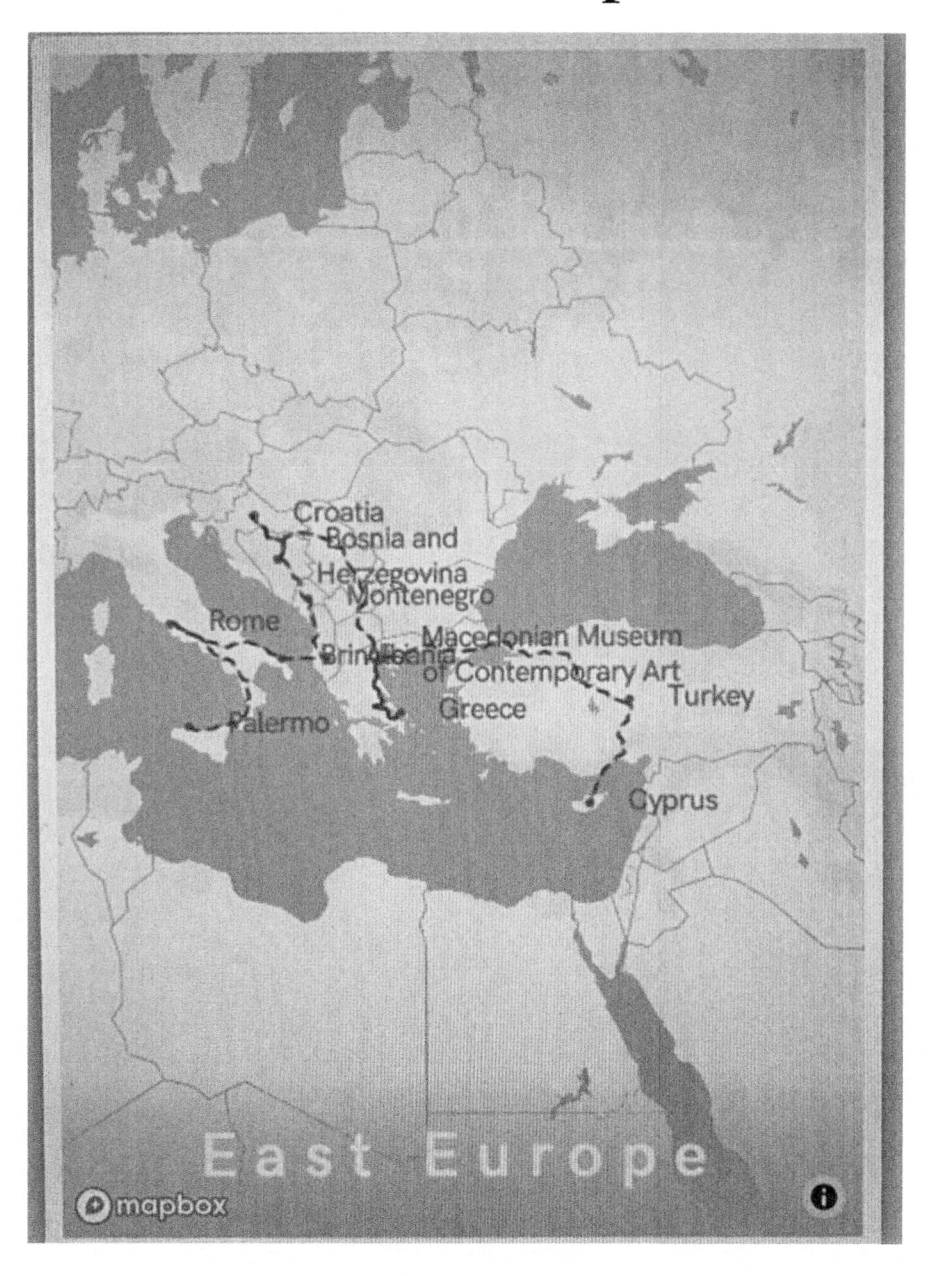

Approximate route

Italy

2012

Mileage: 56,000

Ingredients: one baptism, one box of tissues, one glass of wine

My first night in Italy, I camped in a vineyard. I saw the owner walking up his driveway and asked, "May I camp on your land?"

"Yes," he said with a smile. "I will even bring you breakfast in the morning."

It was a perfect setting, surrounded by mountains and grapevines lined up in neatly spaced rows. Lush green grass softened the sleeping area. In the morning, the farmer brought eggs, toast, and hot Italian coffee.

Riding up the Amalfi Coast was like watching a slideshow of postcards. Everywhere I looked was picturesque, with multilevel stacked houses painted different colors, built vertically up the mountainside with the blue Mediterranean Sea as the foundation. It was hard to concentrate on the twisty seaside road and take in the scenery, so I stopped often to photograph and admire the magnificence of the area.

> Recipe: Attend a baptism ceremony. When the baby is christened, use the box of tissues to dry your tearing eyes. Raise the glass of wine and toast the name of the baby.

At every photo stop, I'd hear Italians say one word clearly: "On-d-ah-mo!" Again and again, the only perceptible word I recognized was on-d-ah-mo. I had to consult my Italian-English dictionary to see what this fantastic word meant. I thumbed the dictionary as kids yelled it, parents yelled it, Vespa-riding teenagers yelled it. Surrounded by a blurred motion of people but audible clarity of voices, I couldn't find the spelling in my dictionary.

Like an aggressive detective questioning witnesses on the crowded boardwalk, I entered a small ice-cream store. Behind the glass counter was an authentic Italian guy wearing a pointy soda-jerk hat, offering every flavor of gelato imaginable. "Señor, what's this word 'on-d-ah-mo' mean?" I asked.

His laughter turned smile confirmed the magic of the word. "It's a great word," he said. "It means, '*Let's go!*'"

Instantly, I decided the name of my motorcycle. That warm, sunny day on the Amalfi Coast, *Andiamo* was born. I held a small ceremony in my mind. In his baptism, he was wrapped in a blanket, caressed in my arms. I tilted him backward, dunked his headlight in gelato, and said, "I christen thee *Andiamo*."

Henceforth, my motorcycle was Andiamo!

~ ~ ~

The town of Amalfi has always been my first choice to spend a night on the Amalfi Coast. The three-star Hotel Amalfi is my preferred hotel. It was once a pasta factory, now a hotel. It's moderately priced and the only hotel right on the water. You can step out your door and swim in the Mediterranean on a clean, private beach. It's far enough from the hustle and bustle, but close enough to walk into town for dinner. Dinner out is like a fashion show with smartly dressed, stylish people, all from different areas of the world, eating at cute little outdoor cafes, sipping red wine and chatting about everything while looking up at centuries-old buildings built in beautiful coves.

The Hotel Amalfi is also the only hotel in the area that offers underground parking. I asked Giuseppe, one of the owners, if I could leave Andiamo in his covered parking area. I was delighted to hear his answer.

"Si, señor!"

Awesome guy. Andiamo covered and tucked comfortably in an underground parking area, I started my trek back home.

To avoid traffic congestion, the fastest route to exit the Amalfi Coast is by boat. I hopped a fishing boat to Salerno, then a train to Rome. I set a personal record for touring Rome's biggest attractions: the Colosseum, the Roman Forum, the Pantheon, the Trevi Fountain, the Spanish Steps, Vatican City, St. Peter's Square, Castel Sant'Angelo, and Roman aqueducts all in one hour and fifty minutes on a rented Vespa from Bici & Baci. Then a flight home to work for a month.

Back in the States, I was faced with new challenges to maintaining this world expedition, which had become my way of life. It caused the demise of several relationships. If I met someone, the first two questions I would ask were "Do you like motorcycles?" and "Do you like to travel?"

I learned my style of travel and what my life was about didn't appeal to everyone. It requires a certain level of wanderlust, the lust to wander the world experiencing everything life has to offer. It may seem like an easy and attractive characteristic. Unfortunately, it's difficult to find someone who truly is a modern world gypsy.

Girlfriends didn't understand my goal of riding around the world. The ride was more important than anything or anyone in my life. Some women could appreciate my endeavor, and others couldn't accept my commitment to traveling for two weeks every other month.

I took a train back down to Amalfi and was reunited with my friend. Andiamo was covered in dust and looking tired from all the Amalfi splendors. I cleaned him off and headed eastbound.

I don't always visit the east side of Italy, the Adriatic coast. One town I had horrific memories of was Brindisi. In the '80s as a college student on my study abroad semester, Amsterdam was a frequent weekend destination for recreation. I was never a huge indulger, but I had carried a small amount of a questionable substance hidden in a secret compartment in my backpack for a special occasion. I traveled Europe's borders in and out with no problem.

On one ferry crossing from Yugoslavia to Brindisi, I was walking down the gangplank of the ferry. The customs officials had all the passengers' bags lined up. I had just seen the movie *Midnight Express* and feared a terrible outcome. I tried to blend in with the older travelers. The police instructed me to put my backpack in the lineup, and all the passengers were ushered away. The police brought in dogs, who sniffed up and down the rows of luggage. Immediately, a dog hit on my bag. No other bags were singled out.

The officers took my bag and called out for the owner. With a slight pause for contemplation, I reluctantly claimed ownership of the backpack. I was led to a private room with my backpack sitting on an inspection table. The officers completely emptied my bag. They went through pages in my books, emptied my toothpaste tube, and searched everywhere. While they searched my backpack, another dog raced over to my bag, signaling a positive to the handler. He had his nose pasted to my secret compartment in my backpack. I was terrified, with visions of an Italian prison and the unfair treatment Billy Hayes had received in that Turkish prison. They pulled the dog away. After they had torn my bag apart and found nothing, I was let go without further incident. I discarded the problem as soon as I could.

Here's an explanation: I attribute the officer's oversight to a technical fact. In 1978, the original patent on Velcro expired. Wide use of hook-and-loop fastening wasn't yet commonplace. My secret compartment featured a Velcro strap covering the internal frame of my backpack, a perfect hidden compartment to unaware officers.

Andiamo carried me to the east coast port city of Bari. I hopped a ferry across the Adriatic Sea to Albania.

Albania

2012

Mileage: 57,000

Ingredients: fourteen C-Band satellite dishes, one square mile of land

Recipe: Place fourteen C-Band satellite dishes upside down, equally spaced within the one square mile. It resembles the surface of a pockmarked golf ball. Imagine yourself walking through the one square mile cluttered with the huge satellite dishes. Now imagine snipers under each satellite dish.

One common sight in Albania was large cement disks every few hundred yards, sometimes clustered in groups. The disks were heavy concrete lids about ten feet in diameter placed on top of underground concrete cylinders with access slots, for military purposes. As I rode by the bunkers, I envisioned snipers aiming at Andiamo and me. It was an eerie feeling thinking how a country needed so many military outposts, seemingly for intimidation.

Research revealed the bunkers were built during the Communist government of Enver Hoxha from the '60s to '80s. He had a total of 173,371 bunkers built, averaging fourteen bunkers per square mile. Literally everywhere, from empty country roads to city centers, they were never used for their intended purpose. The cost of construction drained Albania's economy.

The collapse of Ponzi scheme investments in 1997 also contributed to the demise of Albania. People had invested their life savings in unproven new companies promising great returns. When twenty-five such schemes collapsed, the people were left penniless and hungry.

In a despondent state, I rode north to the town of Shkoder, famous for the centuries-old legend of Rozafa Castle. Perched high on a hill, the castle is the most prominent feature of the area.

According to legend, three brothers were trying to build a castle. Each night, the walls of the castle would fall down. The brothers sought the advice of an elder in the community. The elder's resolution: swear on *besa*, which is Albanian for "word of honor," not to tell your wives. He said the wife who brings lunch the next day must be sacrificed and buried in the walls of the castle to keep them from falling down.

That night, the two eldest brothers quietly told their wives about the plan. The younger brother kept his besa. The next day, the three brothers anxiously awaited lunchtime. When Rozafa, the youngest brother's wife, walked up with a basket of lunch, the young brother told her the deal. She was to be sacrificed and buried in the walls of the castle.

She agreed under these conditions: that her right eye, her right arm, her right foot, and her right breast be exposed from the wall so she could see, caress, walk with, and feed her infant son. "May my son become a great hero and ruler of the world," she said, her last words.

So goes the legend of Rozafa Castle. After walking the grounds searching for exposed body parts but finding none, I headed north to Montenegro.

Montenegro

2012

Mileage: 57,000

Ingredients: one Albanian besa, one French double agent, one US Navy lieutenant

Recipe: Tell a secret to the French double agent. Tell the same secret to the US Navy lieutenant. Make them swear on an Albanian besa not to tell anyone else. Wait one month. Guess which one held to his besa.

I have three stories about my tour of Montenegro I'd like to share with you.

The First Story: Part One

In 2007, before this around-the-world motorcycle ride started, I took a trip to Vietnam to explore the country for two weeks. As I was walking down a street in Da Nang, I passed a pristine 1960s US Army jeep outfitted with all the US military equipment. It was parked in front of an outdoor cafe, where a man wearing a loose linen shirt, khaki pants, and tortoiseshell sunglasses sat alternating between sipping a cup of coffee and smoking a cigarette.

I approached the man and said, "Excuse me, is that your jeep?"

"*Oui*," he replied, his nose raised and his head turned in arrogance. He was outwardly French.

"Bonjour," I said. I needed to learn more about this enigmatic man.

"I'm Herve," he said. "Hop in the jeep, and let's go."

We whisked off to his compound. Speeding through the streets, scattering villagers, he seemed unconcerned about running over one. Heels of fleeing people barely missed the jeep's wheels. Herve flicked his cigarette with his thumb, blowing smoke over his shoulder, skidding around corners with a smile.

Two miles outside Da Nang, we came to rest at his compound parking area. We entered the bamboo-fenced yard, with three ancillary grass huts on stilts and one central large home with covered patio. Near the patio was a sectioned off area with a sign: *Distillerie Clandestine*. I was yet to fully comprehend the duplicity of the name for his personal distillery.

The outdoor patio had indoor couches, like a bachelor pad. As I sat on a couch, a monkey jumped on my shoulders, grasping my hair with both hands, gyrating like a fraternity pledge on his maiden voyage. The monkey was one of many exotic pets Herve possessed.

Herve sat down on a couch opposite me, and in his French accent, formally introduced himself. "I am Major Herve Gourmelon. Bonjour. I am a former French military officer." His skeletal hands slid a tin box across the table, full of strange devices. "Do you like opium?"

Laughing, I replied, "I have a career that requires random drug tests. I don't partake."

Major Herve Gourmelon had a strong propensity to partake. The effects of prolonged drug use were painfully evident on his frail body. "Me, my father, and my grandfather were career military officers in the French Foreign Legion," he said. Herve was intelligent and had graduated from Saint-Cyr, the elite military academy in France.

I walked the musty, cluttered house, a museum of military memorabilia, inspecting unique items of war. Muskets and machine guns hung from the walls, while photos of Herve in military uniforms filled in the wall space between swords and knives. Each item had a story, which Herve told. We took pictures of me wearing his old uniform while he fed me shots of his homemade snake wine.

Herve seemed a lonely man needing company. "Let's go out to eat," he said.

As we walked out a small gate in the bamboo fence, I asked, "What are the three huts on stilts used for?"

"I keep my girlfriends in them," Herve replied, "while my wife has a downtown apartment."

My mind computed the mess, like an abacus. His compound was on a river, where he had a blacked-out Jet Ski tied to a dock, like a villain in a Bond film. The outdoor cafe adjoined his property, like it was his personal kitchen. It was a simple cafe on a bamboo platform above the river. Herve spoke to the waiter in Vietnamese, who hung a fishing line in the water and pulled out a big fish. Minutes later, the waiter brought us a platter with the big fish barbecued and sliced. We picked around the bones and organs still in place.

I was astonished when Major Herve Gourmelon revealed he was a French double agent exiled in Vietnam, unable to return to France. My mouth wide open, shocked by the afternoon exchange and doubting every bit of his wild tale, I said, "Bullshit, Herve!"

He portrayed no guilt or innocence, just a fact-filled face. "During the Bosnian War, I gave NATO secrets to the enemy dictator," he admitted. "The night before NATO forces planned the arrest of Bosnian Serb leader Radovan Karadzic for war crimes, I divulged the plans, and the mission failed. I had access to a lot of information, and I leaked it for my own benefit."

"How could you accept personal profit from helping the Beast of Bosnia?" I asked.

"*C'est la vie.*"

Conflicted but fascinated, I listened to him and asked questions.

He continued on. "The *Washington Post* featured an article corroborating my story. Bill Clinton told French president Jacques Chirac, 'You have a snake in the grass.' Jacques conducted a French military investigation and found me, Major Herve Gourmelon, was the snake in the grass, along with another double agent."

Herve was an absorbing individual, having read the Bible, the Koran, and the Torah, and able to speak five languages and carry on several parallel conversations without falter. My mind was adrift with discord as he drove me back to my hotel in his opium-induced haze, without regard for pedestrians.

In the hotel lobby, I asked the concierge for the business center computer to substantiate Major Herve Gourmelon's stories. I found complete verification of his tales, exactly as he told them, including a local one of him forced to adopt a child after killing the mother with his Jet Ski one night in an intoxicated state.

Dear Herve,

If you read this, thank you for the lucky US silver dollar. I still have it. I hope you realize a man is lonely without his country. I will fight for and never betray my country, and that feels good.

Sincerely,
Robert

The First Story: Part Two

The air temperature gauge indicated minus fifty degrees Celsius at thirty-nine thousand feet. To my right was First Officer Mike, who asked, "Where is your next motorcycle ride going to be?"

"Andiamo is on the Amalfi Coast," I said. "I'll return there to ride the Amalfi Coast, Albania, Montenegro…"

He cut me off midsentence. "Montenegro?"

"Yes, why?"

"I flew many navy missions over Montenegro," he said. "I was stationed there for twelve months."

Intrigued, I asked, "What was your most interesting mission?"

"I did a bombing run to destroy the Podgorica Air Base," Mike said. "Radovan Karadzic, the dictator during the war in Bosnia, was alerted of our intentions to destroy his air force. That night, he sheltered his airplanes in a tunnel accessed by a three-kilometer-long taxiway. I bombed the tunnel, trapping the airplanes inside."

This led to the end of the war in Bosnia.

I told Mike I had met a double agent in Vietnam who leaked NATO secrets to Radovan Karadzic during the Bosnian War. Mike and I surmised the double agent, Major Herve Gourmelon, could have compromised Mike's own missions. Another unusual aspect about this story of coincidence: the tunnel Mike bombed was converted into a wine cellar for the Plantaze Vineyard.

"Come hell or high water," I declared, "I'm going to visit the ground you bombed and witness the evolution of bomb site to wine cellar."

In Podgorica, Montenegro, the next month, I searched for the tunnel. It was difficult to find, riding through cornfields and countryside with wrong turns and incorrect directions. I did manage to locate it, but it was closed for the day. What I saw was scarred with biohazard signs posted and crumbled buildings like a typical bomb site. Prominently displayed on the front gates of the entrance was a sign for the Plantaze Vineyard.

I sat on Andiamo a moment to reflect the compound complexities of my visit. I had met the man who bombed the tunnel trying to save the world from genocide. Conversely, I had met the man who personally profited from the furtherance of genocide. The encounters with both men collided in my mind with bewilderment. I thought of "snaky Herve" and "honorable Mike" and how each man should be judged for their actions. Perhaps a "medal for Mike" and for Herve, "life without a country."

Dear Mike,

Thank you for your service. You fought for the betterment of humankind and saved many people from gruesome genocidal death. You should feel tremendous honor for this. I wish peace and happiness to you and your family.

Sincerely,
Captain Dolven

The Second Story

The most expensive hotel I have every stayed in was Sveti Stefan in Montenegro at $2,700 for one night in a private villa. One of my sponsors paid for this extravagance. Brad Pitt and Angelina Jolie had stayed in my villa the month before. The five-star resort is an exclusive 1.2-square-mile private island separated from the mainland by a rock bridge called a tombolo. My villa was part of eight villas forming Queen Maya's summer residence. It was like a private village reserved for dignitaries. I strolled along rock paths with tiny cafes that cater exclusively to guests only. There were two secluded infinity pools overlooking the sea, with large decks and lounge chairs. Very elite and very private, it was once in a lifetime for me.

The Third Story

I had heard about a town called Kotor in Montenegro, a one-hour ride from Podgorica. Sometimes referred to as the "fjords of the Adriatic," it rivals Norway in fjord-like beauty.

That night, I had dinner and chatted with three red-faced jolly locals. The older, roundish men were celebrating life and welcomed an American to their country and table. They taught me the local toast word, *zivjeli* ("cheers" in Bosnian). We hugged, did the European cheek kisses, and shared an evening of mutual respect for happiness and peace on earth. Their having been recently engaged in deadly warfare spiked my compassion for the three men.

As we "yucked it up," I philosophized. "Wars should be fought individual versus individual," I said. "One on one, opposing persons sit down and try to understand each other's differences. Believe me, common ground can be found, even with enemies."

After many toasts with beer and hugs, I walked back to my hotel. The now-drunk men had high-sided their black SUV in the parking lot, stuck until morning.

The Adriatic coast from Montenegro to Croatia isn't as well known as the Amalfi coastal route, but worthy of recognition. Split by lush, steep mountains and blue sea, the road twists through age-old towns, some scarred by wars. It's like a baby Amalfi Coast. I was headed for Dubrovnik, Croatia.

Croatia

2013

Mileage: 58,000

Ingredients: one box of building blocks, one large mallet, one accomplice

As I neared Dubrovnik, Croatia, I could see an outcropping of land with large walls of stone surrounding a city of red-roofed buildings. The road led me through a deep slit in the mountain, with a series of bridges above, then descended into the walled city entrance, defended by a huge wooden drawbridge over a moat, operated by crank-wheels and large chains.

I parked Andiamo and walked across the drawbridge into the grand rock-walled city of Dubrovnik. It felt enclosed by stone, like a modernized cave. The atmosphere was medieval and tranquil as a guitar player's music echoed through the stone hallways. I walked the worn-smooth limestone-paved streets with shops on either side, aged wooden doors and windows displaying goods for sale. Romantic sidewalk cafes gave off aromas decadently tempting me inside.

I noticed each building had carved stone drain spouts protruding from their foundations. Called maskerons, they're made in the shape of owls, gargoyles, and lions. Rainwater is directed down pipes and ejected out the maskeron's mouth. A legend connected to one maskeron depicting an owl, found near the Franciscan monastery, has it that if you can balance on the head of the owl facing the wall, you will be lucky in love. The fine print of this legend states that you must remove your shirt. I'm not sure who started this additional custom, but it's in the guidebooks.

Like a circus tightrope walker, I was atop the eighty-foot-high walls of Dubrovnik, trying not to fall into the Adriatic Sea to my right and the city to my left far below, my arms outstretched for the two-kilometer saunter through time. Originally, the walls were made of wood, some portions still visible through cracks. As technology improved, rocks were used, then chiseled stone blocks, then iron was incorporated. I had a sensational view of the Adriatic Sea and Old Town, with its terra-cotta roofs, historic buildings, and churches. The walls have never been breached, making it one of the most successful defense structures in Europe.

High on the walls, the wind blew steady off the Adriatic. I photographed a beautiful woman gazing into the sunset. Her hair blazed in the wind like flames of passion. Her emerald eyes were like elegant glass spheres. Her smile of complete happiness shadowed the sun. Her beauty was etched in the walls of my mind. My heart melted.

Recipe: Construct a historic city using the building blocks. Pay attention to the details of each structure. Make them architecturally intricate. Hand the large mallet to your accomplice. Instruct him to destroy your project. How does that make you feel?

A map within the walled city displayed dots indicating where mortar shells had exploded in 1991–1992, launched by the Yugoslav People's Army (JNA). I was saddened to think that an army could destroy this stunning UNESCO World Heritage site. I wanted to wrap my arms around the wall's circumference to show my appreciation for its historic magnificence. I met survivors of the bombings.

One sixty-year-old man described what happened. "In November 1991, I had just walked outside my two-hundred-year-old home to check on an elderly neighbor. As soon as I closed my front door, a mortar shell destroyed my home. I lost everything. I was devastated." He showed me a newspaper article detailing the bombing and a picture of him wrapped in a blanket, crying in front of his historic home, now in flames.

I couldn't imagine this man's pain as he watched, defenseless and suffering, his home being destroyed.

Dubrovnik was the destination for that month's ride. Since it was a rather small town, I knew it would be difficult to find a hotel, private residence, or BMW shop to look after Andiamo for a month.

The Hilton Imperial Dubrovnik, imposing and splendid, sits elevated on a hill overlooking the Old Town. I parked Andiamo at the entrance, walked into the lobby, and asked the question.

"Parking is twenty-seven euros per day," the manager said. "Thirty days is eight hundred ten euros just for parking. Come back in an hour, and we can negotiate a more reasonable price."

I returned, and we sat down at a conference table as if at a business meeting. He produced a folder. Inside was a contract stating the terms of my parking in their garage. He reduced the daily rate to five euros and signed off his responsibility for damage or theft of Andiamo. I signed the contract and headed for the airport, home for a month.

Bosnia

2013

Mileage: 59,000

Ingredients: one Olympic dream, one large cauldron, one life

Recipe: Put the Olympic dream and one life in the large cauldron. Simmer for thirty years. The hopes and disappointments evaporate. All that's left is one life to live. Forget past failures, concentrate on future goals, and live each day full of happiness. If you succeed at this, tell me how.

Climbing the mountains into Bosnia, I was sad to leave Dubrovnik. I had visited Bosnia when it was called Yugoslavia and hosted the Sarajevo Winter Olympics in 1984. It was then at age twenty-one that I realized I would never compete in the Olympics as a ski racer.

I come from a "ski family." As a young engineer at Rosemount Engineering, my father helped design the "world's worst" ski boots. Rosemount ski boots were built from a plastic resin material similar to concrete. They were revolutionary, but failed. When I was three, he skied with me between his legs and taught me to balance on the boards. In 1969, after his tragic fatal plane crash, my mother fostered the spirit of skiing in my five-year-old soul. She denied herself new cars and fancy clothes, opting to spend her money on family ski vacations for my brother, sister, and me. Skiing became a way of life.

Ski racing was the only activity I could beat my older brother at. He was five years older than me and only respected me when I won a race. It became my identity, my validation. I desperately craved his acceptance, as he reluctantly filled the void of my father. At age ten, no child should be expected to be a father and a brother, although Tom was. I believe this obligation fermented him into a better husband, father, and brother himself. I didn't recognize these compound complexities until I matured into self-sufficiency.

Ski racing was my only aspiration as a young boy. On school days, my mom wrote notes to the school principal excusing me from class so I could train. I would arrive at the hill a few hours before team practice, set up my own race course, and work it. I dreamt of one day racing in the Olympics. I imagined the love and acceptance Tom would give me with a gold medal around my neck.

The highest level I achieved was fourth place in the 1982 State Ski Championship. I went on to race my freshman year for a college in Colorado. Those guys were good. There were eleven racers on the team; I was number eleven. The top five racers each week were selected to compete in the weekend races. We won the national championship, no help from me.

I loved skiing until Saturday, February 19, 2005, when my brother was killed skiing a Double-Black-Diamond avalanche chute in Colorado. After his death, skiing wasn't the same. I had no one to share the joy with. Part of my physical being was disembodied. My lifelong love of skiing vanished in an instant. I stopped skiing entirely.

The same mind-set that motivated me to ski race motivates me to ride my motorcycle around the world and endure the hardships, safety risks, logistics, financial commitment, and all the other painful possibilities. I know I won't get a trophy at the end, but I need to distinguish myself from other riders. I'm not content unless convinced that I'm not just an ordinary motorcycle rider. I like this about me.

The personal significance of Bosnia left me with mixed emotions: Should I wallow in recognition of failure or head toward sunshine? I decided sunshine was better for me. I took up a southerly heading out of Bosnia into Montenegro, Albania, down through Macedonia, and out to the Greek Islands.

That was my plan.

Macedonia

2013

Mileage: 59,000

Ingredients: one martini shaker, two ounces vodka, plenty of ice

Macedonia's flag is one of my favorites. It features a yellow sun on a red background, with eight broadening rays to the edges. It was adopted in 1995 after the first design caused Greece to impose a year-long embargo on Macedonia. Greece claimed the sun used was a Greek symbol and a registered trademark. Macedonia settled on a more generic sun rather than the Greek sun. This new Macedonian flag was raised high on the flagpole at the border as I approached. Entry procedures were pretty easy and informal.

> Recipe: Pour two ounces of vodka in the martini shaker. Fill with ice. Shake violently for two minutes. Place shaker in freezer for one hour. Remove and feel the sides of the shaker. Pretty frigid. Imagine your body feeling that cold.

I gained altitude, riding up the mountain pass toward Bitola, Macedonia. Fifty miles ahead, my GPS indicated a hotel with a nice name like Mountain View Resort or Riverside Palace Hotel. I don't remember it exactly. I just remember that finding suitable accommodations became a daily event as darkness approached.

The temperature dropped, and it started to snow. I plugged in my heated vest. When I have a goal set, I push, sometimes to my limits. Reaching the town of Bitola and a nicely named hotel was my goal. As the snow accumulated, the flakes, as big as maple leaves, erased the road. I could no longer see the road markings. Gradual slopes, blanketed in white, made the road indiscernible from the soft shoulder. I had to use the tree canopy above to identify where the road went.

Six inches of untracked powder covered the road, then seven, then eight. Ten fresh inches combined with my uncontrollable shivering made it difficult to steer. Not only my arms, but my entire physical being was shivering, rattling the bike. My fanny jiggled the seat, as my helmet shook like a bobblehead. My body could not heat itself. My electric vest set full blast could not combat the cold.

In twelve inches of axle-deep snow, Andiamo stood upright unassisted. It was unquestionably the coldest I had ever been. My trembling arms shook the handlebars like a martini shaker as I commenced a U-turn. I had reached my limit. I could not continue and possibly be stranded high in the mountains of Macedonia in a hypothermic state. I remembered a town at the base of the mountain pass that most likely would have a hotel. My new goal in mind, I descended into relative warmth.

Feeling like a stovetop snowman, I rolled onto the slushy streets of Ohrid, Macedonia, my knees brittle and stiff. I couldn't walk. Mitko, the proprietor of the Hotel Aleksandrija, emerged to see I was struggling. My frozen jaw made it difficult to ask him for a room. I was unable to walk without assistance. Mitko carried my numb, rigid body to a massive fireplace, where I thawed.

In my heated hotel room, I completed my defrost with a scorching shower that restored my pliability.

The hotel had a lakeside terrace and a nice cozy fireside restaurant specializing in wood-fired pizza and red wine. Mitko was my waiter as well. He gave me a lot of information about the town. It was delicious pizza and great conversation. He smiled when he received my tip, which expressed my full gratitude.

The next day, I needed an ATM for some Macedonian currency. To find an international ATM can be a challenge. I rode up and down the streets of Ohrid and eventually found one in an enclosed glass structure. I used my currency translation app to determine the amount of denar I needed. I always withdraw $200 amounts to set a pattern with my bank. I couldn't see the numbers on the faded screen clearly. I thought I pushed 10,000 denar ($175). I accidentally pushed an extra zero, making it 100,000 denar ($1,750). I didn't need all that. At a bank, I attempted an exchange back into US dollars or euros. The bank teller refused, suspicious I'm sure, of me and the origin of the large sum of money.

The need to ride and make my goal of Greece by sunset made me leave town, thinking I could exchange the $1,750-worth of denar somewhere down the road.

That serendipitous deviation (U-turn) back down the mountain pass to experience Ohrid gave me an EAR (Extreme Adrenaline Rush). It made me glow over the now-snowplowed mountain pass into Bitola, which had only one very rundown hotel. If I had made it over the snowy pass the night before, this hotel would have been a disappointment. Instead, I met Mitko and toured a wonderful little town. Sometimes things work out the way they should.

Macedonia and Greece have a contentious relationship, so I tried to be an impartial bystander on this border crossing.

Greece

2013

Mileage: 60,000

Ingredients: $1,265, one butane lighter, one large ashtray

It was a five-hour ride to Keramoti, Greece, where I planned to take a ferry out to the historic Greek island of Thasos. I arrived a little after sunset and checked into a nice hotel that overlooked the ferry port.

It was a short ferry trip to Thasos. Being the off-season, most hotels weren't open. I finally found one open with a traditional Greek bar and restaurant across the street. The bar was packed with Greek men doing shots of ouzo. The waiter delivered trays loaded with small shot glasses full of the licorice-flavored aperitif. I don't think any other drinks were available. The atmosphere was festive and cheery. Heat was provided by a huge natural fireplace, and my table was in front of it. I was still cold from Macedonia. I joined a group of Greek men hovered over a backgammon board. Games can be a great icebreaker. The rules are the same the world over, so connections are easily made. We played, laughed, and drank shots of ouzo until late that night. *Opa!*

> Recipe: Put $1,265 in the ashtray. Spark the butane lighter with a tall flame. Ignite the stack of money. Watch the bills burn. Run your fingers through the ashes, dreaming of what you could have done with $1,265.

Back on the mainland, I rode toward Turkey. I crossed the border, having forgotten to exchange my $1,750-worth of Macedonian denar. I planned to wait until Istanbul. Surely, they would exchange it at the airport. Turned out they didn't accept Macedonian denar at any airport anywhere.

I called my US bank. They wouldn't exchange it. I contacted internet currency exchange sites. They wouldn't do it. I finally called the Macedonian embassy in Washington, DC, to see if any diplomat going to Macedonia was interested in an attractive exchange rate. Yes, one of the consulates was leaving for Macedonia the next week and was interested. Three days later, he called to say his trip was canceled. I carried the Macedonian denar for months.

At every airport currency exchange office, I would ask, "Do you exchange Macedonian denar?"

The answer was always no. Money exchange businesses deal with the common currencies that are valued against the US dollar and readily traded around the world. Unfortunately, no one trades Macedonian denar because it is devalued and the country is somewhat unstable. I considered filing an insurance claim to recover the loss.

Six months later, I was on a flight to Dubai when I met a Macedonian girl headed to Macedonia. "Would you be interested in a very profitable exchange of Macedonian denar for US dollars?" I asked.

She said yes. She didn't have much cash, so between her US dollars, euros, and a few Dirhams, my 1,700 bucks turned into $435. It was better than zero. I had started to fear. Like the Macedonian flag becoming null and void in 1995, what if their currency also became null and void?

Near East

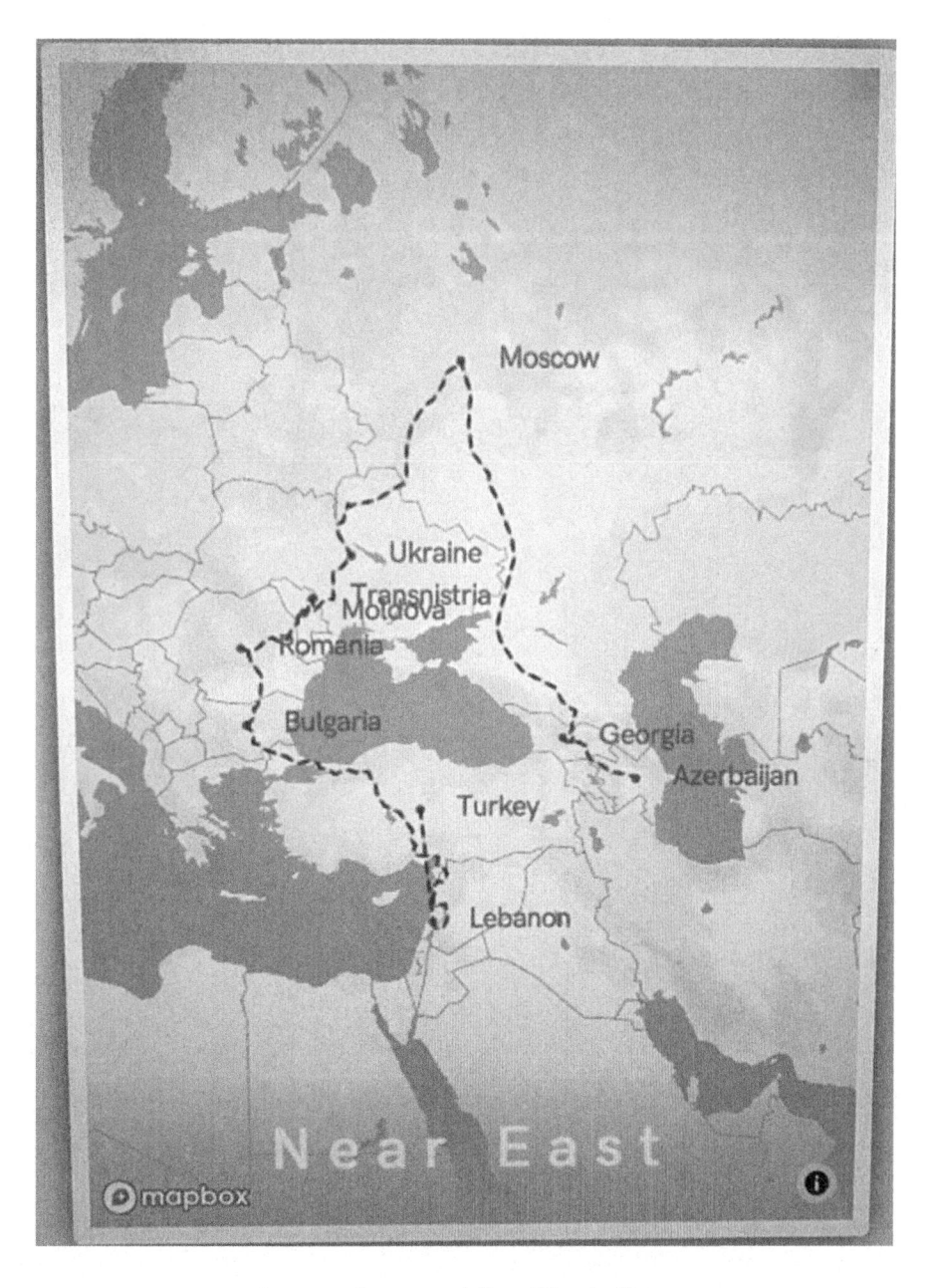

Looped around the Black Sea

Turkey

2013

Mileage: 61,000

Ingredients: one dozen spinning tops, one dance floor

Next time you're driving from Thasos, Greece, to Istanbul, Turkey, I recommend taking the E90. Cross the border into Turkey near Ipsala, then it's a straight shot to Istanbul. Watch out for the speed trap. It's right before the uphill.

Dang that uphill. Andiamo coughed. *Chug, chug, chug.* My boy was a bit under the weather. I didn't know if I could make it to the top. Summiting the hill in the pouring rain felt great because it was all downhill to BMW Istanbul.

I was greeted at the shop by Muhammad, a slender Turkish man with neatly trimmed beard, tight-fitting clothes, and shoes with pointy toes. It was 2:15 p.m., and I was completely drenched. I changed clothes in their dressing room, stuffed my wet gear in my side boxes, and gave my key to Muhammad with a list of items needing attention. Within minutes, I was in a taxi to Istanbul's Ataturk Airport for a 4:15 flight home. I asked the taxi driver, who's name was Muhammad as well, if I looked okay for the airport.

He handed me his personal comb and said, "You better comb your hair."

~ ~ ~

Back at work, I stacked my work flights heavy the first two weeks of the month to have the last two weeks off. The next month, I stacked days off the first two weeks and worked hard the last two weeks. This grueling schedule allowed me time to travel every other month. Colleagues questioned how I endured the self-punishment. Looking back on it, I wonder myself. Mystically motivated, I couldn't wait to continue. My life had become "The Ride."

~~~

On my return to Istanbul, I stopped in Paris for a couple days. I love seeing Paris through the eyes of a Pari-virgin. What made this trip different was that my heart led the way. It didn't matter where I had been or where I was going, my heart was floating on a cloud like a modest mouse. When I saw the Eiffel Tower again for the first time, it seemed to have more detail, more history, and more love. The Latin Quarter sparkled with childlike wonderment. Notre Dame was an enigmatic religious experience.

Eventually I made it to Istanbul. At BMW Istanbul, I was greeted by Muhammad, my service adviser, who immediately had Andiamo front and center. I opened the side boxes to ready my gear—and stared in horror.

I had hastily stored everything wet the month prior. Green mold covered the contents. My leather document folder I handmade at the beginning of my world tour was molded shut, each page a mossy green mess. My rain gear was green, nasty, and smelly. When I tried to put on my gloves, they evaporated into disgusting fragments, floating to the floor. The gloves were eighty-dollar BMW gloves. I laughed, thinking my most expensive BMW gear sometimes was the least reliable. I have since discovered the best alternative gloves. Knucklehead gloves used by US postal workers for ten dollars a pair. I bought five pairs and am currently on my last one. When I find something that works, I stick with it.

Reference Aerostich and Andy Goldfine (the founder) for some of the best motorcycle gear ever made. My favorite piece they've shared is the combat touring boots. I've used many different motorcycle boots, and these are the best. The soles are grippy, like Doc Martens. They're made of high-quality thick leather that rigidly forms to your feet. I got a street-corner shoeshine in Morocco. After the shine, the leather looked brand new. Thank you, Andy, for making the best motorcycle boots in the world.

BMW Istanbul fixed my red warning light that had signaled an ABS fault code since Germany. BMW Nice, France, had wanted $3,374 to fix the fault.

Muhammad at BMW Istanbul said, "Dude, the ABS fault was due to a burned-out light bulb. That'll be twelve bucks."

Dear Muhammad,

Thank you for your honest service and for not exploiting me. I hope you are well.

Sincerely,
Robert

Turkey splits two continents, Europe and Asia. With confidence in a mechanically sound motorcycle, I headed for Asia. Andiamo and I crossed the Bosphorus Bridge from Europe to Asia and replaced forks with chopsticks. I felt like a real world traveler, having ridden seven countries and two continents within two months. Our current destination was Cappadocia, Turkey, home of the fairy chimneys. We had a flawless nine-hour ride to Goreme, the main town, which means, "You cannot see here."

Cappadocia and the fairy chimneys were formed by volcanic eruptions millions of years ago and look like gigantic cones crammed together to form a mountain range. As the lava eroded, tall mounds remained. Fearing persecution, Christians fled to the mounds and chiseled out homes, churches, stables, and sometimes entire cities. Some fairy chimneys are now open to the public. I explored their soft-stone tunnels. Ventilation is provided by holes bored into the depths of the dwelling from the top. I walked, crawled, and climbed through tunnel after tunnel, getting lost in the maze of mountain caves. The soft-stone lava left a powdery dust on my jacket and pants from my scraping the walls.

One tunnel opened up to a huge room like a chapel. I could hear the *ting, ting, ting* of a spoon stirring sugar into a glass of Turkish tea. In the corner was a mustached man wearing a down jacket and Turkish fur hat, sitting quietly on a stool at a small wooden table. He had a burner heating a pot of water and motioned for me to sit down. With generosity, he tinged the spoon on my tiny glass of Turkish tea. We shared silent gestures of friendship, hands over our hearts, bowing our heads, and hands clasped together in a praying fashion. No words were spoken, since we had no common verbal language. He peacefully shined a big Turkish smile, as I bowed to his generosity.

Interacting with the kind stranger in this isolated chapel, sharing only nonverbal signs of acceptance, left me full of gratitude toward different cultures. Moments like that convince me the world is filled with wonderful people, all wanting the same thing in life—happiness. I eventually crawled into sunshine, where Andiamo patiently waited to hear stories from the fairy chimney.

We found a hotel inside the mountain with natural walls, ceilings, and floors carved flat. The walls even had etched details, like a picture hanging. The living area, sleeping area, and bathing area were one continuous cave, air provided by a hole bored to the top of the mountain like a submarine periscope. To avoid the musty cave humidity, the hotel provided a dehumidifier, which kept it comfortable.

Dinner was a local specialty, the renowned "testi kebab" or "pottery kebab." A small ceramic jug filled with lamb, beef, chicken, and vegetables sealed closed, then placed directly onto coals of a fire and simmered for hours. My waiter used thick fireproof gloves to retrieve the pot from the fire. He placed the blazing jug on a pedestal in front of me, handed me a small saber, and instructed me to crack the jug open with its blade. If I hit too low, the contents would spill. If I hit too high, I wouldn't have access to the smoldering stew. Precision was key.

I took a couple of practice swings, then *whack*, I cracked the top off, exposing my boiling meal. My waiter quickly grabbed the saber from me, recognizing my whacking enjoyment. It was a culinary experience and delicious, but I blistered my tongue with my eagerness.

> Recipe: Twirl the dozen tops on the dance floor. As the tops spin in hypnotic synchrony, imagine them gaining significance, enlightenment, and becoming closer to their maker. That's what the whirling dervishes do.

After dinner, I attended a Sema Ceremony of the Whirling Dervishes. Their religion is Sufism, the mystical branch of Islam emphasizing universal love, peace, and acceptance associated with a spinning dance. Dervishes wear tall felt hats to symbolize a connection with heaven. They wear short, tight white felt jackets and long, wide felt skirts to help them spin nonstop and enter a meditative trance, which they believe gets them closer to God. Twelve whirling dervishes spun symmetric circles for hours, poised with their arms bent and head tilted back. It was a strange presentation but interesting to see how they expressed their beliefs.

Speeding down a Turkish highway, I saw a cop pointing a speed gun at me. Yes, I was speeding. A mile later, I saw three cop cars signaling any guilty drivers to the side of the road. I parked Andiamo as one cop approached me to ask for my driver's license, passport, and motorcycle documents. He took them to his police car, did some checking of my records, and returned with a ticket. It was a ticket for 500 Turkish liras, about 70 US dollars.

"You must pay at a post office in the next town," he told me.

I rode through several towns and saw no post offices. As I type this, I wonder what the statute of limitations is for a Turkish speeding ticket.

I spent my last night in Turkey at the Butik Hotel Gelibolu. The owner, Alaeddin, a handsome Turkish gentleman with salt-and-pepper hair, wearing a pressed button-down collared shirt and suit pants, greeted me with a smile. His son lived in Binghamton, New York. My room was on the top floor of the quaint Turkish boutique hotel. Its slanted, three-foot-high ceiling required me to walk hunchbacked.

In the hotel's kitchen, I watched Alaeddin prepare dinner. In his soft-spoken voice, he said "special" this and "special" that. Everything was "special." Whatever he was doing at the moment was the most important thing in his world. He paid acute attention to detail as he served his intricately carved vegetables shaped like flowers, meats sliced evenly, and garnishes too pretty to eat. Now everything became "very special." Dessert was fried ice cream with a sweet cheese topping. "Very special."

Dear Alaeddin,

Thank you for your kind hospitality. You are a true gentleman. I hope you and your family are well.

Sincerely,
Robert

I was in bed by 10:00 p.m.

Up at 8:00 a.m., I packed Andiamo. Locals offered me small wrapped candies symbolizing goodwill. This actually happened everywhere in Turkey. It was a custom I found endearing. Men and women, old and young, handed me treats and welcomed me to their country. I was inspired.

As I waited for the ferry to Cyprus, a young man said, "*Merhaba*, welcome to Turkey." He handed me a cherry-flavored Jolly Rancher piece of hard candy.

Humbled, I thanked him. At that moment, I decided to hand out small gifts of my own to people I would meet while traveling. A work colleague, Captain Chris, has a laser cutting machine, and he made me a thousand wooden coins with my logo on one side and my name on the other side. I hand these wooden coins out to people I meet as a small greeting gift similar to the Turkish tradition I had experienced.

It was a short ferry ride to Cyprus.

Cyprus

2013

Mileage: 62,000

Ingredients: one Motorola flip phone

Cyprus is an island in the eastern Mediterranean, south of Turkey, divided in two almost equal halves, one half claimed by the Republic of Cyprus and the other half claimed by Turkey. Crossing the border, I went through customs and immigration, even though Northern Cyprus is considered part of the Republic of Cyprus. It's a political power struggle that can be dangerously close to war at times. I just nodded my head and complied.

I had a couple interests in Cyprus. One was to visit some long-lost family friends, John and Shirley, who had moved to Cyprus from England after retirement. John was an engineer and had worked with my dad on the failed ski boot project. I used all possible means to locate them, but nobody knew where John and Shirley were. I determined they had relocated and left no forwarding address. I was disappointed, since I hadn't seen them in decades.

> Recipe: Open the Motorola flip phone. Prepare to send an old-style text message with it.
> Press 9;
> 6 three times;
> 7 three times;
> 5 three times;
> 3;
> space;
> 7;

3 two times;
2;
2 three times;
3 two times.
Put the flip phone in a bottle and throw it in the ocean. Hope the Goddess of Love makes your wish come true.

My second interest in Cyprus was to see the birthplace of Aphrodite, the Greek goddess of love and beauty. Petra tou Romiou is a rock on the beautiful beaches of Cyprus, where Aphrodite was born. The Greek myth goes like this: Aphrodite was an image similar to a mermaid, wandering island to island until she found the beaches of Cyprus, where she decided to start her life in human form. Emerging from foamy waves crashing into the large rock, she was born. I saw her rock and definitely felt love and beauty surrounding me. I put a message in a bottle and threw it out to sea, hoping my wish would come true.

I looked for my bottle floating while I took the ferry to Lebanon.

Lebanon

2013

Mileage: 62,000

Ingredients: one garden shed, one shovel, one AK-47, one chore in your yard

It was supposed to be a seventeen-hour ferry trip to Lebanon. The ferry was old and moldy, and there were only a few women and children, not a good sign. I had booked a stateroom with private bathroom. For starters, the tiny stateroom had a broken entry door. When I got inside, I found the bathroom walls were stained and discolored, the lower bunk was tattered and lumpy, and the carpet was prickly and faded. Not quite what I expected.

I stowed my gear, washed up, and lay down on the bunk. There were no sheets covering the mattress, only an old tiger-print fleece blanket. In the morning I felt an itch on my lower back and on the back of my knee. I scratched them both. I twisted my leg to see the source of the itch. A slimy leech-like creature had burrowed into the back of my knee. I tried to pull it out, but parts of the creature remained under my skin. With tweezers, I extracted most of it. It was very difficult to extract the same type creature from my lower back, but I tried my best. Most of the gooey mess came out, but some remained. Progressively over the next period of time, the itching continued. Doctors later identified the creature as a parasite similar to an Amazonian bot fly.

Needless to say, the ferry was delayed because the engines operated at reduced speed in an attempt to save money. The seventeen-hour trip took thirty-two hours.

When I disembarked in Tripoli, Lebanon, I was faced with attempted extortion from a customs official, who reclined in his chair, feet on his desk, smoking a cigarette. "Temporary importation of your motorcycle will cost a thousand US dollars," he told me.

"I've researched the cost, and I know there's no fee on a temporary basis!" I exclaimed.

After a heated discussion, he acquiesced to my pleas. I paid nothing and was free to ride Lebanon.

I needed a place to stay and keep Andiamo for a month. My GPS directed me to the Radisson Blu Martinez in downtown Beirut.

I was kindly greeted by the front desk manager. "Do you have a room for the night?" I asked her. "And can I leave my motorcycle here for a month?"

She answered yes to both questions without hesitation. It was a very nice welcome to Lebanon, a country that has intrigued me since the '80s.

A beautiful underground parking spot and a taxi to the airport. Back in a month.

～～～

Upon return, I toured Lebanon for two days. Cosmopolitan and hip, Beirut is the Paris of the Middle East, a melting pot of religions and cultures. Lebanese people celebrate living each day, instilled by witnessing life taken in an instant. Everywhere I went, I was welcomed with enthusiasm.

I got invited to a hilltop residence, a four-hundred-year-old old home handed down from generation to generation. The entrance had two ten-foot-high solid wood doors with huge metal hinges. Inside were sixteen-foot ceilings held up by a series of thick wooden beams. The owners were a newly married couple renovating it for their personal home. During the civil war bombings in the '80s, sandbags were piled around it to protect six families seeking refuge inside. In my romantic mind, the cute newlyweds reminded me of "The Lebanon," a 1980s song by the Human League. The song describes the conflict of that time and the horrors of a humanitarian mission entangled in war. It describes a woman looking down on Beirut from a similar hilltop residence as she watched her city bombed and destroyed. The song forced my consciousness to live in the now. I was transcended into the lyrics:

> She is awakened by the screams
> Of rockets flying from nearby
> And scared she clings onto her dreams
> To beat the fear that she might die.

The song goes on to describe her man fighting for conflicting reasons. It was like my new friends had lived the song, making our connection even more fascinating.

They recommended the top sites. I tried to see them all. I walked the Corniche (beach boardwalk). Visited Baalbek, with its ancient Roman ruins. Toured Byblos, a seven-thousand-year-old old city. Took a cable car ride up to overlook Jounieh Bay and the gorgeous coastline at sunset. I took an underground boat trip to Jeita Grotto, considered a finalist in the seven wonders of the world. There I saw the world's largest stalactite: the length of three men hanging hand to foot, dangling to the water where my small boat navigated the cave.

> Recipe: Hang the shovel and AK-47 on the wall in the garden
> shed. Close the door. Return the next day with one chore to do
> in your yard. Which of the tools will you need most?

The next night, we visited some other friends, who owned a printing business. The owners were brothers, one social and one businesslike. It was a very professional operation and the region's largest printing company. Their clients included entire countries, airlines, and some real bigwigs. The office was hidden high in the hills, camouflaged by brush cover. They had just invested $250,000 in a huge offset printing press. Behind a mahogany desk in the office, an AK-47 rifle hung on the wall.

"What's that used for?" I asked the social brother.

"It's just a tool," he nonchalantly replied.

"Oh, you mean like a shovel?" I asked.

"Syria is just over the mountain ridge," he explained. "We need to protect ourselves."

A total head-spin for me. I was shocked, thinking of them having a shootout in their yard.

I told them I was headed over the mountain to Syria the next day. They told me stories of Syrian refuges showing up on their property with all sorts of intentions. I'd been warned not to visit lots of countries, always with pleasant surprises. I was not deterred by their warnings.

Later that night back at my hotel, a strange man approached me. He was Syrian and had just snuck into Lebanon for safety.

"Please, sir," he said, "I haven't eaten in days. I need food."

I gave him a loaf of bread I had and a bottle of water. He snatched the bread and literally shoved the whole loaf down his throat, chewing violently, then sat on a rock wall and guzzled the water.

The next day while I was preparing my bike, another man struck up a conversation with me. "Where are you headed?" he asked.

"Damascus," I replied.

"I am Syrian," he said. "I just came from there. Yesterday I was walking down the street in Damascus, arm in arm with my brother, when he was shot in the back of the head and died. It's unruly at the moment and is not safe, especially for an American."

This story clinched the deal. Syria had to be postponed. I was very much looking forward to seeing all the historic sites. One too many bloody stories, and I headed back to Turkey on a ferry to ride up to Bulgaria.

Eastern Europe

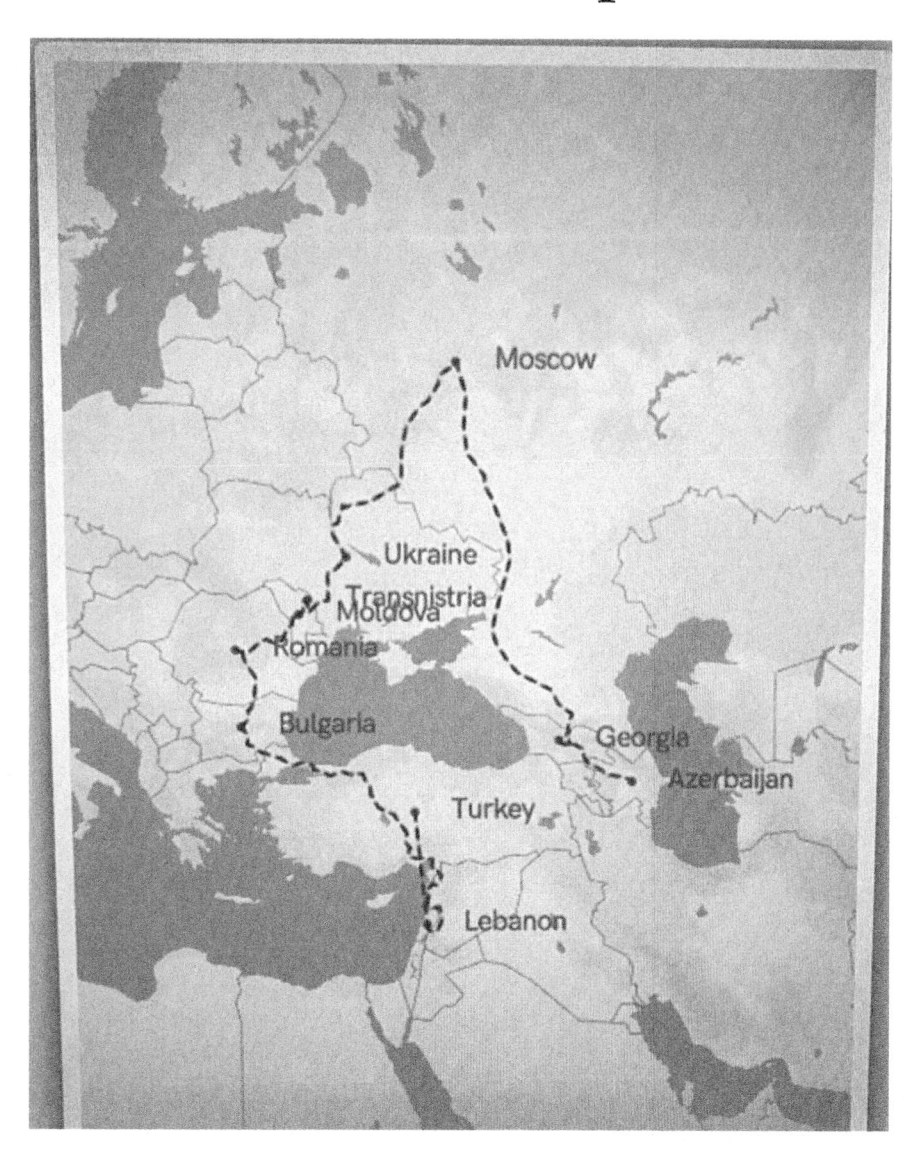

Caspian Sea next to Azerbaijan

Bulgaria

2014

Mileage: 63,000

Ingredients: two housewarming party invitations, one waste can

Recipe: Admire the two invitations to the housewarmings. Plan to attend at least one. Rip up both invitations and throw them into the waste can. Feel terrible about not attending either.

I had recently flown with two first officers who were both from Bulgaria. Here's how the introductions went:
"Hello, First Officer Yuri. Where ya from?"
"Sofia, Bulgaria."
"Can I park my motorcycle at your family house?"
"Yes!"
Next flight:
"Hello, First Officer Grigor. Where ya from?"
"Varna, Bulgaria."
"Can I park my motorcycle at your family house?"
"Yes!"
I had two solid potential parking spots before I had even left for that month's ride.

The ferry out of Lebanon was a quick overnight to Turkey. I took a quick ride up through Turkey to cross the border into Bulgaria. I then sewed the Bulgarian flag on the back of my jacket.

At 10:00 a.m., I entered Sofia. It was days before the end of that month's ride. I kept riding to Varna. I made Varna by 5:00 p.m. and spent the night there. I woke up early and wanted to continue the ride. I had made such good time and was ahead of schedule, so I bypassed both my potential parking spots for the unknown country of Romania and another new flag sewn on my jacket.

Bulgaria is a country riddled in strife left over from the Soviet era. I got the feeling everyone wanted to just go about their own business and not stand out. The people seemed fearful of "Big Brother" watching them, ready to discipline them for any wrongdoing.

Friends on an Indonesian ferry

Lobster Gondola

Andiamo Full Circle

Balinese cremation ceremony

Indonesian cultural dance

Sydney Opera House

Indonesian boys

Runway 24 Lukla Airport, Nepal

Tasmanian devil

Swing bridge Peru

Uros Indian woman

El Camino de la Muerte, the Road of the Dead.
No flags on my jacket.

Bolivia

Bolivian gas station

Ben and I

Andiamo Full Circle

Salar de Uyuni

North Korea

Arbol de Piedra

Kissing the bitch-man

Hand of the Desert

80 mph winds

Azerbaijan

Straps started, for future flags

Camping Moscow, Russia

"What?"

Randy and I Fez, Morocco

Randy and I Sumatra, Indonesia

Fez

George, Maurice, friend, me, and Michael, Romania

Greg, me, Kathy, and John

"End of the World" sign

This is a fun way to watch some videos I have made of my trips.
1. Open your phone's camera
2. Point it at the image (you don't need to take a picture, only point your camera)
3. Tap the link on your phone to watch each video

"Unique Accommodations" in New Zealand

"Bucket List"

Bob Dolven

"Lemonade"

"Budget Travel"

"Believe in Yourself"

Andiamo Full Circle

"Cheers Australia"

Romania

2014

Mileage: 63,000

Ingredients: one fluorescent green T-shirt, one pair of fluorescent green sunglasses, one pair of fluorescent green sneakers, one pair of green plaid shorts

After a quick tour of Bucharest, I changed the month's destination to Bran, Romania. My new goal was to park at Dracula's Castle. I was sure they would have parking accommodations. I could ask to park Andiamo in some kind of maintenance shed or something. That was my plan.

I was transfixed by the Transylvanian architecture. The wood-built homes, churches, and buildings featured curved tiered roofs covered with thick wooden shingles and pointed steeples. They all looked like something out of a Dracula movie. I had an eerie feeling being shadowed by their shapes.

> Recipe: Put on the fluorescent green T-shirt, green glasses, green sneakers, and green plaid shorts. Stand on a busy street corner with friends. Wave at passersby. What are their reactions? How many people take you seriously?

I rolled to a stop at a red light. There was a group of young people on the curb. One young man stuck out. He was wearing a florescent green T-shirt with yellow trim bands. Yellow-and-green sneakers and green sunglasses completed the outfit. In the crowd, he was the one my eyes could not deviate from. His T-shirt read *You looked better from behind.* I knew he had to be friendly, sporting a shirt like that. I wanted to ride the train from Romania to Budapest, Hungary, and needed the schedule. Mr. Green

T-shirt gave me directions to the train station. The stoplight turned green, and I was off.

I got information on trains to Budapest. There were plenty to choose from. It was going to work out perfectly. Now all I needed was a place to park Andiamo for a month.

To park at Dracula's Castle in Bran, Romania, was still my goal. I plugged Bran into my GPS. It was only a thirty-minute ride.

As I exited the train station parking area, a shiny blue Audi stopped alongside me. My immediate reaction was, *He's too close!* Then I saw it was Mr. Green T-shirt.

"Vear yu heedet?" he asked.

"Bran," I said.

"Follow me."

"Ya live there?"

"Yes," he said.

"Do you have a garage there?" I asked.

"Yes."

"Can I park my motorcycle there?"

"Yes," he said.

"Let's go," I said.

That's an actual transcript of our first conversation.

I followed his blue Audi for thirty minutes to his house in Bran. We parked outside his large gated yard, which enclosed a three-story house and a two-car garage. He introduced himself and his then girlfriend, now wife, as Michael and Simona. Simona was the quiet side of Michael and kept him in control.

"Hello, I'm Robert," I said.

We entered the tall metal gates and walked back to where two younger men and a fatherly gentleman were seated at a picnic table full of fruits and vegetables and bottles of homemade wine. We all introduced ourselves. George was the father, a very kind and soft-spoken man. Maurice, one of the two younger men, spoke perfect English and explained a game they were about to play. This was a traditional Orthodox Christian game during Easter. One person holds a hardboiled egg in their fingers while another person has one chance to deliver a pound to crack the other's egg. The person with the uncracked egg will receive good luck. Maurice and I tried it, and my egg cracked.

Having lost the game, I cheered in triumph. "I've already received good luck by meeting all of you," I said.

My trifecta of personal needs were met when Michael said yes, I could spend the night, yes, I could leave my motorcycle for a month, and yes, Dracula's Castle was two kilometers away, where Michael's cousin was the marketing manager and would give me a special tour.

Ahh, serendipity.

Michael, Simona, and I drove two kilometers listening to Major Lazer's "Be Free" blasting on the car stereo. We parked in front of Bran Castle, and out walked a handsome Romanian gentleman from the administrative offices. Michael introduced me to Alex, his cousin. Alex spoke perfect English without an accent. He was thirty-something, well dressed, and about to allow Michael, Simona, and me VIP access to Bran Castle, aka Dracula's Castle, aka Vlad Tepes's Castle ("Vlad the Impaler").

Since Vlad's actual castle is in ruins, people have associated him with Bran Castle. Bran Castle fits the description of Dracula's Castle featured in Bram Stoker's fictional work, *Dracula*.

Bran Castle is a tremendous example of grand structures. Passed down to various occupants since 1388, it has served as fortress, royal residence, and tourist attraction. I passed through the rooms, chambers, and tunnels imagining the historical events that preceded my VIP tour. The furniture was massive and made with rare materials and craftsmanship.

With great anticipation, we were led into the restricted access point. The more infamous parts of the castle are it's medieval instruments of torture. As we descended deeper into the dungeons, the instruments of torture became more gruesome, cleverly named and used for punishment or deterrent.

This punishment or deterrent, whatever you want to call it, was administered publicly and for different durations. I pictured Vlad the Impaler sentencing a criminal to five days on the "Gridiron," four days on the "Witch's Billy Goat," three days on the "Guided Cradle," two days of wearing the

"Iron Boot," or an afternoon enduring the "Spanish Tickle Torture." Thank goodness, we're rarely subjected to cruel and unusual punishment in America.

That night, Michael, Simona, George, and his wife prepared a wonderful meal. George produced a thirty-year-old bottle of his homemade wine he had been saving for a special occasion. We toasted and celebrated our connection. They were so nice to invite me into their home and provide me with meals, accommodation, and a place to keep Andiamo for a month. I knew I would miss them, but I'd be back in a month.

The next morning, Michael and Simona drove me to the train station, where I boarded the train to Budapest, Hungary. As the train slowly pulled away from the station, they blew me kisses over and over. I filmed the exchange. It was charming to see them expressing a sincere farewell. This newfound bond between random strangers left me knowing the world is full of people wanting to be happy, show love, and enjoy life. In the middle of Romania, I trusted strangers with Andiamo and my gear. My instincts had taken over. It felt good to truly trust and believe in humankind. That moment seeing Michael and Simona on the station platform blowing me kisses is one of my profound memories to describe love and peace on earth.

~~~

While back in the States, we kept in contact through Facebook. I freed up my schedule and was back in Romania in short order. The average duration between riding segments was fifty-three days.

Michael had parked his Audi outside while Andiamo was parked in their garage. The family had planned a festive feast for my return. We spent the evening eating, drinking, and sharing stories of our lives. I felt so welcomed and warm.

Since Michael's favorite author was Dan Brown, I brought him a Dan Brown book filled with US dollars as bookmarks.

George gave me a three-foot medieval sword, which I have adored since.

Andiamo Full Circle

Dear Michael, Simona, and family,

I am so grateful for your kindness. I miss you all. I thank you for your generous hospitality and I wish all of you the very best in life.

Until we meet again,

Yours truly,
Robert

We said our tearful goodbyes, and that was that. Northbound to Moldova.

Moldova

2014

Mileage: 64,000

Ingredients: one corn maze, one case of wine

Recipe: Place the case of wine in the middle of the corn maze and exit. Walk miles and miles in search of your prize. Find it and be rewarded.

I parked in front of the world's largest wine cellar, hoping I had enough gas. You can self-drive the labyrinth of underground streets, which have a total mileage of 200 kilometers, or 120 miles. I opted for a guide as my designated driver, since I was doing some wine tasting and would have hated to lose my balance and break one of Vladimir Putin's personal bottles. (He stores his wine there.)

My guide drove me in a golf cart along the underground roadways named after wine varietals, like Merlot Avenue, Chardonnay Street, and Cabernet Cul-de-Sac, all categorized and organized. We stopped for a view of a hundred-year-old bottle covered in dust. Evidently the dust proved the age and added to the value. The underground streets went on forever and provided the perfect environment to store wine. Bottles were stacked to the ceiling along the streets, so close we could have crashed into them and caused a tidal wave of wine. Later in the tasting room, I purchased a few bottles to tote with me.

I stayed at Château Vartely, which had a fantastic restaurant. There I met five US embassy diplomats, who begged me not to go to Transnistria, my next country. They said there would be nothing the US embassy could do for me if I needed help. They told me Transnistrian currency was worth less than a piece of toilet paper (not true in 2020).

They actually pleaded with me. "Please don't go, for your own safety."

Were these like my warnings about Syria? Would I be in danger? Should I travel in fear and limit my horizons?

I had to witness the oddities of the country.

Transnistria

2014

Mileage: 64,000

Ingredients: Two hundred slices of Swiss cheese, one Matchbox toy car

The next morning, I readied Andiamo for departure: destination Transnistria. With so many warnings not to visit, I had great trepidation. I had done research to verify the rules and regulations of Transnistria, a small body of land between Moldova and Ukraine they call a country. A minuscule 1,600 square miles of disputed territory under a ceasefire from the last unresolved war with Moldova, it was a breakaway state from the former Soviet Union and trying to disassociate itself from Moldova with Russian support.

Border entry procedures were conducted in four blue construction-site temporary-type cargo containers. I have found that the more insignificant a country is, the more convoluted its entry procedures are. The four cargo containers were stuffed full of uniformed officials sitting behind small desks and shuffling papers like burned-out Las Vegas card dealers. The wood-paneled walls were discolored from air vents blowing black stains. The government posters were faded from years of Soviet cigarette smoke. The filth film on the windows filtered what gloom was let in.

I was guided to a slouching, red-faced, round man with bags drooping under his bloodshot eyes that were too heavy to meet mine. His neck barely had the strength to support his head upright. He thumbed through my credentials, and with practiced deliberateness, wrapped his sausage fingers around the lacquer handle of the rubber stamp, blotted the ink pad twice, checked the orientation, then stamped a small sheet of blank paper. He then extended his arm and grunted in the direction of the guy sitting behind him.

Andiamo Full Circle

This man was a cloned version of the first. He grabbed the small sheet of paper from me, produced a larger sheet of blank paper, and stamped it with dismal professionalism. He grunted and motioned me to the guy sitting behind him. That guy took the larger stamped paper as the ink was drying and slid it into a pile of papers stacked like dusty old newspapers. He then stamped my motorcycle documents.

I was forced to endure this painful waste of time again for immigration with my passport. I could not fathom how grown men didn't see the tremendous uselessness of these gyrations. It was sad to see how completely numb and unmotivated the flabby Communist men had become. I did notice most of them had a bottle of vodka stashed in their desk drawers like worn-out downtown detectives. It was a three-hour border entry followed by a thirty-minute transit of the country.

They have their own banking system, government, and military/police force. I have my personal theory about the purpose of the latter's existence. I believe that to bypass arms sanctions, Russia uses Transnistria to store weapons. The residents are mostly in favor of Communism and the former Soviet way of life.

The unambitious locals thought it was great under the Soviet Union and Communism. Most people could collect a small paycheck for leaning on a shovel and could live in provided cinder-block-stacked housing projects with three generations of family sharing a one-bedroom apartment with no running water. It was a great lifestyle, if vodka was your only need.

> Recipe: Place two hundred slices of Swiss cheese in a continuous line like a straight yellow-brick road. Roll the Matchbox car over your cheese road like a child playing. Notice how the wheels sink into each hole of the Swiss cheese. Imagine the occupants of the Matchbox car and how they are jarred like jackhammers.

No residents cared to improve the infrastructure of their country. The neglected roads fell into terrible condition. Any repairs were done cheaply and quickly by laying tar on top of tar, which created potholes like Swiss cheese.

It was obvious that Communism had destroyed these peoples' pride in their country and left them unmotivated to improve things. I was deeply saddened by their uninspired acceptance of substandard systems, leaving me even more thankful to be an American. I appreciate the pride Americans take in our country.

The few buildings occupying the country were decrepit examples of projects built in haste by citizens only wanting government handouts.

I collect foreign currencies and exchanged a few dollars for their colorful paper. Ironically, the police officer used a form of math to benefit himself and dispose of his Transnistrian paper, acknowledging the worthless currency.

Exiting Transnistria was as difficult as entering, like taking the SAT twice. One guard wanted to search my side boxes. I demonstrated how difficult it was to gain access. My carry-on roller bag was strapped on top of my side boxes, restricting access to them. Securing my gear is a complicated process of balancing the gear, then weaving the jack straps through the correct tie-down loops, then covering the pile with my rainfly, then covering that with my cargo net. The pile ends up taller than I sit and must be secured tightly to avoid shifting while riding turns and bumps.

In his vodka trance, the guard shrugged and waved me on to Ukraine.

Ukraine

2014

Mileage: 64,000

Ingredients: one town of the future, one dinner table, one abandoned amusement park, one happiness meter

At the border, I changed ten dollars into Ukrainian hryvnias. On the forested outskirts of some nondescript country town in the middle of nowhere, I searched for a place to sleep. I had little money, it was late, and nothing looked safe. For protection, I chose the back of a truck stop next to a small, fenced-in, algae-filled pond that smelled like a garbage dump. The nasty pond was actually a fish farm for locals. I couldn't spare the money for a shower, so I tried to enjoy the blended scents.

I set my tent up near the pond, upwind from the overflowing dumpster. The toxic fumes in the outside pit toilet penetrated my nose and filled my throat as if with physical force.

The cracks in the pavement met the cracks in the foundation. Inside the truck stop cafe, I didn't know what to make of the items on the menu, which were handwritten in Cyrillic characters. I felt illiterate looking at etchings on paper. Even the prices posted in Ukrainian hryvnias dizzied me. None of the busy babushka women spoke English. Nor did they offer me help. One startled me, towering over my table. I looked up to see a wrinkled, round woman wearing a stained apron that covered her large bust, knee-high stockings, and heavy-heeled black shoes. No words spoken, she sneered at me with a notepad in her left hand and a pen in the other. My starving finger pointed to scribbling on the menu. The stated amount was less than the hryvnias in my pocket. My torso growling with hunger pain, I held up one finger. She jotted on her notepad as her dress twirled toward the pan-rattling kitchen. I had no idea what it was going to be.

Ten minutes later, with thumping footsteps, the babushka woman smacked a garnish-free beige plate in front of me. On the plate was a jet-black charred fish. She handed me a set of flimsy tin utensils, then retreated to the kitchen.

I stared the fish in the eye and whispered, "Ten minutes ago, you were swimming in the algae pond out back, right?"

No response from the charred fish. A few tasteless bites was all my empty stomach could handle.

I slept like a bug on an electric fence. Morning arrived late. I held my breath as I packed my gear, and I was outta the unpleasantness.

Kiev, the capital of Ukraine, was my destination. My GPS directed me to the Hotel Riviera, the base for my operations out of Kiev. Around the corner was the funicular, a cable car climbing a steep hill to Upper Town. From there I walked to Independence Square, at the confluence of downtown streets, an area sectioned off with a peaceful center court with benches to meet friends. I kept seeing young people with megaphones and signs protesting something. I wanted to ask one of them what they were saying, but I didn't think much about it at the time.

The main attraction was the fabulous flower clock. The colorful fifteen-foot circle of flowers told time and cleansed my nose with fragrant beauty. A few months later, it was destroyed, along with most of Independence Square, during the Ukrainian Revolution when the freedom fighters fought the freedom fighters. My eyes filled with tears when I watched news reports showing the flower clock destroyed by flames and rioters.

The following day, I arranged to see a Russian tank-driving school. Disappointingly, the tour was canceled due to a military conflict. Things were heating up between Ukraine and Russia. The organization's alternative was Russian rifle shooting in an underground firing range.

Forbidden to film, I was driven to an undisclosed location, escorted into a dark bunker, and told to sit on a bench and wait. The bunker had long-range capability for sniper target practice.

In stormed Uri, a thin-faced, muscled militia type. He handed me several high-powered Russian weapons, the coating on each weapon worn thin from years of service, smelling like gunpowder and oil. "Riddy, sit, fir!" he said.

I fired each weapon in rapid succession like some kind of action hero. I demolished anything downrange, exploding mannequins, paint cans, and armor-plated human silhouettes. I wanted to rip off my shirt and pound my chest with my conjured Rambo persona. Hundreds of spent shells smoking at my feet, I thought of the Ukraine-Russian conflicts these weapons had been used in.

Uri escorted me out of my playpen and urged my silence for his protection as he drove me back to my hotel.

Outside the front door of Hotel Riviera was Ukraine's longest zip line, a half-kilometer cable stretched over the Dnieper River. I had to try it, even though the equipment was well used and perhaps less maintained than other zip lines I've enjoyed. It was interesting to see the difference in safety regulations as the pimple-faced boy handed me a hard hat and palmless gloves, clipped me to the cable, and shoved me off the ledge. My feet dangled high above the river as I let out a thrill seeker's scream. The gloves were to be used as brakes to stop before the concrete wall at the end. Cable burns on my palms were my only injuries sustained on this high-energy event.

That month's ride had come to an end. I asked the front desk manager the question, and "yes" was the answer. Five dollars a day parking at the hotel. I returned home for a month.

~~~

Recipe: Move your family to the town of the future. At the dinner table, promise your children a trip to the amusement park that weekend. With the happiness meter, record how happy the children are. Now destroy that promise and record their happiness.

The next month, ready for more adventure, my guide briefed me in the Hotel Riviera lobby on what I could touch and what was still radioactive in the town of Pripyat and the Chernobyl Nuclear Power Plant. He assured me all necessary precautions would be taken to provide a safe, close-up view of the devastation caused by the "world's worst nuclear disaster."

The seat cushions provided little comfort on the van ride to the Exclusion Zone. Seventy kilometers north of Kiev, at the heavily guarded outpost, I was issued protective clothing and was ushered through a vintage metal detector contraption used to record my radioactivity. The operators intended to compare my readings before and after the tour. I was issued a Geiger counter to identify hot spots where water had drained into pools of radioactive sediment.

We drove deeper into the Exclusion Zone, the haunting aftermath frozen in time when life ceased. In a vegetation-covered abandoned home, with glass shards on the living room floor and toppled appliances in the kitchen, my Geiger counter frightened me. I had taken an alarmingly high reading on a child's stuffed animal. I thought of the child reaching out for her stuffed animal, crying, with tears gushing as her mother carried her and fled the family home to evacuate the city. Material possessions were insignificant. Only survival mattered to this family. This emotional experience shocked my blessings into the forefront of my mind.

I imagined the young family living in their house. Instantly, they were forced to gather what they could and leave the rest of their lives behind. At that moment, they weren't worried about the latest iPhone or flashy car. They just wanted to keep breathing.

The deeper I went into the Exclusion Zone, the greater the devastation. Less living foliage, more damage to homes and buildings, increasing amounts of paralyzed ghostly images.

The movie theater had a *Now Showing* poster partially hanging on the wall next to a ticket booth occupied by specters from that day. The Olympic-sized swimming pool filled with gymnasium debris made me think of Olympic dreams destroyed.

In the city center of Pripyat, I gasped in shock at the town of the future, offering only unfulfilled promises. All the young families had been coaxed there with high-paying dangerous jobs at the Chernobyl Nuclear Power Plant. An amusement park, scheduled to open the day after the meltdown, was a view into dreams obliterated. I sat in a rusted-out radioactive bumper car, envisioning children's anticipation exploded into a mushroom cloud.

The nuclear meltdown occurred April 26, 1986, inside reactor #4. During a test simulating the exact event that caused the meltdown, the reactor redlined and exploded. Thirty men were immediately vaporized. Sixty more perished within hours. Families waiting for their loved ones to return from work were left wondering what had happened. Children shaded their eyes as they pointed and cried out, "Mommy, what is that huge plume of smoke coming from Daddy's office?"

Pripyat and Chernobyl were under Communist control of the former Soviet Union. The Soviet Union did not provide an immediate public response. Instead, they forced the men of the city to clean up the devastation before the world found out. The cleanup crews were issued only rubber face masks, rubber boots, rubber gloves, and a shovel for safety equipment. They were forced to work in fifteen-minute shifts, dousing the surrounding fires before the soles of their rubber boots melted. They tried to use robots, but the electronics could not withstand the extreme temperatures.

After a number of days spent concealing the disaster, the Soviets changed their initial statement that there had been an electrical fire, to one stating there had been a nuclear meltdown that threatened the entire European continent. Twenty-seven countries from around the world contributed financing to assist in the cleanup and containment effort.

The death toll is still under examination. Estimates range from four thousand to sixteen thousand. I'm morbidly fascinated by the evolution of societies. Stories of rags to riches to rags, like Pripyat, Cuba, Easter Island, Machu Picchu, and the Roman Empire, intrigue me like football intrigues a fan during the Super Bowl.

It was time to leave Ukraine. Andiamo carried me across the border into Russia.

Russia

2014

Mileage: 64,000

Ingredients: one Russian paparazzi, one Russian cop, one jack-in-the-box toy, one VI explanation, one tattoo artist

The Russian border guards were familiar with my carnet (an expensive motorcycle passport that indemnifies me against tax liabilities if I don't correctly export the motorcycle and must be renewed every twelve months). They completed their portion of the perforated sheet, retained half and stamped my half, and with an entry stamp in my passport on my three-year, multi-entry Russian visa, I was now authorized to ride the largest country in the world. Russia bordered fourteen other countries along the then eleven time zones.

One hundred and fifty miles north of the border, with no Russian rubles to my name, Andiamo and I veered from the road into a grassy field. The level ground was surrounded by a thick hedge of trees. The tall grass provided cushioning for my tent. I saw no visible signs of life other than the disappearing sun. Setting up camp was a race against daylight. Rain began to complicate the process. With my rainfly pulled tight over my tent, I dove inside and quickly zipped the door closed to prevent soaking my gear.

The next morning as I stood up outside my tent, I felt as if the grassy muddy ground was sinking. I reached for the blinding sun to stretch my stiff body. Startled, I focused on a man's wrinkled face and worn straw cowboy hat. His heavy ears caused his expressionless face to droop in a weathered way. His overalls had holes in both knees as he stepped over my gear and continued to walk by without a smile or acknowledgment. Perplexed, I wondered what this man's purpose was. Miles from signs of life, I had no idea where he was going. In less than ten seconds, he floated through my personal space and exited without the slightest reaction. Bewildered, I packed up my gear and headed toward Moscow.

I had a special reason to visit Moscow. A year prior to that morning, while touring Pompeii, Italy, I saw a good-looking couple walking near the coliseum of the ancient city. The man carried a BMW Rallye 2 Pro jacket. It's not just a motorcycle jacket. It's an iconic piece of adventure-riding gear. Those who own one know its significance.

I had to engage this man. "Do you ride motorcycles?" I asked.

"Da," he responded, Russian for yes. His name was Anton, and he had a handsome, slender, Russian look, with fair skin and chiseled face.

His wife introduced herself. Natalia was a gorgeous Russian woman who spoke perfect English. She translated my conversation with Anton. We chatted about adventure riding. Anton was humble about his long-distance riding to exotic locations. I told them I was riding my motorcycle around the world and would be in Russia in a year and needed a place to park. We exchanged contact information and continued our separate tours of Pompeii. I thought it would be cool to contact Natalia and Anton when I eventually made it to Moscow.

Riding within range of Moscow, I emailed them. Natalia responded with an invitation to their home the following day. She gave me the latitude/longitude coordinates for where to meet. It's easier to navigate to a position on Earth than to read the Russian street signs.

My GPS led me to a pinpoint on the map of Moscow. At the arranged location, Anton flashed his headlights like a KGB agent meeting his handler. We exchanged pleasantries with a mix of English and Russian. I followed him to their beautiful downtown-Moscow high-rise, which resembled a gigantic Jenga structure.

I unpacked my gear with Anton's help. Our presence was sensed by thick automatic doors as we approached the entrance to his building. A uniformed security guard submissively bowed his head to Anton, who inserted a key into the wall and twisted. We took Anton's personal elevator to the penthouse, where the doors mechanically opened to their private residence. I felt like a dignitary visiting a royal palace, my eyes immediately drawn to the most striking feature of their palatial home: a six-foot-wide perimeter garden surrounding the whole interior. It felt like living outdoors. Various floor-to-ceiling plants and trees filled the living room, family room, and kitchen with a rain-forest feel. I imagined exotic birds flying from tree to tree.

Natalia greeted me with Russian warmth. It was like long-lost friends being reunited. We hadn't seen each other since our chance encounter in Pompeii the prior year. She had booked us reservations at a traditional Russian restaurant and for an evening performance of the Russian National Ballet. It's a good thing I travel with a dressy travel blazer folded up in my bag for such occasions.

With me dressed as formally as I could, our evening began. We drove in their blacked-out Land Rover on historic cobblestone streets, while Natalia pointed out interesting sights. We parked near the KGB headquarters and walked the remaining two hundred meters.

Anton opened the heavy antique wooden door for us to enter the homestyle Russian restaurant, with its wood floors, hand-peeled log walls with huge wooden corbels supporting the beamed ceiling. Checkered tablecloths matched the curtains. The aroma of old-fashioned home cooking warmed my stomach. Natalia fastidiously preordered a complete five-course meal comprised of traditional Russian foods. She gave detailed explanations of each item as she heaped mashed potatoes on my plate. It was simple comfort food and made me feel at home. My belly swelled as Anton refused my offer to pay the bill.

It was a short distance to the impressive theater, where patrons of the ballet were impeccably dressed. We sipped pre-show cocktails at a stand-up table. A polite announcement, given in five languages, requested no flash photography. Thankfully, Natalia had purchased a DVD of the performance in advance. We had a VIP booth above the stage with a close-up view of the dancers. The show began with a bang from stage-side flamethrowers that sent a flash of heat to our faces. The dancers' movements seemed to hover above the stage. I had to imagine these were Russia's best dancers, as they defied gravity. The warrior-like masculine men tossed princess-like feminine women without fear of gender stereotypes or political correctness. The crowd stood with thundering applause as the show concluded.

Afterward, we had post-show drinks at a terrace bar overlooking Red

Square and the Moscow Kremlin. Natalia spoke of Russia like a college history professor. I envied and admired her knowledge, appreciation, and respect for her country.

In the morning, steam came from the shower head in the bedroom-sized guest shower. Natalia had breakfast prepared as I stacked my bags in the entryway. Anton had spent part of his night highlighting a map of the most important sights I should visit in the region.

Anton recommended a service shop that worked on BMW motorcycles at half the price of the BMW authorized service center.

Dear Natalia and Anton,

Thank you for the generous gifts. You made me feel like royalty, treating me like a king. You both went above and beyond to make my visit a true pleasure. You are such a kind and lovely couple. I hope to see you both again to return the hospitality. I hope you are well.

Sincerely,
Robert

I left the bike at the shop Anton recommended because their service was half the cost, while I returned to the States. Later, you'll find out why, in this case, saving a few bucks wasn't such a great idea.

"Southbound in September" became my mantra to escape the dropping temperatures up north near Moscow. I had reached the temperate shores of the Black Sea near Crimea, in a town called Kerch, Ukraine. While waiting in line for the ferry to Russia, I needed an exit stamp in my passport.

One customs official approached me with physical disdain and contempt. He glanced at my United States passport and said, "Follow me," his arm rigid with a clenched fist around my passport.

I followed him into the customs building and down a hallway to a dimly lit private room.

This large man's mind was fixated on something. His demeanor was that of a guilty suspect. His voice reverberated in the corners of the yellowed ceiling and beige walls. "Ten euros," he demanded.

"For what?" I asked.

His answer? "Ukrainian exit fee."

I showed him my passport with multiple entries and exits of Ukraine. Never had I been charged this phantom "exit fee." My blood curdling with rage, I kept my body poised in restraint.

His inflated chest emphasized the importance of completing our transaction, since the ferry was leaving in ten minutes. "*Ten euros!*" he repeated.

"*No!*" I said.

I observed his sagging pants and untucked shirttail as he huffed outside. Holding me back, he allowed all the other vehicles onto the ferry to ensure I was last to board. The gangplank was at the point of being raised when he eventually waved me through.

As I rode past him, I stared him in the eye. "Karma is right behind me," I said.

Twenty minutes later, I rode off the ferry into Russia. One officer waved me to the front of the line. I feared reprisal. Instead, this blue-eyed boy shook my hand and congratulated me on riding from the United States. He stamped my docs, and once again I entered Russia. Up and down, good and bad, pleasant and unpleasant experiences like these make my ride a "Full Circle."

I rode farther down the Black Sea Coast to Sochi, Russia, where I was denied entry into the Republic of Georgia because of disputed border territory. There was another breakaway state similar to Transnistria, except Georgia wouldn't let anyone cross the border in this area called Abkhazia, formerly owned and operated by Georgia, now separated with the help of Russia. The disputed territory prevented my planned route into Georgia, so I took a left turn and headed eastbound. The border was like riding parallel to a fence line, looking for an opening. The high Caucasus Mountain range was the fence line without a gate into Georgia, forming a mountainous barrier to my destination.

I kept riding eastbound, paralleling the border with no entry points. A mountain pass into Georgia was becoming a dismal desire.

Wilted and drained like the sunflowers in the field off my right, I felt isolated in disputed land, out of touch with peaceful people. I was unsure where I could climb the Caucasus Mountains into Georgia. If there was a "barrel of emotions," mine would have been in the bottom. I wondered when things would get better. Like a spinning wheel of good and bad, I knew it wouldn't take long. When things are at their worst, they can only get better, proven to me many times.

Then it happened, as it always does: serendipity.

Raging along at 150 kilometers per hour, out the corner of my eye I spotted three old Russian airplanes parked in a field. As I passed them, I thought of missed photo ops that I regretted not capturing. I spun a U-turn and headed back for this portrait of Russian aviation.

Three aging Antonov AN-2 bi-wing airplanes bathed in the sun. My tires crackled up the gravel access road where a man toiled at a shack guarding the entrance to the grass airstrip. The faded windsock drooped to the tall weeds. To the hardworking Russian, I made a pinching gesture, requesting permission to photograph the amazing Antonovs. He responded affirmatively.

Then, like a Russian mafia movie, I heard music then a tricked-out black VW with tinted windows drove up the gravel road.

Their blaring music stopped, and the two young men inside barked at the worker, then started on me. "What are you doing here? What do you want? These are personal airplanes, not yours."

I fearfully recognized serendipity had started.

The two young Russians and I used iPhone translation apps for clear communication. Griig wore a tight tank top, skinny jeans, white Adidas sneakers, and greased-back hair. His father owned the airplanes and operated them for anyone or anything needing transport. The other young man, named Timur, was quiet, with a cautious intelligence, shaved head, and cherry-red track suit with stripes on his arms.

"I'm a pilot," I explained, "and I'd like to photograph the three airplanes."

It was 4:00 p.m. I had about three hours of valuable daylight left. Either I continued to make time on the dry straight road or get invited to spend the night with my new Russian friends. *Stay with them!* my mind screamed.

Initiating Operation Houseguest, I inquired about hotels, then asked leading questions inspiring them to invite me to their house. I was excited at the possibility of interacting with a Russian pilot and seeing the family's way of life. My self-deprecating humor broke the ice. One mutual chuckle after another was all it took. Griig invited me to spend the night with his family. I followed the black VW twenty kilometers to their apartment building.

We parked in front of the unpainted cinder-block apartment complex. The main entrance had a blue metal door that squeaked like a coffin lid as Griig opened it. Like sandpaper, the abrasion of my boots powdered the decaying cement floors and chipped stairs. I hoped I wouldn't pull the rusting railing from the wall as we climbed to the third-floor hallway, dimly lit by sunlight creeping through window slots. A black rubber mat was placed outside the door of their apartment. A slice of sunlight helped Griig identify which key to use on the deadbolt lock. Mother, Father, and two sons lived wedged into a Soviet-era two-bedroom, one bathroom apartment. Inside, Mother was waiting, her hands still wet from washing vegetables as we shook hands. She gave me a tour of their apartment from where we were standing. She pointed to the kitchen area, dining area, TV watching area, and sleeping area. Our feet still planted, she smiled and offered me vodka.

They were Muslims and didn't drink alcohol but insisted on me drinking. Mother relentlessly tried to force Russian vodka on me, but I didn't take a drop. I was still a bit on edge and needed all my faculties at full strength. Mother said that it was the pilot's day off, and he was at a local cafe with friends having vodka himself, so it was okay if I drank vodka.

Recipe: Sit in front of the Russian paparazzi. Have them ask you offensive, insulting questions about your country as they film every statement and show it to the world on social media. Do you feel like a victim under interrogation? Do you defend your beliefs or acquiesce to choose other battles?

I was startled when ten thirty-something Muslim men burst through the door claiming they weren't Russians, but Adygeans. Adygea is another breakaway state trying to distance itself from Russia. I was sitting defenseless on the couch as the ten men surrounded me. Each pointed a cell phone at me, filming "The American Motorcyclist," like I was about to do a backflip in the living room.

We talked about the world, which created disagreements that could have intensified, but thankfully, I refrained from correcting their misconceptions of 9/11, past/present presidents, Syria, and America's place in the world. They all thought G. W. Bush contrived 9/11 to improve his public perception. They claimed the USA invented Osama bin Laden to blame 9/11 on him and improve the USA's world acceptance. They also said the Boston Marathon bombers, who grew up in the area, were invented by President Obama to improve his ratings. I wouldn't have been concerned about a few isolated opinions, but everyone in the room, including the quiet mother, agreed with these false statements and expressed negative opinions of the USA. I feared for my safety, spending the night as a perceived enemy. The guidebooks recommend avoiding political discussions while traveling in foreign countries. Good advice.

The group was proud of the Kardashians because they're of Armenian descent, and they valued the quality production they produced.

Amorck, the father and large-bellied pilot, threw open the door around 11:00 p.m., yelling. He had drunk three bottles of Russian vodka. He boisterously greeted each friend and family member in the room, saving me for last. He didn't speak English, and I didn't speak Russian. We communicated with common pilot terms, like runway, taxiway, and emergency procedures, finding a comfortable commonality. He was a former Russian air force pilot who violated the Muslim no-alcohol policy with great zest.

The dreaded bedtime had arrived. In their cramped quarters, I slept on the couch, while Griig and his brother snuggled in a twin bed. Amorck and wife shared a queen bed. Amorck's snoring like an untuned bassoon rendered my earplugs ineffective.

In the morning, Grigg was in the kitchen with his mother. Our previous night's heated discussion didn't deter them from preparing eggs, sliced sausage, and small slices of toast for us.

After breakfast, we exchanged some gifts. Amorck gave me an Armenian necklace still in my jacket pocket. Griig gave me his Russian military belt. Mother gave me a quince (local tart fruit). The entire apartment building came out to watch the American motorcyclist pack and ride away.

Dear Amorck, Griig, Timur, Mom and Brother,

I would like to thank you for allowing me to spend the night with you. Thank you also for the generous gifts. I appreciate you allowing me to experience your life. The anti-American comments you all made were offensive, impolite, and incorrect. Americans are not, as you said, "hamburger-eating, Coke-drinking, lazy blanks." I tried to see the positive side of your Communist habitat and hope you can see the positive side of Americans. I have only stated factual observations without judgment here. Please accept my gratitude. I hope you all are well.

Sincerely,
Robert

Still riding parallel to the Caucasus Mountain range, looking for a border entry to Georgia, I saw five bikers and their bikes having cigarettes roadside. I had just had a break myself but hadn't seen many bikers, so I pulled over to chat with them. It started again: serendipity. The bikers were from Chechnya and asked where I was headed. Coincidentally, the leader of the group was named Timur. He invited me to his home in Chechnya.

"Is Chechnya safe?" I asked.

"Follow me and see," he said.

I asked him if I could spend the night at his place. He said yes and off we went.

Military checkpoints were of concern to my five biker friends. They called for support to arrange safe passage through the many checkpoints. I wasn't sure who they called. I just know that minutes later, a gang of intimidatingly loud motorcycles met us to outnumber the officers at the checkpoints like a swarm of killer sharks.

The group got bigger when we met more Chechen bikers downtown. They were all part of the "Wild Division," a Chechen motorcycle club named after a former cavalry division of considerable strength. All the Wild Division members welcomed me with open arms. Ready to ride, we started our bikes. The rumbling bass line of a motorcycle group ride always gives me shivers. Each rider revs his engine like a musician tuning an instrument. I get choked up inside. Being welcomed by "warriors" of a disgruntled nation willing to lay down their lives for their brothers and beliefs intensified my emotions.

The powerful gang led me to a secluded restaurant in the mountains that served as their clubhouse/hideout. Inside was a long table, bar area, and stage for club meetings. East European music blared over the loudspeakers. They showed me their weapons stored in a locked safe room. They had racks of daggers, knives, swords, AK-47s, pistols, and some medieval instruments of torture to round out the display. They also had body armor, helmets, face masks, and ancient uniforms made from buffalo hide.

We all sat down at a long table to eat. Timur gave a speech in Russian, which seemed to rally the crew. We had soup with a shank of meat in it, potatoes, and bread. Being Muslim, they didn't drink alcohol in public.

Two male club members did a traditional dance with two females on the dance floor. It was interesting to see the dramatic male dominance and the female submission in their traditional Chechen dance, similar to a peacock spreading its feathers to attract a mate and strutting around with an inflated posture. In the dance they were doing, the female actually never submitted, leaving the male hungry and strutting onward.

The night wound down, the group disbanded, and we were on our way home to Timur's apartment. Timur's place was very similar to Amorck's the night before. In the bathroom, water was provided by a fifty-five-gallon drum and ladle. When he showed me the toilet and said they didn't use paper, I ceased all possible urges.

In the morning, Timur, who was chairman of the Wild Division Grozny Motorcycle Club, received a phone call from a TV station requesting an interview with me. Running behind schedule, I hesitated but thought it would be an honor to see what would happen next.

The station director said it would only take an hour or two. The dreary Eastern European rain made my mounts, dismounts, and many city shots look ominous. After two hours of filming, they pulled over and said it was time for the formal part of the interview. I was led into a cafe, where cameras and lighting equipment were set up.

A veiled Muslim woman interviewed me in English, asking questions fed to her by the director. I felt like a celebrity.

The interview went overtime, and I needed to ride. I thanked them and hit the road.

Dear Timur,

Thank you very much for your hospitality.
I admire your dedication to your motorcycle club and
your love of motorcycles. I wish you all the best,

Sincerely,
Robert

I knew daylight over the icy-cold, fogged-in Caucasus Mountains would be a challenge. I tried to make up the lost time. The pressure of getting to Tbilisi, Georgia, and all the flights home in time for work weighed on me like an elephant.

I was getting very comfortable with Russia and had a number of words committed to memory. In every country I visit, I learn at least four expressions: *hello, goodbye, please,* and *thank you.* I use those four expressions with varying inflictions to assist in communicating my message. It portrays a small attempt to learn about the local culture and respect it.

I accelerated faster, trying to make up time, but "Cardboard Cops"

Andiamo Full Circle

(a term I coined to describe the countless life-sized billboard cutouts of a policeman pointing a radar detector at oncoming traffic) slowed my pace. They're an actual photograph and appear to have a personality. I would always slow for them because after every ten or so "Cardboard Cops," a real cop appeared, ready to hand me a ticket.

> Recipe: Have the Russian cop stand still. Allow him to put his nose against the jack-in-the-box toy. Unlatch the lid, springing the clown out of the box. Watch him jump back with anxious surprise. He will not perform at his best from then on.

Preemptively for safe passage, Timur alerted the police checkpoints along my route to let me through without hassle.

At one checkpoint with a line of cars, I filtered to the front. An angry cop stomped in front of me with an arms-crossed pull-over signal. His stiff epaulettes (shoulder boards) reflected his boyishly smooth face. You can generally determine the experience of an officer by the age of the uniform. The other tattered-uniformed officers were in the car chatting. Clearly, they let the kid do the work.

My mind was crushed as the young cop used a phone translation app to exclaim, "You are very bad. The ride is over." He typed, *The bike will be impounded, and you are going to jail.* His trembling hands struggled to hit the keys of his iPhone translator app.

I pretended not to understand what his message said. That bought me time as he worked me for money.

His message was crystal clear. "You need to pay me fine of one thousand US dollars."

I grasped his phone as I gestured for clarity. "*One zero, zero, zero US dollars?*"

"Da," he affirmed.

Without pause, I flared up like a cobra in a jack-in-the-box, ready to strike, "*Nyet!*" I yelled in his face.

Spittle launched from my lips, and the word hit him like a punch from Mike Tyson. He jumped back, swallowed, and understood I was vehemently opposed to his request. There was no way I was going to forfeit one thousand US dollars. Out of principal, I'd rather go to jail.

He was visibly shaken by my jack-in-the-box response. "*Skolko?*" he mumbled.

I turned away and walked a few steps. Elated, I continued a few more steps for dramatic effect. I knew the meaning of that precious Russian expression, "How much?" I turned to face him, reduced our distance, and forcefully sneered. "*Nyet.*" I showed him a zero sign with my hand against his nose. Unbeknownst to the young fella, he had opened negotiations. Like a pressure cooker, my strategy could go either way: contained success or explosive mess.

Every country around the world has a less tolerant justice system than the United States. Not all police procedures are as fair, as equal, and as regulated as in the United States. In other countries, you're guilty until proven innocent. These accepted bribes are commonplace and how the Russian police actually make their money, forcefully pressuring people to pay them bribes.

I had learned years prior, in the interior of a country, one way to handle such traffic stops is to attempt to use false identification to reduce your exposure. I gave the cop an expired driver's license with a wrong address.

His thousand-dollar request, his boyish face, his trembling hands, convinced me this would be resolved successfully. I just needed to satisfy him financially.

"How much you pay?" he asked again.

"Zero," I reiterated. After a lot of back-and-forth posturing, I needed to expedite the conclusion and get on my way. I conceded, with a devilish smirk. "Five hundred."

"Five hundred?" he gleefully clarified.

"Da," I said. From my money clip, I handed him a fresh five-hundred-ruble note. My driver's license hit my chest as he disgustedly grabbed the money from my hand. I collected my things and left. Five hundred rubles is about seven US dollars at today's exchange rates. The money I saved in the altercation later went toward a hotel for the night.

Recipe: V1 or Velocity sub-one is "takeoff decision speed," the speed at which a pilot is forced to make a decision whether to abort or continue a takeoff. If an emergency occurs before V1, the takeoff is aborted. If the emergency occurs after V1, the pilot continues the takeoff and handles the emergency airborne. Every decision in life has a V1 moment: yes, no, left, right determines your destiny. Have the artist tattoo *V1* on your body as a reminder to make your best decisions in life.

The next morning, south of Vladikavkaz, the high Caucasus Mountains fiercely looked down on me. I looked up with fear at the angry peaks I needed to conquer to reach my destination and get a flight home to show up for work on time.

Andiamo's scorching-hot engine began stuttering. I needed to assess the situation. His kickstand sank into the soft shoulder as I stopped to contemplate this V1 moment. I had to make a decision to abort the climb and ride back to Vladikavkaz for service or ride a questionably running motorcycle over the now-freezing glassy mountain roads. Either decision churned my stomach. I needed help. With what I wasn't sure.

My ears were funnels of joy receiving the unmistakable hum of a BMW boxer engine descending from the mountain fog. A minute later, three BMW motorcycles appeared, like angels from heaven. They pulled over, and I greeted them enthusiastically. I showed them my service order paperwork from the cheaper Moscow BMW shop Anton had recommended. My last service and oil change was done there. I asked them to check the paperwork for anything unusual.

I felt like a Russian roulette winner as one man announced he was the service manager at the Moscow shop. He had refilled Andiamo with mineral oil because it was cheaper. I use $18-per-quart synthetic oil. It handles my abuse much better than mineral oil at a buck ninety-nine per quart. They gave me an extra quart of their mineral oil. I was appreciative for this fortuitous meeting. Now aware of why Andiamo was scorching and acting strange, we climbed the mountains for an icy ride into Georgia.

Georgia

2014

Mileage: 66,000

Ingredients: the letter B, the letter F

I knew the authorities were watching as South Ossetia passed off my right within a few kilometers. It was yet another disputed territory claimed by Russia, owned by Georgia. To comply with sanctions, it's rumored Russia stockpiles weapons there. It was like walking a tightrope along the Russo-Georgian border identified by barbed wire.

Clearing my eyesight, I blinked rapidly to verify entry procedures were actually written in English. The customs agent welcomed me into Georgia with a three-month temporary importation permit for Andiamo.

I parked underground at Kopala Hotel in Tblisi, Georgia. The next day, I booked a flight home through Baku, then Doha, then to the States on Qatar Airways.

Upon return to Georgia, I packed five quarts of synthetic oil, an oil filter, and one heavy-duty garbage bag in my checked luggage.

I bought a ticket on Pegasus Airlines out of Istanbul. Pegasus is a ULCC (ultra low-cost carrier) in Turkey. They charge additional fees for anything and everything. This was before the ULCC model was adopted in the States. I handed the agent my boarding pass.

"You need to pay extra for your carry-on bag," she said.

"What!" I protested.

"We charge for carry-on bags."

Fuming, I paid the money. "I'm never flying this airline again," I said. *Hilarious*, I thought. *Their website, FlyPGS.com, looks more like FlyPigs.com.*

Andiamo Full Circle

The next month, FlyPigs.com offered a ticket ten dollars cheaper than the competition. I booked it. "I'm never flying this airline again" is the most fickle statement an airline passenger makes.

At my Georgian hotel, in the dim and dusty light of the underground parking area, Andiamo looked terrible. A cat had taken up residence under Andiamo's cover, and it now had a certain cat-like urine smell. I changed the oil right there, using the heavy-duty garbage bag to contain the old oil.

Recipe: Attempt one of your bucket list items. Realize it won't happen. Replace the letter *B* with the letter *F* for your new spelling of said list.

Georgia is supported by the United States, and Azerbaijan is supported by Russia. The border is constantly disputed.

I hoped to find Davit Gareja Monastery. Deep into the mountains I rode. On a dusty gravel road, I spotted a group of soldiers. "Howdy," I said naively to the US Army sergeant in charge of guarding the road leading up the mountain.

The sergeant's jaw flexed as he screamed, "What in the hell are you doing here?"

"I'm looking for Davit Gareja Monastery."

A United States Army unit protected this road at the base of the isolated mountain range.

"Get the hell outta here." Like whiplash, the sergeant's head directed me.

I rode outta there quickly, albeit up the dirt road. From the top of the mountain, I looked down the other side, where a Russian army unit conducted their own maneuvers. I rode by them and didn't stop. One kilometer later, I saw the blue helmets of UN Peacekeepers huddled in a group, waving metal detectors. They appeared to be mapping a minefield grid with roped quadrants. There were a considerable number of *UXO* signs with skull and crossbones posted in the area. UXO stands for unexploded ordnance land mines. Sign after sign, like telephone poles along a country road, caused me to wonder why.

My brain was in neutral, as I had not yet connected the dots to this puzzling portion of Earth. Then "war zone" catapulted into my brain as I realized what the signs meant. My bucket list *B* became an *F* as I kicked Andiamo into gear to escape the war zone.

I retraced my route past the UN blue helmets and their minefield, past the Russian army conducting maneuvers, up to the top and down the other side, where the Americans were now on the ground doing the belly crawl. That seemed peculiar.

Then the road disappeared. It had been blown up by an IED. A large crater replaced the tire tracks. It felt like my tonsils had regrown, as I blazed a detour around the crater. Distancing myself from the war zone couldn't happen any quicker as I rode to safety. It was one of those "wow, that just missed me" experiences. I craned my head backward as I rode the heck outta there and waved goodbye to my time in Georgia.

Asia

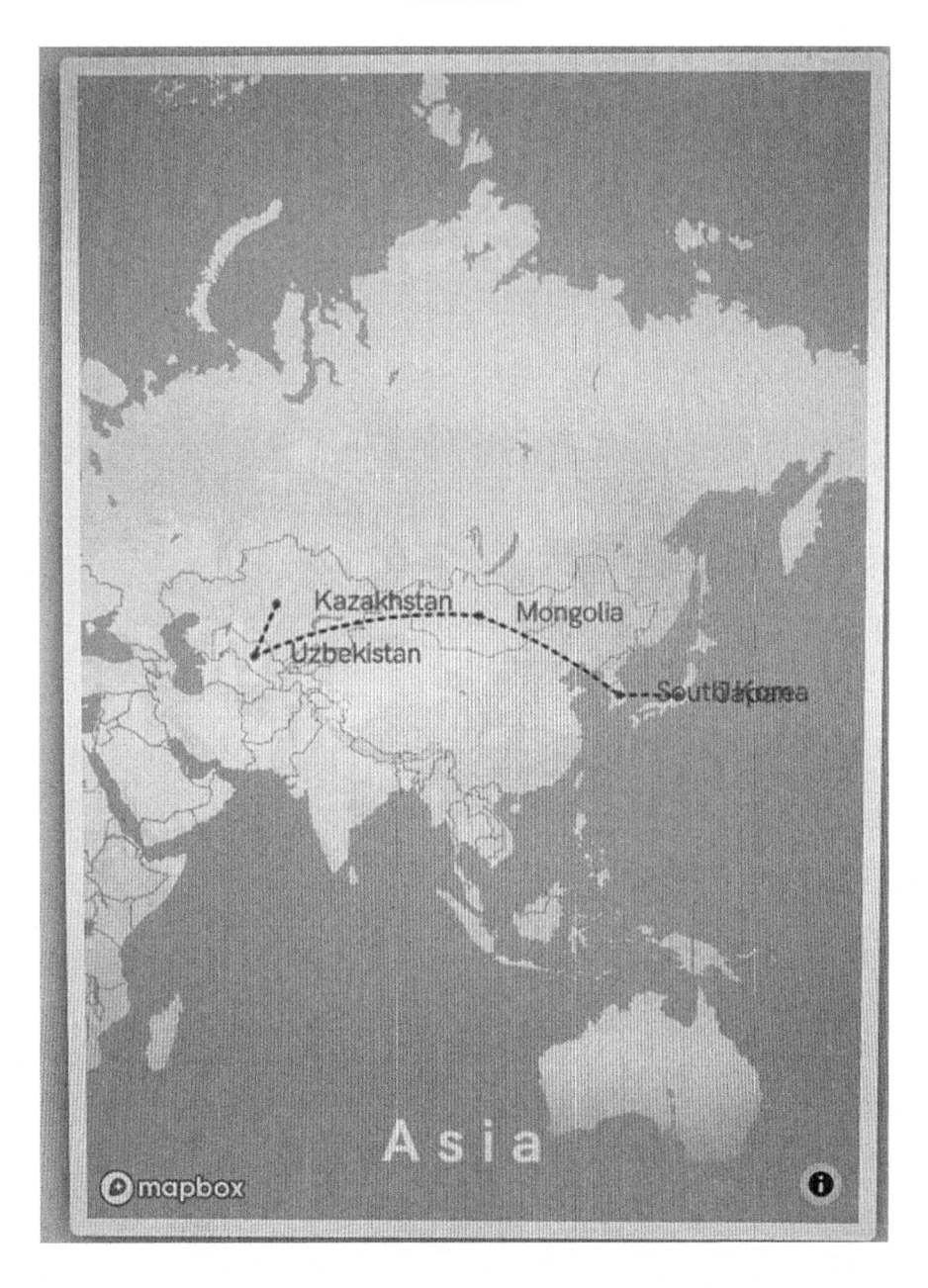

Azerbaijan

2014

Mileage: 66,000

Ingredients: one gallon lighter fluid, one match

Recipe: Pour one gallon of lighter fluid in a straight line in the sand. Light the match. Throw it on the line in the sand. Watch it burn for days.

Azerbaijan means "Land of Fire." Baku, the capital city, is the lowest city in the world sitting at 92 feet below sea level. The top site I saw was Yanar Dag, wonder of the world near Baku, Azerbaijan. Flames jet nine feet into the air as it burns. Natural gas has been seeping slowly from the porous hillside, causing a slow, steady burn since the '50s when a shepherd accidentally ignited it. Standing next to it melted my riding suit.

The next day at the sea-port of Baku, I purchased a ticket for me and one for Andiamo for the thirty-hour, roughly day-and-a-half journey across the Caspian Sea on a cargo ship. Vika the sales agent pointed me in the direction of the ship.

Riding the dock area, I spotted my ship named *Carag Carrav*, an '80s vintage German-built ship originally manufactured for military transport and listing to the starboard side. Waiting to ride aboard, I made friends with the ship's electrical engineer, nicknamed "Cnapkn." He was a spotted-skinned, seafaring fifty-one-year-old with a smoker's voice, who definitely had job security, as the ship's aging electrical systems would often fail.

A line of diesel trucks drove up the gangplank with me. Four men wearing dungarees, hard hats, and rubber boots shouted over the thunderous noise of the trucks and signaled me into the cargo ship. Rusted slick with seawater and truck oil, the swaying drawbridge made balancing tricky.

The noise intensified. Fumes blackened my lungs inside the lower deck loading area. Undecipherable Russian instructions were yelled at me. A burly worker grabbed my jacket, raised his fist, and pounded my helmet, explicatively identifying the descending fifty-foot platform elevator used to raise and lower semi trucks between decks. I was directly beneath it as it closed down on me from above like a car crusher ready to pancake me. There were no safety zone markings painted below this massive hydraulic elevator.

I had narrowly escaped death once again. The way it works in the rest of the world, each person takes responsibility for their own negligence, i.e., funeral costs would have been paid at my own expense and not a lawsuit windfall.

That elevator loaded the upper deck stuffed full of trucks as the lower deck filled with diesel smoke. I waited for my cabin assignment.

Finally a woman yelled to me, "Ver joom rridy."

Down the hall in my room, I found two Georgian men. Pablo looked like a dark-skinned snowman with spherical bald head, coal eyes, and carrot nose. The other man's name was Tremer, tall and thick with a deep-bass voice that sounded like he was talking into a fifty-five gallon drum. Tremer didn't say much, but when he did, the walls rattled.

With introductions complete, Pablo forced his homemade chacha on me (a cognac-type strong distilled liquor made from grapes). Pablo poured a few drops into a jar lid. The chacha produced a twelve-inch flame when he lit it inside our cabin. His eyelids only opened halfway over his snowman charcoal eyes. He insisted I drink his chacha as he stared into my forehead. He became belligerent when I declined.

Then Tremer growled, "Drrrankkk."

Reluctantly, I tried Pablo's chacha, chased with juice from a large jar of homemade stewed tomatoes that each of us drank from. Pablo only spoke broken English but knew American pop culture and politics. He recited the names of past US presidents with ease and was shocked when I couldn't name the current Georgian president. He had opinions on each

US president and called Obama a "nixxer" and couldn't believe America would allow such a thing.

Like Gilligan's Island and their three-hour tour, my tour was scheduled to be a day and a half and hadn't started well.

I hoped only Pablo, Tremer, and I would have the six-passenger cabin to ourselves, but in walked three large-bellied drunk Georgian truck drivers. A man nicknamed Wolf had a thick black mustache that served more as a toupee. Yuri was short and quiet in a passive-aggressive way. Ivan was young and old, with a pronounced hunchback, and appeared to be on death's doorstep prematurely. They were carrying plastic bags full of wiener strings, tomatoes, bread, and a rusty old propane tank. Like Mom bringing in the groceries, they unpacked their plastic bags. They were roughly my age but looked weathered from years of smoking and chacha.

I knew they were talking about me. I recognized a few words such as *America, motorcycle, BMW, wealth,* and derogatory gestures. Pablo made up a song, "Goodbye, America," which concerned me. How could I sleep and trust my belongings unattended for the night?

It was then Pablo displayed animosity for my American wealth. He grabbed my iPad as I typed, giving me a toss-it-overboard motion. Yuri pulled him away from me and calmed him down.

Pablo was mad that Georgia was fighting in Afghanistan alongside the Americans but claimed America would not protect Abkhazia and South Ossetia or any other disputed breakaway states in Georgia.

Tremer empathized with Pablo's point with resounding bass tones. "Ya, Pablo, ya," he said.

Yuri nodded in agreement.

I argued with them. "Last month I was nearly blown up by an IED while the US Army was protecting the border in Georgia. So don't tell me we aren't protecting you!"

"The US is ungrateful and should send more help," Pablo said.

Hunched over, Ivan agreed and yelled at me in Russian, his words bouncing off the floor.

Tremer bellowed in with disapproval. "Fucking American."

It was pointless to argue with them to defend myself. I was outnumbered.

They all agreed that the Soviet era was better for them. They were proud of Stalin being from Gori, Georgia.

Pablo called Communism "good because we didn't need to work as hard."

Ivan struggled to straighten his back as he nodded in agreement with Pablo.

The man nicknamed Wolf told me stories of the Kazakh Steppe, where the bad roads and wolf attacks had killed three Turkish truckers in recent months. He'd received his nickname by shooting a wolf attacking him. He strung the wolf on the hood of his truck as he drove the Steppe. From that day forward, he was called the Wolf.

They called me crazy for thinking I could ride the Kazakh Steppe and cautioned, "Do not camp or ride at night."

After their warnings, I washed my face in the room's washbasin with a trickle of brown water and climbed into my top bunk to write until I fell asleep. My earplugs could barely drown out the five Georgian men's pontification. I typed and fell asleep with a finger on the *A* key to find five pages of *AAAAAAA*s.

Morning came, and we had only moved a few kilometers to anchor in deeper water. I went to the ship's bridge to inquire about our progress. I slid the rotting wood door open to find the bridge empty.

In the salon (cafeteria), no one had any information on why we had moved only a short distance and anchored.

That afternoon on the bridge, I found the chief officer, a uniformed young ambitious man interested in advancement to captain. He spoke a bit of English, had neatly trimmed hair, and wore stylish glasses that made him look smarter. I hung out with him on the bridge, asking questions about maritime rules. I read through the manuals on ship systems and emergency procedures just to kill time.

The trip was going on forty-eight hours. It was scheduled for only thirty.

In bed early on the second night, I fell asleep as the ship's engines rumbled, indicating we were on our way. Hopefully, I'd awake to a new country and the end of this tumultuous trip across the Caspian Sea.

In the morning, I found us anchored only miles from our destination. On the bridge, no one could explain why we weren't docking. Any ship officer I asked repeatedly answered, "Dunt no, druup an-kar."

It was a frustrating mystery. I adjourned to my bunk.

Days three and four were extraordinarily mundane. The sea was still, and the ship was anchored. My time was spent avoiding my cabinmates and scrounging for food in the salon, which was running low on supplies. The thirty-hour trip was going on ninety-six painful hours.

The engines idled, and the ship slowly moved locations again, Kazakhstan only five kilometers away. I returned to the bridge.

The chief officer greeted me by asking, "Vear vu yistrdee? I nut si yu?" Then he muttered the ever-so-familiar words, "Druup an-kar."

Oh shit, here we go again.

He went on to say, "Vee cont git tu purt. Meybee tumoroow."

All the horror stories I had read about this ship were coming true. I allowed seventeen of my days off to attempt this sea crossing. I returned to my stuffy smoke-filled cabin to plan out my "murder of time." "Killing time" seemed too moderate of an expression.

My cabin was filled with smoking men, so I walked the deck.

In the salon, the busy Russian woman, the only female aboard, was being hit on by aging truckers.

"Lunch?" I asked her.

"Cheekin vith reece," she replied.

"Fabulous," I said and sat down at the only available place, a small wooden stool and wobbly table. I asked to purchase a bottle of water.

She handed me a half-empty opened bottle.

"Is this all you have?" I asked.

She replied, "Eit's mine. No mur un chip."

Great news! Running low on provisions and stranded here indefinitely. This trip made Juárez, Mexico, seem like a desirable vacation destination.

As the days went on, the tension built among the men as we sat anchored and motionless. Yuri snapped at Ivan to straighten up. The Wolf growled at Tremer, who answered with a boom. Pablo gave me a strangling sign while I looked away to write.

This alleged day-and-a-half journey across the Caspian Sea was now on day five and counting. I spent the fifth day in my bunk, only to visit the one horrendous pit toilet shared by all forty men aboard the ship, not all of whom had accurate aim.

My bunk was tiny. Feeling claustrophobic and stir crazy, I borrowed a cigarette and went out on deck for a paradigm shift. The flame of the match transferred to the cigarette. As I drew in gently, the cherry glowed. I inhaled deeply, and the smoke swirled down my larynx, warming the sides like an exhaust pipe from a '74 Ford. The joy of this deadly tube couldn't brighten my day. Everything seemed so hopeless. I counted the ships anchored on the starboard side, then the port side, for a total of twenty ships anchored offshore from Aktau, Kazakhstan. It was a terrible situation of helplessness.

Reentering my cabin was like entering a sáuna. The thick heat from five men smoking with no fresh air covered me like a vacuum-packed blanket.

Food was everyone's concern. With forty men in tight quarters for six days, there's bound to be fighting. The last wiener was missing from the Wolf's plastic bag. He accused Yuri of taking it. They yelled back and forth. Yuri's passive demeanor flared up to aggressive. Pablo landed a solid right hook to Yuri's mouth, twisting his neck toward his bunk. Blood dripped to his chin as Yuri admitted the theft. We all stayed out of it until the tension cleared.

At dinnertime, only slices of *salo* (sliced pig fat) were available to eat in the salon. I wondered if my body could continue absent nutrition. After my few bites of salo for dinner, I retired to my bunk. In my cabin, the party accelerated as other truckers filed in. It was a catch-22 between leaving the cabin door open to allow the smoke to escape and unintentionally inviting passersby in to join the harassment. The five-gallon bottle of homemade wine was empty, but the chacha still flowed as my cabin mates sang to a video featuring a veiled man playing a high-pitched Arabian stringed instrument and singing anti-American propaganda.

"*Robert!*" yelled Pablo.

I leaned my head over my bunk to see what he wanted.

Like a third-grade tattletale, he mockingly told the other partiers, "There is an American!"

Immediately, a husky, greasy-haired man with a decades-old scar from his forehead to his chin, like he had tried to eat a chainsaw, invaded my bunk space. He wore a dirty white tank top and pointed his finger at my nose. "You imperialist pig," he said repeatedly.

"Scarface" shouted other derogatory comments toward America and me. He was a guy who had nothing to lose and was willing to bet it all.

A dark Turkish man played a video on his phone of a child singing, "Fuck America, ya ya ya. Fuck America."

These drunkards in my cabin were out of control, singing, dancing, and threatening me while I pretended to read in my top bunk and ignore them. The present situation would pass, although I found it terrorizing while it happened.

Scarface started lifting my bunk like a Russian power lifter. "Imperialist pig," he yelled. "Death to America." He gave me the jugular vein cutthroat death sign. "Yankee, go home."

I tried to remember what I'd learned in my travels. *Remain calm. I will emerge from this painful encounter and survive.*

Scarface spat, then with a hushed voice, whispered, "I'm gonna kill you!"

I snapped. I needed immediate intervention. I pressed the red button. Using my satellite emergency locator transmitter/receiver, I contacted GEOS Worldwide Search and Rescue and explained my situation. I was in imminent danger and needed extraction. This was February 2014, the height of the Russo-Ukrainian War in the area, and the US was tangled in the modern-day cold war. I explained it could be an international incident, complicating things politically.

GEOS immediately contacted the US embassy in Kazakhstan. Ingrid, my savior, a diligent consulate representative at the US embassy in Kazakhstan, contacted the port authority. The port authority contacted the ship. The ship was categorized as emergency status and moved from number fifteen in line to number one with high priority. We were docked within thirty minutes of me contacting GEOS Worldwide Ltd. I had never been so proud and relieved to be an American.

Once the ship was moored, my shipmates and I were told to muster in the salon and await further instructions. Forty men crammed into a closed room, all smoking nonstop.

Five Kazak soldiers burst into the salon. They asked some questions in Russian I didn't understand.

Pablo then violently pointed and yelled out, "There's the American."

The soldiers rushed back to me, asked questions about my satellite communications, took me ashore, and placed me in a quarantine cell for the night until immigration staff arrived in the morning.

The immigration officials were clearly acting on orders from above but wanted to know my importance. The procedures took about two hours with questions of who, what, where, and why Ingrid at the US embassy in Kazakhstan had contacted the port authority for my immediate rescue.

I explained that with onboard fistfights, food and water shortages, my death threats, and a complete feeling of helplessness anchored at sea, "I needed my country's help, and it responded swiftly and appropriately."

Several other guards took my key and rode my bike off the boat and parked it near my quarantine cell. I was worried they would damage the bike. However, they professed understanding how to operate and ride a motorcycle. I let fate take its course.

I'm not sure what happened to Scarface, but I know threatening the life of an American has consequences and perhaps inclusion on a terrorist watchlist.

I would like to thank the United States of America and Ingrid at the US embassy in Kazakhstan for saving my life. Without either, I could have been victim of a horrible destiny.

My trip that month was seventeen long days. I clocked a distance of seventeen miles on Andiamo's odometer. In summation: one mile per day.

I'm often asked, "How many miles on your motorcycle?" People often guess a million miles.

I answer in relative terms. "The present-day odometer reads roughly three times the equatorial circumference of Earth." This makes it sound longer than the actual seventy-seven thousand miles of the ride. I need to explain the complexities and difficulties of each mile I've ridden, like that the seventeen miles for this month's ride were not all beer and Skittles. Each mile on Andiamo has been earned the hard way.

Kazakhstan

2014

Mileage: 66,000

Ingredients: one Fisher-Price See 'n Say The Farmer Says version

Upon clearing immigration into Kazakhstan, my screen went black as my malfunctioning GPS entered dead-battery mode. I just wanted to put miles between me and the terrible Caspian crossing. Relying on my internal compass, I searched for a hotel. Aktau's Soviet-style architecture stifled my amazement with identical World War II memorials, military monuments, and block housing painted a single shade of gray.

I spotted a suitable hotel with a circular driveway and covered entry. The uniformed bellman helped me hoist Andiamo onto his center stand, averting a hernia.

A friendly "*Dobryy vecher*" (good evening) to the front desk girl and explanation of my needs initiated "Project Parking."

The girl turned to speak with a thick-bodied maintenance man. He firmly shook my hand as we were introduced. When I requested a place to store my motorcycle for a month, he stepped aside.

A man wearing a pressed shirt and shiny jacket stepped up. "I'm Hendrick, the manager." Hendrick's explorative mind kept denying my needs. "No, no, no, no, no, nothing. I'm sorry, we just can't accommodate your request. There simply is nowhere for your bike."

I've learned that if no is the initial answer, they just don't have enough information, so I explained the importance of my needs.

Hendrick's mind kept searching the property, still saying, "No, no, no" in his German accent.

With each no he gave, my hopes grew stronger. I didn't give up on him, and he didn't give up on me.

The maintenance man's expression changed. He suggested a way to solve the problem. "We can clear an area in the toolshed."

Leaning against the hotel's north wall was an enclosed shed built with chicken-wire fencing and a corrugated tin roof and cluttered with dingy bedsprings. The three of us cleared a spot, and I pushed Andiamo in for the month. It was the perfect mediocre parking spot.

At dinnertime in the hotel lounge, I ordered a beer. I was alone at the bar, except for one other guest relaxing in a cushy chair. His pilot's uniform contrasted with his glass of wine. As if posing for a proud dating website photo, he gave me the finger-gun "let's do lunch sometime" wink. I couldn't believe my eyes.

My shock reentered the lounge, as his Chiclet smile flashed. "Hello, I'm Dimitri. I'm a captain at Air Astana."

It's strictly forbidden to be seen in uniform consuming alcohol. My mind, like a wavering teeter-totter of conflict, wondered if it were poor judgment or lax regulations. I said hello.

Sensing my disapproval, he said, "Don't worry, I fly out late tomorrow."

Pilots respect their occupation, but this was an obvious display of self-esteem by uniform. I excused myself to search for the business center computer. I booked a flight home through Moscow for $750 and got on it the next morning.

~~~

Back in Phoenix, I researched my upcoming ride.

"Scorched earth" describes the Kazakh Steppe, a horizontal windswept bleakness, with villages separated by five hundred kilometers, dotted with wandering wolves and wild camels. I would need to carry extra food, fuel, and water over the Steppe. From my cushy couch in Phoenix, I questioned why I would leave this comfortable life in the United States to experience the hardships ready to capture me on the Steppe. I worked hard for two weeks to have two weeks off. It was a grueling schedule, but the only way to complete the ride.

~~~

Then it was back to Kazakhstan.

Before takeoff out of New York's JFK Airport, a taxi delay caused excruciating pain, as my liter of water filtered through. The minutes ticked like a sledgehammer on my bladder. We were on an active taxiway. Having forbidden myself to be "that passenger" who gets up to use the lavatory just before takeoff, I squirmed in my seat as I considered using a blanket to disguise refilling my water bottle.

With two JetBlue A320s and two American 737s in front of us, the captain said, "We're #5 for departure."

I clenched my fists, bit my knuckles, and flexed my quads. Airborne, we climbed into smooth air. The seat-belt sign being extinguished was like my number had been called at the DMV. I dove into the lavatory, overcome with a turbocharged sense of relief.

At my hotel in Kazakhstan, the shed's chicken-wire door fell off its hinges when I opened it to confirm Andiamo had survived the sub-zero temperatures and gale-force winds off the Caspian Sea in his makeshift parking spot.

The next morning, Andiamo started with slight battery hesitation. I left him running at the supermarket while I stocked up with enough food, fuel, and water to conquer the Steppe.

Andiamo raked forward as his front wheel entered the first pothole of the Steppe. Camel herds and wild Arabian horses scoured the dust for food. Rusty oil rigs sucked fuel for Russia. The ugliness was attractive. Over the flat and roadless terrain, trucks cut a straight line to their destination hundreds of kilometers away, coloring the air with a dusty hue.

I followed in the worn path of heavier trucks that created a resemblance of road. The occasional downpour troweled portions smooth and slippery. Balance was challenging, with my gear cinched to my rear rack stacked higher than my head. My center of gravity out of safe limits ready to topple me, I fishtailed around craters like I was twerking. Somehow, I've become allured by this sadistic pain.

The sun became a convex disk of blaze-orange on the western plain as my eyes oscillated the reddish-yellow air for a safe place to sleep. Immersed in nothingness, all I could see was the delightful dust-glow. My cabinmates on the ship had warned me about rabid attack wolves ready to devour me on the Steppe. I needed safe shelter for the night, so I kept riding to reach my destination of Beyneu.

A scattered settlement of adobe buildings appeared on the now dark-green horizon. One building capable of sustaining life was a cafe for the occasional hungry trucker passing by. On the doorstep were three small crumbling stairs leading to a doorway. When I spread the wool blanket door aside, the smell entered me like steam from Mom's kettle.

The female owner sitting on a stool resembled a statue waiting for a customer. Her apron stained from wiping her hands, she asked, "What you need?"

Attempting clear language, I asked, "How far Beyneu?"

She held up two fingers. "Doo huirs."

I didn't have two hours of strength in me, so this outcrop of adobe buildings was home for the night. "Hotel?" I asked.

"Nyet," she said.

I put my hands together to form an A-frame tent symbol. "Camp?" I asked.

She pointed anywhere outside.

In search of a spot to pitch my tent absent camel poop or debris, I found shelter from the wind near a garage occupied by an old Russian van. I had the nightly camp setup perfected to a five-minute magic act.

The cafe owners' son, a roundish boy-man, approached me. He held a gun whose stock was oily and chipped. "Vor de vulves," he said, apparently worried about wolves attacking me. "Du vu na how to jooot?" He set a plastic milk jug thirty yards away and handed me two shotgun shells. "Von priktiss chot."

I blew the bottle away.

"Purvect, de seacond sheall fur de lead vulf. Jooot heam. Vrest vill scatta." He turned to leave. "Zleep vell." He left the shotgun for me to snuggle with.

The wind over the Steppe fluttered my tent throughout the night. The sun had switched horizons. My right eye was bloodshot from sleeping with it open all night on wolf-watch. I used a mouthful of water to brush my teeth and a hand wipe to wash my face. I took the shotgun shell out of the gun and walked into the cafe. The mother/cafe owner was still on the stool waiting for life to happen. I handed her the gun and shell, bought a bottle of water, thanked her in Russian, and walked out the blanket doorway.

The two-hour ride to Beyneu took me four hours of battling the terrible terrain. As I entered town, a longnecked wild camel jumped in front of me. I squeezed hard on the brake lever, activating my antilock brakes. The Kazak camels were different from other camels. They had adapted to the harsh, cold, windy conditions, growing long fur hanging from their necks and thick skin that wobbled as they walked. Some had humps that slumped like wilted flowers. The town was merely a gas stop for truckers crossing the Steppe.

I rode four additional hours. The terrain turned into pavement as I accelerated toward civilization. More sustainability appeared. Land turned green. I spotted a tree, then a river with water in it, then a house. Grass now covered the ground. I increased my speed to a hundred miles per hour on the now-smooth surface to notice my teeth had stopped chattering.

The air was fresh, the altitude was higher, and things turned beautiful again. In a small village, I stopped at a roadside shop to ask for a place to camp and get some supplies for the night. I grabbed a plastic container from a dusty shelf. Its name written in Russian Cyrillic characters, the shaded green bottle looked like lemon-scented Palmolive dish soap.

The shopkeeper's cigarette twitched in his mouth as he said, "Nuting eelse drrink."

I bought it and some canned fish.

Back on the road, lush green fields weaved into sharp, snowcapped mountains surrounding me. The valleys became saturated with horses, goats, sheep, cows, dogs, and cowboys. The backdrop was stunning. I inhaled the fresh air.

Two stocky and nimble cowboys were working with a muscular show horse adorned with satin socks. The horse's savage horsepower demonstrated as Andiamo made him rear up, hooves high in the air, ready to crush the cowboys. They nervously authorized camping in the groomed setting, swiveling their heads between me and their horse.

Camp was magically set up in five minutes. Awestruck in the setting, I considered myself lucky to travel this way. I swallowed some canned fish and chased it down with a swig of the lemon-scented Palmolive dish-soap-type drink.

Recipe: Dial the arrow of the Fisher-Price See 'n Say to the cow setting. Pull the string. It says, "Moo." Repeat this for all the animals on the dial, resulting in "Old MacDonald's Symphony," moo, quack, baa, neigh, and so on.

The rolling hills were like separate amphitheaters of animal sounds from herds segregated into groups of horses, cows, donkeys, goats, sheep, and roosters, all making their characteristic calls simultaneously from their divided sections. The combined calls created a unique acoustic experience echoing through the hills. The sheep would baa from the sheep section, the horses would neigh from the horse section, the roosters would cock-a-doodle-doo from their section. They were all in different spots, either on a hill peak or in the deep valley. The dogs seemed to bark for encores, and the whole symphony would start from the top. I coined it "Old MacDonald's Symphony."

Uzbekistan

2014

Mileage: 68,000

Ingredients: one used washing machine, one used microwave oven

I made it to the border of Uzbekistan on May 1. My visa started May 2. My front tire touched the red-and-white striped gate blocking the border crossing.

A broad-shouldered guard with a devilish look said, "Gum beek toomaroo."

There was not a hotel for hundreds of miles. I parked Andiamo outside a cafe a hundred yards from the border. The pale-white cafe building had two primitive windows split by a low doorway that I smacked my head on as I entered.

Recipe: Strap the used washing machine to your back like a backpack. String the microwave oven to your front side. How far would you walk with these items for two dollars?

Inside the Uzbek-style cafe, I sat on the floor, using pillows as chairs at the knee-high table.

A Brillo-haired Uzbek man wearing an ikat robe and sporting a thick beard sat next to me and introduced himself. "I'm Murat. I'm a transporter." Murat carried items across the Kazakhstan-Uzbekistan border for a small fee.

Each person was allowed to carry two bags across the border per day. Bags were full of clothes and household items and stacked up in the backyard of the cafe waiting for transport. Sometimes Murat would carry an appliance that qualified as one bag. He told me he could walk across the border with a washing machine strapped to his back and a microwave in his arms, meeting the "two-bag" limit. He earned a small commission selling the items to awaiting hawkers on the other side. The hawkers would take the items to poverty-stricken villages with a marked-up price. Murat would bring the proceeds back to the cafe owner. Being a transporter was a good job in the area.

Karott owned the cafe. He wore western-style clothing, appeared well fed, and had a powerful loud voice. He issued assignments to awaiting transporters, like traders bidding stock prices on the New York Stock Exchange. The elderly transporters, restricted by strength, could only carry small bags, while Murat, being younger, could carry heavy, expensive items and earn more in commission.

This cafe operation was an illicit business. I believe more than clothes and appliances were being transported across the border. A group of whispering transporters cautioned Murat. They told him I was a spy and he shouldn't talk with me. This warning occurred often as I traveled the "Stans." I lust for the mystique of intense cultural differences like this one.

Since there was no hotel, Karott allowed me to set up my tent out back among the piles of used items. It was like a junkyard of old appliances, clothes, and other discarded articles waiting to be carried across the border. On a filthy heap of old clothes, I saw a T-shirt with the imprint, *I Heart Wisconsin Dells*. I fell asleep thinking about the compound differences between the T-shirt's previous owner and future owner. How many hands had touched this impulse purchase from a gorgeous Wisconsin resort town to end up on this impoverished border between Kazakhstan and Uzbekistan?

The next day as I was crossing the border, the broad-shouldered Uzbek guard with a devilish look wanted to see my iPad as I was clearing immigration. Sitting at his desk, he asked, "What's your password?"

I had never had any border guards look through my phone or iPad.

"Unlock it," he demanded.

I did, and he thumbed through my files. I wasn't sure what he was looking for, but I could speculate. Disappointed he didn't find any contraband, he stamped my passport and shoved me through the border.

The dictator of Uzbekistan controlled the natural gas industry like a recluse miser. All cars run on natural gas. He only allowed petrol (gasoline) to be sold one day per week, so the black market gas business was booming. I carried five extra gallons in this land of no gas stations. Masked men in dark back alleys, like drug dealers, sold gas stored in one-liter water bottles. One hotel operator brokered me thirty liters of the "best gas in Uzbekistan," according to him. I'm disappointed I don't have footage of me pouring thirty water bottles of gas into Andiamo, but he feared being filmed. Like during Prohibition, getting Andiamo something to drink was illegal.

Payment was cash only. One US dollar equaled 10,130 som. There were money counters, human and mechanical. I was able to film a money-changer guy as he flicked the stack of bills quicker than money-counter machines featured on drug dealer films. I changed a hundred bucks. He counted out 1,013,000 som in less than ten seconds. The audio portion on my video sounds like a playing card in bicycle spokes.

Seventy kilometers off-road into the desert was the Aral Sea. Large ships that sank in the sand are rusting miles from any water, run aground when Stalin of the Soviet Union built two major dams to irrigate his cotton fields, thus choking off the water supply to the Aral Sea. The shoreline receded, to leave the ships where they were. Decades later, they rot in the dry desert. It created the world's largest eco disaster. It also left tens of thousands of people devastated without the sea to live off. It was a ghostly scene I was glad to leave.

Riding through the next village, I heard a semi-loud "psssst." Perplexed, I suspected a front shock seal had blown. At the next stop, oil gushed from my left shock, another suspension problem due to my overloaded motorcycle. I had to ride at slower speeds to avoid bottoming out the suspension.

As I assessed the situation, six Belorussian motorcyclists on big adventure bikes stopped next to me. "Where can we find gas?" they asked.

"I don't know," I said. "I only have thirty miles left in my tank. Then I'm out."

"There is a rumor that in the next town, one kilometer after the bridge, on the right-hand side, a guy may sell gas," they said. They told me to watch out for bad gas tainted with semi-volatile liquids that would destroy

Andiamo Full Circle

my engine. Two of their mates had been completely stranded, with bad gas seizing their engines.

I thanked them and wished them luck. I felt like Mel Gibson in a Mad Max movie. The desperation left me alone in this collapsed world, depending on fuel to save me. I hadn't eaten anything for a day, but I wasn't worried about fuel for my body, only Andiamo. He was my master, and I needed to find him fuel to save us both.

The odometer was a countdown to an empty tank. With five miles left, the engine quit halfway across a bridge.

An inconsiderate cop whizzed by in his car and saw me straining to push Andiamo. "Get off the bridge!" he yelled.

Moments later, a Russian adventure rider named Serge, with a red plastic gas can strapped to his bike, asked me for gas. I told him about the rumored guy one kilometer ahead on the right, and Serge went to look for the "gas guy." Fifteen minutes later, Serge returned with five liters of liquid in his red plastic gas can. It was an act of humanity to save a fellow rider. Adventure riders were mutually dependent on each other. We were part of the same gang fighting against the dictator of Uzbekistan, who limited the amount of gasoline used in his country. I gave Andiamo five liters to sip on until I could acquire more from the "gas man" ahead.

I followed Serge to the "gas man" and bought thirty liters of the yellowish liquid contained in separate one-liter dirty water bottles. Serge transmitted his location on the two-way radio attached to his helmet and confirmed he had found gas. Minutes later, Micheal came to a stop on his bike among my thirty empty bottles scattered around me. Micheal had a CB radio antenna attached to his rear rack that looked like a flagpole. He had all the additional accessories attached to his brand-new BMW 1200GS adventure bike. He looked like a rolling NASA space center. Serge and Micheal were riding Uzbekistan together and asked me to join them. The three of us rode two hundred miles to the next town of Bukhara.

Two thousand years ago, Bukhara was a main trade hub on the Silk Road. Camel caravans carried silk, cotton, leather, gold, clothing, and food from Central Asia to Europe along this network of trade routes.

Serge, Micheal, and I rolled into a modest hotel with grand gates and a traditional courtyard.

"No availability," the owner said.

Micheal spoke Russian and negotiated our stay in a room with a solo guy. The room had two beds, but this other guy, named Adam, was an adventure rider as well and didn't mind us crashing on his floor.

Adam wore a Muslim taqiyah on his shaved head. There was strength and hardship in his large, muscular body. He beat his chest like Tarzan and said, "I'm a Chechen warrior." He extended his arm into my chest like a politician pointing into a crowd. With a certain deliberateness, he declared, "I know you!"

This frightened me as I wondered how. It turned out he recognized me from my Chechen TV documentary done months prior. He was friends with Timur, leader of the Wild Division Motorcycle Club, whom I stayed with up in Chechnya. Timur had told Adam about me and the flashlight I gave him. It was another crazy coincidence in this shrinking world.

We unpacked our gear and settled into Adam's room. Serge and Micheal spread two thin mattresses on the floor and gave me the unoccupied extra bed. Four tired motorcycle riders sleeping together in a small room rattled the windows with testosterone.

The next day, the four of us rode to the only national gas station in Bukhara. We all had extra gas cans and a few empty water bottles to extend our fuel range. Filling Andiamo from an actual fuel pump was a novel act in Uzbekistan and made me feel human.

Inside the gas station market, a woman dusted her merchandise. I spotted a unique item. It looked liked a pipe for smoking tobacco, with a thin, hollow stem with a bowl chamber on one end. Naturally, my examination required I take a mock drag to test its functionality.

The woman slapped it out of my mouth. "For da child pee pee."

Like a physicist solving an equation, I realized this device connected to a child's penis to direct urine into a receptacle similar to a tiny funnel. She also offered a slender female version. From then on, I decided not to put unknown things into my mouth.

Having filled up with gas, it was time to head for the cooler tempera-

Andiamo Full Circle

tures awaiting me north in Siberia. I thanked each man for saving my life, then waved goodbye to Adam, Micheal, and Serge. I headed north into the unknown, solo again.

~ ~ ~

Exhausted, I made it to a hotel in the capital city, Tashkent. I showered and went downstairs for dinner. At the hotel bar, I typed on my iPad and had a cold Osterbrau beer. A woman wearing a business suit sat at the next table with a glass of red wine. I learned her name was Helen, and she was married to a California Highway Patrol motorcycle cop who lived to ride and rode to live. She was part of a delegation from Washington, DC, in Tashkent teaching responsible oil and gas extraction methods to avoid further earthquakes. The Uzbeks suck oil and gas without thought of negative effects. She asked why I had decided to ride my motorcycle in Uzbekistan, of all places.

"Uzbekistan isn't the only country," I replied. "I left Phoenix years ago. I rode through Kazakhstan…,"

She interrupted me "Were you trapped on a cargo ship months ago and enlisted the help of Ingrid at the US embassy in Kazakhstan?" Her question seemed like a laser beam of coincidence.

"Umm, yes," I said with a skeptical tone.

"I work closely with Ingrid," Helen said. "She's the only embassy representative capable of what she did for you to get that ship ashore."

As Helen spoke, I typed her words. The Osterbrau beer clock on the wall read *7:27*. Helen had a meeting scheduled at 7:30 and ordered another glass of wine to go.

I was still feverishly typing when into the bar walked an amber-haired young man in western clothes. An American-looking guy with a pink polo shirt and plaid pants, he ordered a beer and cheeseburger.

"Are you the motorcycle guy?" he asked.

"How do you know that?" I asked.

He raised his beer to salute. "You're quite a legend." He introduced himself as Steven, and in a slightly perturbed voice, said, "Helen disrupted the meeting by telling the group about the Kazak embassy woman who helped you get off the ship in the Caspian Sea." He had a lot of questions for me. "Who pays for your ride? How do you get the visas? How do you stay out of trouble?"

"I pay," I said. "I carry two passports for visa issues, and I get into trouble, but eventually things work out fine."

Steven had traveled as much as I, but he had the US government doing the logistics, ensuring his safety each step of the way. He called me crazy as he sat at my table. He was a brilliant twenty-seven-year-old Georgetown graduate ready to start his PhD at Yale that fall. He did seismic work to predict when, where, and why earthquakes hit certain regions. His head swiveled as he surveyed the room like an owl.

"Uzbekistan is irresponsible. This very building could crumble at the slightest tremor."

That knowledge will keep me up all night, I thought.

At closing time, the bartender reached into the ice-filled cooler for his last two beers. Steven and I carried them to the cushy chairs in the lobby.

"Steven," I said, "the events this evening need to be documented. Can you please type a synopsis like you typed the term paper for the pretty girl in college?"

He grinned. "How'd you know about that?"

"Lucky guess."

The keys of my Bluetooth keyboard were smoking as his fingers typed a recap of our entire night's conversation. He finished the recap, and I thanked him and said good night.

The next morning, I rubbed my eyes open and pawed for the ibuprofen bottle on my bedside table. My eyes barely focused, I saw that my iPad book writing app was still open and had a bubble message on the screen. I clicked "yes," not knowing what the message said. The iPad fell. Realizing I had accidentally deleted Steven's synopsis, I was devastated for several minutes. Then I remembered hearing, "Notes can immortalize bad ideas. The good ideas stay with you." Therefore, I retyped the highlights from my conversation with Steven and Helen.

Upon checkout of the hotel, I looked for Steven to get his contact info again. He was nowhere to be seen. I had to leave.

Dear Steven,

If you read this, get in touch with me and let me know how you are doing. You are a fascinating individual, and I hope you are well.

Sincerely,
Robert

I rode hard for ten hours that day and was nodding off around sunset. My technique to scare myself awake is to ride with my eyes closed and count as high as I can before opening them in fear. I usually get to about six seconds before my heart is beating with reenergized adrenaline.

That evening upon check-in, the hotel proprietor asked for my passport. He recorded my information as I asked for dining options.

Russian hip-hop music punctured my eardrums from the occupied but lifeless party room near the lobby. Most attendees at the celebration were older and in a plump-belly vodka haze. In contrast to what one would expect from the loud music, every chair in the room was occupied by stagnant old Russian family members. Having no option of dining elsewhere, I ordered borsch and bread.

The space was cramped, with tables smashed together except for a small square clearing for a dance floor. Bottles of Russian vodka, sliced meats, bread, and potatoes were equally divided on each table. Actually, mostly vodka bottles covered the tables, allowing wedding guests personal guzzles. Small glasses were scattered around. Everyone in the room grabbed a glass, poured a shot, and toasted the newlyweds.

An aging uncle of the young bride slowly and silently poured two shots of vodka. He raised his glass, gesturing the other glass to me, and said, "Nice driveway." Actually, he said, "*Na zdorovie*," which sounds like "nice driveway" when pronounced in Russian.

All the raised glasses in the tiny room had the appearance of a human chandelier.

After many "nice driveways," it was time to dance. I pulled the father of the bride out of his chair onto the dance floor, eliciting laughter louder than the music, as two fifty-something men danced together. Like a flood of bodies, the dance floor filled. We did the chicken dance and played musical chairs.

The microphone was passed between each person to make personal toasts. I used the audio speak-back feature on my phone's translation app and typed the message, *Congratulations. May you enjoy a long, happy marriage.* I played it, translated into Russian, over the microphone sound system. The crowd went wild. I ended my evening on that high note.

My ears rang into my pillow.

~ ~ ~

Back on the road the next morning, I shifted cheek to cheek frequently. My butt had saddle sores from the ten-hour ride the previous day.

I crossed into Siberia, ready to ride the epic Trans-Siberian Highway, the longest national highway in the world, extending 6,800 miles and crossing seven times zones from St. Petersburg to Vladivostok.

My right-turn signal blinked onto the AH6, the Trans-Siberian Highway. Siberia is endless. I mean endless. I could almost see the thick forests generate oxygen for the region, scattered with sparse villages and traditional Russian log cabins. Each village had Russian Orthodox churches featuring magnificent onion-shaped pinnacles on top of tapered steeples. The onion domes had various decorations and textures covering them. Some shiny ones reflected the sun like advertisements for divinity.

Chugging down the Trans-Siberian Highway was another bucket list item. I felt like a real adventure rider. I had read reports of the unpaved sections being terrible and sometimes impassable. I was ready to experience the hardships on this vacant road.

My ABS braking system activated as I slammed on the brakes when a herd of cattle crossed in front of me. Andiamo stalled. I restarted him, but he coughed without combustion. After several attempts, he struggled to run. This was not good. As he idled sporadically, I removed the oil filler cap to witness plumes of smelly black smoke spit out like mushroom clouds from his engine. This meant with each combustion stroke, oil was being burned. Eventually, I'd burn it all. I had 800 milliliters of emergency oil remaining and 296 kilometers to ride to the nearest BMW services.

The pressure built while I contemplated what to do. I had several options. Try to stop the Trans-Siberian train on the tracks running parallel to the highway. Try to stop a truck that could carry Andiamo and me to Krasnoyarsk, where there was a BMW service center. Or ration my remaining oil and ride it out. For contingent comfort, I checked my work schedule to verify how many days I had remaining on this month's ride. I decided to continue riding and hope for the best.

I gently twisted the throttle above idle and cautiously tapped through the gears until I had accelerated to an adequate speed. I simmered at that speed. If I revved too high, black smoke clouds appeared in my rearview mirror, burning more oil. I attributed this current nightmare to a combination of the Moscow shop using mineral oil compromising the pistons during my extreme riding style and Uzbekistan's bad gas.

Every seventy-five kilometers or so, I would stop roadside to ration another 200 milliliters of engine blood into the rough-running engine. My mind void of other thoughts, I fixated on making it to Krasnoyarsk BMW. This predicament had my undivided attention. Nothing else in my life mattered. For 296 kilometers, the rest of my life was paused.

The badness felt good, like a total escape from reality. Every conceivable outcome ran through my head. I could be stranded and eaten by wolves. I could be stranded and saved by a Russian trucker. I could be stranded and hit by the train while trying to flag it down. I could be stranded and mugged by the Russian mafia. I was under pressure to make it back to work on time. I yearned for retirement when I could ride full time without pressure to return to the States.

With blue skies and tail winds, Andiamo labored into the service area of BMW Krasnoyarsk. Like a marathon runner crossing the finish line, he collapsed. He was done, finished, kaput. There was no more road he could run.

Eight men in the service area frantically gave me the "cut the engine signal." Little did they know my trusty boy and his boxer engine had carried me 296 kilometers on one cylinder. That heroic feat was confirmed when the mechanic showed me the crumbled remnants of the left piston in the palm of his hand. I ran my fingers through the shavings. The tiny slivers cut into my fingertips. The BMW boxer motorcycle engine is the best motorcycle engine in the world, ready to withstand the dramatic environments of riding around it.

I was relieved and distressed at the same time. I had made it to my destination. "What do I do now?" I asked myself.

Krasnoyarsk BMW planned to fly a new engine from Germany and have it fixed in a few weeks.

"Perfect," I said.

Looking at the bright side, this would coincide with my return the next month and allow me an excuse to ride the Trans-Siberian Railway.

I changed out of my riding clothes in the dressing room. Cindi, the polite receptionist, called me a taxi to the train station. I booked a four-day trip on the Trans-Siberian Railway to Vladivostok, Russia.

~~~

As I started to climb up to my top bunk on the train, the Russian woman sharing my four-person couchette shouted from her bunk. "No, no, no!" She indicated I must remove my shoes, then climb the ladder. She seemed to have a negative view of this train journey that I felt fortunate to be on. I guess it could be considered a long, ugly, tiresome voyage.

Conversely, with a positive attitude, one could see the beauty in the land, other passengers, and the neatly dressed crew selling goodies and providing assistance.

The sheets on my bunk were clean and starched. Next stop: "Sleepy Town." Slumbering to the swaying train, I felt a bite on my back. Immediately, I flashed back to the Turkish ferry, where I was bitten by a bot-fly-type creature.

I woke around 10:00 a.m. after sleeping nine hours, gathered my iPad and gear, and headed for the dining car for coffee and to write in my book while I watched Siberia pass by.

Decorated like an old Orient Express dining car, it had wrought-iron accents, red curtains, wood trim, and retractable ornate bottle holders on each table to keep bottles upright through the turns on the longest railway in the world.

Andiamo Full Circle

I was the only American among people from Germany, England, Spain, France, and Russia headed for Beijing or Vladivostok. The menu consisted of olive appetizers, borsch beet soup, and various beef selections. The speed of the train was slower than the high-speed TGV, Deutsche Bahn, or Trenitalia. The picturesque scenery was lush and fertile. Traditional Siberian villages were scattered around frigid clear lakes. I felt like my window was the picture frame of an amazing portrait. The land would be unforgiving in winter, when temperatures dip to minus forty degrees Celsius, making life freeze. The Siberians have adapted, storing goods for the winter and embracing the conditions instead of running from them.

The train was pleasant and full of interesting people. Three young Russian men with chiseled, bruised faces, wearing Mixed Martial Arts tank tops sat at the table across from me. I didn't feel like interacting, but one engaged me. In an uncommunicative state, he searched for verbal darts to throw at me. When that didn't work, we exchanged a set of gestures, trying to understand each other. I realized he came in peace, so our bond began. We toasted and gulped the room-temperature Russian beer from our glasses, sharing each other's supply. Things became good. The three young Russian army men were from a town near the railway named Chita, on their way to Vladivostok for additional parachute training. The dart thrower showed me his Russian army training videos, depicting shooting AK-47s, driving tanks, and detonating explosives.

We would repeat the same understood words: "Mother Russia, beautiful, big, Russia good, USA good, Russia strong, USA strong, Russia-USA friends." We had found the common ground of mutual understanding and brotherhood with only a few words. We took pictures of each other and listened to each other's music. He was proud of his Michael Jackson music, and I was proud of some Russian music I had archived.

Two young French students entered the dining car. We immediately welcomed the young men like long-lost brothers, hugging as the train knocked us around. They were students traveling Russia and spoke perfect English.

I addressed the clean-cut French students. "My Russian friends are drunk. We need to communicate with smiles and gestures."

The most angry-looking of the Russians was disturbed when he didn't understand what I had said, so I hugged him and gave him a thumbs-up.

"*Harasho*," I said, meaning "good," to calm him.

After a drunken exchange of maleness, I paid my forty-dollar bill and plunged into my narrow top bunk.

I typed the following random thoughts during this four-day train journey.

I love being able to recognize accents of where a person is from, then greet them in their language or toast them in their slang!

I pretend I'm on skis alongside the train, getting airborne and landing on the varied terrain, avoiding obstacles and taking the land as it comes.

I love riding the trains in Europe, Siberia, anywhere! They allow you to sit back, relax, and watch the world go by. Each Siberian village provoked new questions: What are the people like? What do they do for fun? Are they happy? Can they afford to buy food? Do they have kids? Are they well cared for? Why is there so much graffiti? Were there hooligans in ancient times? Do they have jobs? Do they stay warm in winter? Do their roofs leak? If they have cars, how do they function in minus forty-degree Celsius temps? Are the roads plowed in the winter? Do they make their own clothing? Is there a Home Depot nearby? Do the trains keep them up at night? Why does the waitress keep looking at me?

As the telephone poles whizz by, I try to time them to the music on my iPod, leaving me with an interactive melodic experience, like living a music video.

As an oncoming train passes, I look at the unfocused images in their cars. I envision and move to the hard beats of the music. When the passing train suddenly ends, I am faced with whatever is in view on the other side of that train, sometimes beautiful scenery, sometimes an oil refinery. Either pleases me!

Andiamo Full Circle

It has been a beautiful day, enjoying the train ride.

The duration of each stop was listed on a poster. Some were two minutes. Others were thirty minutes or longer. At one longer stop, I jumped off the train and ran into a market to buy some noodles and water. The shopkeeper was pleased I left him with the coin change when I ran across the platform to hop onto the steps of my train as it left the station. I twisted the door handle open and pulled myself into the car while the shopkeeper cheered me on.

While I ate my noodle soup, the two French students I had met earlier sat with me. We talked about life, travel, and professional aspirations after their engineering internships would end the next summer. They planned to get jobs or maybe get their master's degrees. Life to the boys seemed unlimited, and they could do whatever they wanted. The world was ours.

One's father worked for the French train company TGV. He could travel France for free and Europe at reduced rates. We agreed Thailand is a wonderful country, especially the people, and especially when they do the "namaste bowing gesture." We said our goodbyes. I sincerely wished the fine young men all the best in their lives.

As I opened the train car door to leave, I looked back as one said to me one of the most validating compliments I could imagine. "Don't stop being you."

As I walked back to my couchette, I felt my life had touched another's, growing my world in a small but significant way.

The train arrived in Vladivostok five minutes ahead of schedule. I booked the Vladivostok-Narita flight on Russian S7 Airlines for $306. My Russian flight landed on time in Tokyo, where I got bumped off my first standby attempt. At the customer service counter, I asked a nice Japanese agent the best flight for a standby traveler.

The kind lady smiled. "There is an additional flight added to Denver and virtually empty."

United operated their Boeing 787 on the Denver-Tokyo route. I was excited to ride the new Dreamliner and all its reputed advancements of a lower cabin altitude of six thousand feet, humidity added to the air conditioning, mood lighting, photochromatic windows, and a first-class lay-flat bed combined to give me the best night's sleep I've ever had on an airplane.

I landed in Denver and ran to catch the next Phoenix flight, home for a month while Krasnoyarsk BMW worked on Andiamo.

~ ~ ~

I returned to Krasnoyarsk BMW to find Andiamo complete and ready to go with his shiny new engine. The shop owner was an adventure rider as well and loved my story, so he did me a solid "*Spasibo*, comrade."

Back on the Trans-Siberian Highway, the air was fresh and pure in the middle of Siberia. I pondered the sum of each tree generating oxygen versus a person's consumption. In other words, I was breathing really fresh air forced into my open mouth like an oxygen mask supplying positive pressure as I rode faster and faster.

I enjoy the ride because I must maintain constant concentration, similar to a golfer who needs to focus all his attention on his swing or he will fail. If I divert my attention, it could be fatal. One afternoon my attention was diverted by my iPod jack coming unplugged. As I looked down, I failed to notice a twelve-inch-deep cutout in the road. My tires hit the edge of the cutout, shifting my weight unexpectedly left. I countered my weight right. A pothole in my path required me to shift back. The inertia kept me going in the wrong direction. The edge of the concrete cutout impacted my kickstand and skid plate with a scraping force.

I regained control and rode at thirty-five miles per hour for a bit to calm down and monitor the motorcycle systems. I stopped and crawled on the ground to inspect the undercarriage of my lifeblood. Under the bike, I saw huge scrapes and bent metal, but the impact hadn't punched a hole in the oil pan. With the new engine and four quarts of fresh oil, the oil should have been circulating through the oil system leak-free. In the oil sight glass, I squinted my eyes to see any metal shavings present. It was translucent and ready to ride into Mongolia.

Mongolia

2015

Mileage: 69,000

Ingredients: one large wall map of the world, one Stretch Armstrong toy

Recipe: On the wall map, affix one hand of Stretch Armstrong to South Korea. Stretch his elastic arms to attach his other hand to the Black Sea. Imagine one government controlling that much territory. The Mongol Empire did.

Riding in Mongolia was similar to Bolivia, with few roads paved or even graded, only dusty tracks in the dirt, creating dust clouds that clogged my lungs. Towns were far apart, and services were few.

Mongolia consists of rolling, barren hills with indigenous houses called gers (yurts) dotting a land full of wild horses, cattle, and sheep. There are no fences to corral the animals. They are free to roam. It seemed the entire country was without confinement, all roaming in nomadic style. I believe this is a trait originating from the Genghis Khan days. I imagined Genghis Khan traveling the Silk Road, conquering the cities as the Mongols moved west to eventually form the largest contiguous empire in history. Genghis would ride westbound unarmed into a village to peacefully negotiate with the local chief, offering the tribe access to the Silk Road trade route and protection from other tribes in exchange for a tax collected twice a year. If the local chief agreed, they became part of the Mongol Empire. If the chief disagreed, Genghis would shake his hand and leave. The following day, Genghis's Mongol troops would destroy the village. Horrific westbound rumors arrived before Genghis, making the nervous chiefs usually willing to accept the terms.

Riding late one evening, I needed a place to camp. I knew Mongolians considered a stranger visiting their ger as a gift from God. They would extend hospitality to the point of starving themselves.

Halfway up a shallow hill, I saw a solo ger, an octagonal felt tent supported by flexible tree spines with a chimney in the middle marking an exhaust for an interior fire used for cooking and heating. I positioned Andiamo so he wouldn't tip over in the soft dirt outside the ger. The felt door slid to one side, and a shiny round face appeared in the slice of opening. I smiled at the face. The face became a head, and the head became a female body wrapped in animal fur, wearing felt shoes. Her smile wide as the ger, she bowed her head, slid the felt door open all the way, and welcomed me inside. The only inside light was provided by coals from a weeks-old fire. Rusty pieces of metal framed a surface where a kettle curdled yak milk.

The round, smiley-faced woman poured a filthy cup of yak milk from the kettle and handed it to me. She gestured for me to "down the hatch." Hesitatingly, I sipped the whiteish liquid. It tasted like a combination of rubbing alcohol and goat cheese. My torso flexed with a northbound spasm funneled to my throat. The face smiled, affirming her pride. I smiled back, fighting the urge to vomit. She shuffled to the other side of the ger to produce a huge round metal tray of rotting food items. Her culture considered me a gift from God, and she was ready to give me her world. She jabbed the tray into my chest.

I felt so humbled by her generosity. I selected the smallest, most-cooked food item on the tray. She set the tray aside to watch me enjoy the piece of chicken foot. She was like a witness at an execution. My teeth severed the tendons, my tongue tasted the skin, and I thought of my digestive system. The profoundness of this encounter warmed my heart, hopefully to the boiling point to purify the chicken foot. I thanked her profusely and formed the A-frame tent symbol, communicating my need to camp for the night. She nodded and slid the felt door aside, indicating Mongolia is one massive campsite.

I started Andiamo to ride the proximity in search of a suitable surface for my tent. I rode in circles, finding nowhere to camp. Farther and farther from the face's ger I went, until it was socially unacceptable to consider the ground hers anymore. I felt bad riding off into the darkened sky, searching elsewhere for a place to camp without thanking her in a manner equal to her generosity.

I eventually found adequate ground to sleep on.

My favorite thing in Mongolia was the Golden Eagle Festival held in October each year. One hundred participants compete, using trained eagles to hunt and catch foxes and rabbits. Prizes are awarded for the eagles' style, precision, and speed, while the handlers are judged on their Mongolian traditions. It's a fabulous Mongolian heritage festival.

The next day in the capital city, Ulaanbaatar, I arranged air freight of Andiamo to South Korea using a local DHL Office. I disconnected the battery and drained the fuel from the tank while they built a wooden palletized crate and said I could meet Andiamo in South Korea in a month. It turned into an expensive logistical nightmare.

South Korea

2015

Mileage: 70,000

Ingredients: two high-speed bullet trains, two hundred yards of fuel line, one quick-connect plastic joint

> Recipe: Cut the two-hundred-yard piece of fuel line in half. Insert the quick-connect joint to the fuel lines and snap together. Tie the fuel lines to the bullet trains. Have the trains travel in opposite directions. Observe the fuel line become taut, then the quick connect destroyed by the opposing forces.

Collecting Andiamo in Seoul, South Korea, was further complicated by the Mongolians destroying my fuel line's quick connectors. In an attempt to drain the remaining drops of gas from Andiamo's tank, they mangled the connectors, rendering the bike unrideable. Also, the expressway bridge connecting Incheon International Airport to mainland Seoul does not allow motorcycles to cross. For these two reasons, I had to find a local company to deliver Andiamo to BMW Seoul.

Thankfully, Andiamo was quickly delivered to BMW Seoul by a local transport service and repaired the next day.

Later that day, I battled three hours of riding in freezing temperatures, icy roads, and construction detours to see the giant golden Buddha in Suwon, South Korea. When I dismounted Andiamo, my legs were so brittlely cold, I fell to the ground. Good thing I still had my helmet on as my head snapped back, hitting the pavement. I stiff-legged it to the ticket office.

"The Buddha is under construction and covered by a giant blue tarp," the clerk explained.

I felt like Clark Griswold at the gates of Walley World. Dang that GBT! Dejected, I turned southbound into warmer temperatures en route to the south coast.

I took the ferry out to Jeju Island. Often called the Honeymoon Island, it's a tropical-type island off the south coast of Korea that caters to newlyweds.

A unique experience on the island was Love Land, a tourist attraction featuring sex exhibits. It's a private park filled with twenty-foot-high statues of male and female genitalia, fountains shooting water from male phalluses, and exhibits demonstrating sex occurring inside a car, in a phone booth, and on a bicycle. You can stroll through the park to see over 140 sculptures, all sexual in nature. The original purpose of the park was to display love-oriented art and eroticism to newlyweds as an icebreaker. It's the most unusual park I've ever seen.

The next month, with my paperwork in order, I left Busan, South Korea, on a ferry to Japan.

North Korea

Year 105

Mileage: Andiamo was not allowed to enter.

Ingredients: one newborn baby, one cassette audio player, one cassette tape, one soldier

Adventurous destinations intrigue me. The more adventurous, the more intrigue. North Korea intrigued me. I had to see for myself if the news reports, rumors, and movies were true about this enigmatic country. The restrictions in place prevented me from riding Andiamo there, but I was satisfied with visiting without riding. I almost had my visa for North Korea approved. Unfortunately, it was denied. This happened in early 2015.

Sony Pictures produced a movie titled *The Interview*, scheduled for release on Christmas Day 2014. In early December, Sony's website was hacked, revealing embarrassing emails, company information, and details about the movie itself. Later, the hackers were identified and confirmed by the FBI to be North Korean. Sony pulled the picture from over three thousand movie theaters and said they were not going to release the film due to North Korea threatening September 11-type retaliation on any theaters around USA that showed the film. America was in an uproar over Sony caving to the terrorist threats. Actors spoke out defending free speech and censorship. President Obama said he would respond proportionately against this cyber vandalism but concluded that it wasn't an act of war.

On Christmas Eve, Sony announced they would stream the film on Google Play, YouTube, and their own website, making it available for rent or purchase.

I downloaded the movie and watched it Christmas Eve. It was entertaining and made me more excited to visit the "Hermit Kingdom" itself.

The border was still closed, with no update. Eventually, the country did reopen its border in 2016, and I did go.

Recipe: Place the cassette player in the newborn baby's crib. Play the tape of child lullabies themed with anti-American propaganda. Repeat this step until the baby grows to be a soldier. What is the soldier's impression of America?

May 2016

Where do I start talking about North Korea? So much material. So little time. I can talk for hours nonstop telling stories about my visit to North Korea, but every story leads to a tangent.

Tangent #1: Just the fact that I'm calling it North Korea violates their rules. They prefer to be called the Democratic People's Republic of Korea (DPRK) because the land is one peninsula—Korea—no North or South Korea, just Korea. According to them, anything south of the 38th parallel, which would be South Korea, is "occupied by the American imperialists and their allies." Per DPRK, they're still at war with America and South Korea.

I worked at getting a visa and eventually was granted one. The visa allowed entry in the year 105. *Wait what?*

Tangent #2: They reset their calendars to Kim Il Sung's birthdate (Grandpa Kim), so year zero equals his birth year of 1912. Year 105 to the rest of the world was still 2016. Last time the world reset their calendars was for Jesus. That's confirmation the DPRK people think, "Grandpa is God."

To get there, I had to fly into Beijing, then take a connecting flight to Pyongyang, North Korea, since there were no flights from South Korea into North Korea directly.

The greasy Tupoluv 204-100 aircraft departed Beijing at 2:55 p.m. From the tarmac, I climbed the airplane's stairway. Two armed guards positioned themselves outside the deadbolt-locked cockpit door. The Tupoluv had fixed, nonremovable seats obstructing the over-wing emergency exits.

An aft smoking section was available, and there were no safety briefing cards in the seatback pouches. Understanding flight safety, I questioned Air Koryo's ability to deliver me to Pyongyang safely.

On the runway of FNJ (Pyongyang), one guy with a snow shovel cleared the snow to help us avoid sliding off into the snowbanks. A few other men with shovels cleared the ramp area where we parked. Nearby, old Air Koryo Tupoluv and Antonov airplanes were missing engines and other critical components.

Inside the terminal, customs officials completely emptied my luggage, logging each item into a ledger, including the SD cards I had. They went through my iPad files, camera, and cell phone photos, and asked for movies on my iPad, all the while questioning me about my intentions. They even counted and logged the bills in all the currencies I carried.

On the other side of customs in front of the airport, my three handlers waited next to their van. A slender male named Gang, with combed tight hair and skinny jeans; a female named Kim, dressed in a puffy down jacket and tight miniskirt; and a male driver who didn't speak. They warmly greeted me with enthusiastic smiles and handshakes. Introductions complete, we drove into the frigid North Korean cold.

The roads had the traction of window glass. They don't plow the roads, so the repeated freeze-thaw snow makes them like skating rinks. I got the impression everyone hated my country after Gang and Kim compared DPRK to America with references to their superiority and America's inferiority, emphasizing how they knew I was envious of them and their paradise.

Thick-trunked trees, like living fence posts, lined the streets from the airport. Tiny twigs grew from the fence-post trees. I asked why so many women collected the small twigs into bundles.

"They are only making it more beautiful for the dear leader Kim Jong Un in case he passes through," Gang replied.

Clearly the scarf-wrapped peasant women were collecting the twigs to heat their homes. That was the first of so many brainwashed lies my guides told me. I had no idea what fabrications they'd say next.

We stopped at a shooting gallery, where Gang was proud to prove his

Andiamo Full Circle

superior marksmanship with ancient .22 caliber rifles. This was a regular stop for Gang. He was delighted to beat the American and notify all spectators like a football player spiking the ball in the end zone after a touchdown. Dinner was at an unlit, unheated, unattended restaurant, where they served duck soup.

As we drove through the desolate streets during a power-outaged darkness, the remaining lights only illuminated mosaics, statues, and paintings of the two leaders: Kim Il Sung, the Eternal President, and Kim Jung Il, the Dear Leader.

"Why is the hospital without power while the leaders' monuments are shining brightly?" I asked Gang.

This provoked Gang to say, "The monuments are more important."

Statues of their dead leaders were more important than the hospital?

In August 2015, clocks were reset thirty minutes earlier than Japan's to mark the liberation of their country from Japan after World War II. Gang told me victory was due "solely" to the efforts and contributions of Russia and China.

I asked Gang and Kim about Hiroshima and Nagasaki, to which they each replied, "Hmmm, I vaguely recall reading something about them, but in no way did those events contribute to the end of World War II or the liberation of our country from Japan."

They expressed no gratitude or acknowledgement for the United States. Their response fueled my contempt for their brainwashed answers.

We parked outside a drab beige hotel with a broken revolving door.

Gang retained my passport and visa. "You may not leave the hotel or go anywhere without me," he said.

The hotel was a Soviet-style unheated, unlit, dreary three-star affair. The front desk clerk was the only person in the vast lobby area. He explained the hours for "hot water." Gang quickly blamed the lack of hot water on the sanctions imposed by the American imperialists and their allies, not on the fact that 80 percent of his country's money goes to the military and not to building a satisfactory infrastructure. In the morning, I had no hot water. I quickly dunked my head under the freezing water and splashed cologne on my body.

Gang and Kim met me in the lobby. Breakfast was a hard-boiled egg, a piece of white bread, and a slice of bologna. They escorted me into a van, and we set out for our first stop: the birthplace of the Great Leader Kim Il Sung. It was reconstructed with antiques and stories that were unbelievable such as his mother boiling one grain of rice in one small pot, then being able to feed ten thousand soldiers. Gang pointed to the actual small pot from this story. By age fourteen, Kim Il Sung had completed his seventh symphony composition.

I questioned Gang's sanity when he said, "This is it. Look." He pointed to a small table. "This is where the Great Leader President Kim Il Sung wrote our basic constitution at age four."

I wondered how Gang could be mentally capable of accepting this as true, unless of course, the constitution was a book of fairy tales.

Back on the streets, every intersection had a shapely woman dressed in a tight blue winter police uniform, watching people to make sure no crimes were being committed, traffic and otherwise.

Next stop was the Grand People's Study House, which I was not allowed to enter due to a military issue.

Next were the big statues. Gang suggested I bring a bouquet of flowers for the Great Leader President Kim Il Sung and Dear Leader Kim Jong Il. Even though Kim Il Sung died in 1994, he is still the current president and will hold the title until someone gains enough mental capacity to question the fantasy.

"Am I required to bring a bouquet?" I asked.

"Everyone brings flowers," Gang said. "It is a sign of respect."

"Gang, when I give a gift, it's from my heart," I said. "I fear this bouquet would not be from my heart. I respectfully decline."

That hit Gang like a third grader being told, "There is no Santa Claus." He asked three more times if I wanted to bring flowers.

I apologized and said no each time. At the big statues, Gang required me to lower the hood of my jacket, exposing my head to the cold, then required me to bow and pay my respects to the statues. I just couldn't see myself doing that because of the oppressive atrocities those very leaders continue to inflict on the people of North Korea.

Andiamo Full Circle

At each site, a local guide was required to explain the highlights. My favorite was the hammer, sickle, and paintbrush, representing the worker, farmer, and intellectual. Built fifty meters tall to signify the fifty-year anniversary of the Workers' Party in Korea, it is the epitome of Communist art and a physical reminder of peoples' places in life. Each person in a Communist society has a job to do, period. Not much else matters.

I requested to drive up close to a modern-looking pyramid-shaped hotel that had been under construction for twenty-seven years.

"It is not possible to view up close," Gang said.

I drew several conclusions why we couldn't, but I thought it was mostly because North Koreans have a tremendous fear of failure. I believe the unfinished building was a magnificent structural failure. That's why it's forbidden to take pictures of construction sites or workers, because they're not at their best.

Gang wouldn't let me use my telephoto lens. "Absolutely no photographs!" he said.

Next stop, the botanical gardens, where two flowers were named after the leaders Kim Il Sung and Kim Jong Il. For Kim Jong Il's forty-sixth birthday, a Japanese botanist cultivated a special begonia called the Kimjongilia, which is designed to bloom on Kim Jong Il's birthday every year. Before that, an Indonesian botanist created an orchid named the Kimilsungia that is featured in a lot of their propaganda.

Tangent #3: You must not refer to them as Sung, Il, or Un. You must say the entire name, i.e., Great Leader President Kim Il Sung and so on… but I need to abbreviate. At the botanical garden I saw photoshopped pictures of Un overlooking Il at construction sites and various other events. In the pictures, one of them would appear four feet taller as they shook hands like it had been photoshoped. I queried the local guide about this disparity.

"Everything good happens because of President Kim Il Sung's oversight," she said, "or the inspiration and oversight of one of our leaders and their in-depth knowledge of every subject there is."

I recognized a pattern of rote memorization when they answered my questions. It became painful for me to listen to the brainwashed recital of every good event attributed to the Great Leaders and every bad event attributed to the USA. I did admire the extreme patriotism they had for their country and leadership, be it good or bad.

Tangent #4: Kim Jong Un qualified as a pilot simply by thumbing through an airplane manual. Minutes later, he was able to fly solo. This was proof to my guides that "he knows everything."

Next stop, the Victorious Fatherland Liberation War Museum, giving yet another inaccurate review of events and atrocities committed by the evil American imperialists and their allies. I was greeted by the local guide, and we walked the corridor full of shot-down and recovered USA airplanes, tanks, armored carriers, etc. It was painfully obvious that the only maintained portion of these destroyed relics was the US markings, so easily identified by museum guests as inferior American equipment. Opposite that side were the pristine North Korean planes and tanks, all intact, with shiny paint in war-ready condition. All weapons were of Chinese or Russian origin. Photos displayed surrendering US naval officers and their signed confession letters and statements of their kind treatment received from the North Korean government under the direction of President Kim Il Sung.

My most anticipated exhibit at the War Museum was the USS *Pueblo*, a 1960s-era spy ship that was conducting "marine research" in North Korean waters. The goal of the captured sailors was to extend a middle finger whenever photographed. The "digit affair" became these navy sailors' entertainment. I researched the story beforehand and knew what I was looking for. I searched and searched every picture in great detail, looking for the "digit." I found it in a picture of the USS *Pueblo* crew seated in two rows. One seaman in the front row had his middle finger extended.

"What does that mean?" I asked my guide.

"It is a sign of peace."

I guess it could be considered that, with a stretch of imagination. Inside the museum, they had more depictions of the crew, and recounts of battles according to their interpretations.

The 360-degree diorama was impressive, with life-sized models of tanks, planes, men, and equipment blended into a mural painted by forty-two artists in "Korean speed," all with significant dimensions, and forty-two thousand paintings of US and North Korean troops. Every picture depicted strong, towering North Korean soldiers clobbering the small, meek US soldiers. I expressed my offense to their continued use of the term "American imperialist" until it became a joke to them. They did a great job with the museum that I did find fascinating.

Our van was stopped at every corner by policewomen dressed in blue, because after 6:30 p.m., it was illegal for cars or vans to be on the streets unless they were military or vehicles with a tourist aboard. At each stop, the lady cops would shine their flashlights in my eyes to confirm I was a tourist. Only 1,500 tourists visit the DPRK each year, and I can understand why.

We stopped at a supermarket that had items for sale but no one buying them. It was called "Department Store One." Allegedly, North Koreans could buy some of the items, but the posted prices were out of reach to even the wealthiest citizens. Chinese knockoffs of Crocs sold for $168. A tube of Colgate toothpaste was $28.

Cars were pretty much out of the question and reserved for sports heroes, celebrities, or high-ranking government officials.

"No one needs or wants a car because of our superior transportation system," Gang said.

The overcrowded, freezing, fogged-up trolley cars broke down frequently. The underground metro covered a distance of thirty-five kilometers with sixteen stations. Each metro stop had a name like Victory, Reunification, Glory, etc. They were identical to the Soviet metro stations with elaborate chandeliers, marble arches, mosaics, and pillars. Their subway has the deepest average depth of any metro system in the world, and has the alternate purpose of bomb shelter.

Over dinner that night, I was out of patience with the negative view they had of America. Gang was unwilling to understand or hear my side of the story. We had some heated discussions about our differences, leaving me with a desire to study the Korean War and the confessions, torture of prisoners, napalm, and biological weapons with insects and gas that both sides used.

We stopped at the foreign bookstore to purchase some items. I bought a Juche idea book, their basic constitution that Gang told me Kim Il Sung wrote at age four, and propaganda posters showing North Koreans stomping on a US soldier. Text translations included, "Never let this happen again" and one stating, "Defend the highest peak for a thriving nation."

That morning, I was thrilled to have a lukewarm shower. Breakfast was two slices of bread, with butter and jam, and with a one-egg omelet.

On the way to the airport, we got into another heated discussion. "Your government selected Dennis Rodman to represent United States and visit North Korea as an ambassador," Gang said.

"It was not the US government," I said. "It was Vice News, an edgy internet news service. I did research the story before I came."

The van's side window had a PPG logo etched into it, indicating it was manufactured by the Pittsburgh Plate Glass company, of which I am a stockholder and am moderately familiar with. "Who manufactured this window?" I asked Gang.

His final rehearsed, brainwashed, and incorrect answer: "It was manufactured in DPRK."

After the "answer" that broke me, I ceased all conversation.

At the airport, Gang slid open the door of the van. "I am going to report our conversations to my government," he said. "It's best you don't return to DPRK."

"Gang, I warned you halfway through our time together to stop offending me," I said, "but you continued without pause. I respect the loyalty you have for your country. Please respect mine. I hope someday you learn what real paradise is and stop being fooled that this is paradise because I assure you, I have seen paradise and this is not it."

With that, Gang jumped back into the van in haste. I would have felt bad for being so brutally honest, but it was warranted and justified.

Going through customs and security was a breeze. I stopped in a coffee shop and sat next to a girl who asked, "Are you the motorcycle guy?"

"How in the world do you know that?" I asked.

"I work at the French embassy," she said. "A colleague of mine spoke with you on the flight from Beijing to North Korea. She told me about an American riding a motorcycle around the world making a side trip to DPRK."

Wow, I thought, *what another crazy coincidence.*

This girl was the director of a program benefitting DPRK handicapped children. She had been in the DPRK for four years and was about to receive her new assignment that was likely to be in Bolivia. She had many interesting stories of her office and apartment being searched daily by the DPRK government, and of censored phone calls and emails and of money being stolen from the funds of the school for the handicapped and directed to the military.

"I don't bow or bring bouquets," she said. "That's the norm for me and my embassy people."

The frequent water, electricity, and food shortages disgusted her to the point of revolt. She was proud that I had spoken my mind to Gang.

"The DPRK people need to know there is a wonderful world outside their oppressive nation."

I flew back to Beijing, then to Seoul, South Korea, thankful that I live in a country where I'm free to live my life as I choose and explore the world, experiencing other cultures so I understand how good I have it living in America. I hope one day the people of North Korea have the same freedoms.

Japan

2015

Mileage: 71,000

Ingredients: one ant colony, one leaf blower

It was a pleasant journey across the Sea of Japan. My ferry docked in Hakata Bay as scheduled. This bay is where the Japanese term "kamikaze" originated, involving two Mongol-attempted invasions of Japan. In 1274 Kublai Khan, grandson of Genghis Khan, dispatched 500 vessels for the first invasion. The night before the Mongol troops were to invade, a typhoon hit, sinking the fleet. The Japanese were saved by the typhoon.

The second Mongol fleet, in 1281, was much bigger. This time Kublai sent 4,400 vessels and one hundred forty thousand soldiers and sailors. They were about to assault the much smaller force of forty thousand Japanese samurai warriors when another typhoon foiled the invasion, once again saved by a typhoon. The outnumbered Japanese referred to the typhoons as "kamikaze," which means "divine wind." Near the end of World War II, Japanese forces were outnumbered. They drew upon history and used their pilots and aircraft as weapons called "kamikazes," hoping to recreate the "divine wind" and defeat the stronger Allied forces. The day I arrived in Hakata Bay, there was no typhoon. We docked without incident.

Andiamo and I invaded the shores of Japan.

My first destination was Nagasaki, where on August 9, 1945, the United States dropped an atomic bomb over the city, instantly killing forty thousand people. Lee, a soft-spoken, kind gentleman, was my guide at Peace Park, which memorialized the hypocenter. Lee's father worked at the Mitsubishi shipbuilding plant, but had taken a train out of town that day.

"How do you feel about Americans now?" I asked Lee.

"I celebrate peace every day," he said, "and hope this devastation never happens again." He tried to turn it around into a positive and learn from it, which inspired me to do the same.

Nagasaki is a smallish coastal city that seems to have less hustle and bustle than Hiroshima. Cute streetcars meander through the downtown streets at a slower pace than the bicyclists, which silently swerve to avoid collisions with pedestrians. Everyone works in concert to create a feeling of cooperation.

Recipe: Imagine the one ant colony built on a scenic sidewalk crack. Imagine the ants within, sleeping in their tiny little ant beds. Now use the leaf blower to blow the ant colony into oblivion. Imagine those ants and their resolve to rebuild their colony.

I got lost trying to find my next destination, Hiroshima. Four Japanese motorcyclists riding sport bikes stopped alongside me on the expressway and said they'd show me the way. Very friendly and curious, they took selfies with me and called friends to come and meet me. The Japanese girls screamed and jumped up and down, while the boys asked questions about the ride.

I followed them to Hiroshima Peace Memorial Park, where I thanked them, thinking, *On my right, I have kind Japanese bikers who kindly helped me, and on my left, I have a memorial to the complete demolition of their city inflicted by my country.*

Hiroshima Peace Memorial Park is one of the most profound places I have ever visited. Hundreds of memorials have been erected, each honoring specific aspects of the world's first city to be annihilated by a nuclear bomb. It's a lesson in life and history to experience this city.

I started at the Cenotaph, a saddle-shaped statue honoring everyone killed by the bomb. Like a sniper, I closed one eye and looked through the saddle statue. In view was the Flame of Peace, which has burned continuously since built in 1964 and will continue to burn until all nuclear bombs on the planet are destroyed. Looking through the saddle, one eye still closed, I saw that aligned beyond the flame is the A-Bomb Dome. Featured in most pictures of Hiroshima, it's the building closest to the hypocenter of the bomb and partially survived the blast. The plaque on its entrance is a pledge for peace. It reads as follows:

As a historical witness that conveys the tragedy of suffering the first atomic bomb in human history and as a symbol that vows to faithfully seek the abolition of nuclear weapons and everlasting world peace...

Like an awakening, I opened both eyes to internalize the Cenotaph, Flame of Peace, and A-Bomb Dome building in the background, horrified to think that two countries provoked and responded in this deathly manner.

Rodney King's simple words came to mind: "Can't we all just get along?"

My experience with different cultures, in different settings, under different circumstances convinces me world peace can be achieved. We all have the same basic wants and needs. If we understand this and work together toward these common goals, we can all enjoy world peace.

The Japanese celebrate peace every day, ingrained from an early age. At one memorial, I filmed fifty schoolchildren who had made origami "crane chains" and connected them to other crane chains displayed at the memorial.

The concept started with Sadako Sasaki, the most widely known hibakusha. Hibakusha is a Japanese term for a person affected by the bomb. She was two years old when the bomb exploded one mile from her house. Her mother found her in a pile of debris. Thinking she was dead, she was later elated when little Sadako survived. At age twelve, Sadako was hospitalized with leukemia and given a year to live. In the hospital, Sadako started a chain of origami cranes. It's believed that if a person folds 1,000 origami cranes, they will be granted eternal good luck. Sadako had folded 644 before her death. Her family and friends completed the rest and buried them with her body.

A statue of Sadako holding a golden crane was unveiled in Hiroshima's Peace Memorial Park with a plaque that reads *This is our city. This is our prayer. Peace in the World.*

My throat lumped, and I had tears of inspiration reading her story. My suggestion: "Let's work toward a common goal of world peace by understanding, accepting, and supporting each other."

~ ~ ~

I headed northbound to Kobe, Japan. It was a spectacular ride—island-bridge, island-bridge, and so on. The country was manicured with flawless pride. It was probably the most beautiful continuous ride I've experienced. However, Japan had the most expensive toll road system I had ever used. Average price was $35.00, with the highest price being $67.50 on this "island-bridge" route. I noticed only one American-made vehicle: a spectacular left-side drive Cadillac Escalade. Every other car was Japanese-built. Clearly, they want to support their country.

I booked a room at the Kobe Meriken Park Oriental Hotel. It resembled a massive cruise ship and had the best steak house serving Kobe beef in the city of Kobe. I sat at the table while the chef prepared the steak in front of me. Over the tall flames, he seared the steak for forty-five seconds on each side, then sliced each piece, neatly spaced in a sushi-like style. Each piece was individually salted and melted in my mouth. For me it tasted more like pork than beef. In other places, Kobe cows are crossbred with local cows to suit the palates of each country. Most often, the United States crossbreeds Kobe cows with black Angus, which is what I'm used to. The cost in US dollars for my 250-gram steak was $208, which works out to be about $400 per pound or $17.33 per tiny sugar-cube-sized bite.

A short ride to Kyoto, and I took a tour of the Zen gardens at the Golden Pavilion. There my tranquility was interrupted by troves of schoolchildren, each holding a pencil and paper, tugging on my jacket. They were assigned the task of asking English-speaking tourists questions to help them improve their English. It was fun fighting off the swarms of kids, all asking me their questions at the same time. I did escape and snapped a picture of the Golden Pavilion.

I loved the geisha women of Kyoto, painstakingly adorned in silk kimonos and painted white faces. Their expressionless faces made me feel they were more like a live statue than a live woman.

Back on the road riding, I focused on Mount Fuji from fifty miles away. Near the base was a paragliding school. In the office, I scheduled a flight with an instructor. In a four-wheel drive van, they drove me to the base of a smaller mountain cliff. I got in a wheelbarrow attached to a monorail train track, powered by a lawn mower engine. As I hung on for dear life, this contraption pulled me up a very steep incline to the top of the cliff. The instructor strapped himself to me. We waited for a gust of wind and ran off the cliff. Run, run, run, jump, and we were airborne, with my feet dangling in the wind five hundred feet above the ground. My eyes targeted Mount Fuji and felt as big as the mountain.

My fear was directed to the tiny strings connecting me to the nylon kite fifteen feet above my head that was going to keep me and my pilot aloft high above the unforgiving landing site. But the fear soon gave way to the completely free feeling I had. Soaring around the sensational scenery of Japan will always be one of my most favorite moments in my life. Plowed fields below were outlined with thick trees and vegetation covered in a thin fog layer. My excitement made breathing effortless. With each inhale, my lungs inflated like balloons and only exhaled half of that, keeping me buoyant with excitement.

~~~

In a little town thirty miles west of Tokyo, I found a hotel. It was September 20, 2015, my birthday, and I wanted to celebrate. After a hot shower, I went out that night with the equivalent of twenty dollars in my pocket, hoping for a place that would accept a credit card.

I bowed my head as I entered a cute old-fashioned sushi bar filled with Japanese lanterns and oriental relics on the walls and cluttered shelves.

I tried to communicate with the bar maid that I had no money. "Will you accept my Visa credit card?" I asked.

She didn't understand, but two older Japanese men next to me said, "It's our treat."

I accepted their generous hospitality, and we drank beer and sake and communicated with my iPhone translator app. They were surprised about my ride and how far I had come and how young I looked, according to them. I showed them videos of me in Hiroshima and at the Air and Space

Museum next to the *Enola Gay*, the American B-29 bomber that dropped the atomic bomb on Hiroshima.

Two physically hindered girls graced the bar, one in a blue satin prom-type dress, the other in a green lace gown, both carrying a basket of red roses, which they offered to the patrons. After they communicated with my Japanese friends, Ms. Blue Dress told me she was single, offered me a rose and winked at me, then kissed me on the cheek and wished me a happy birthday. Humbled by the gesture, I wished her continued happiness in life.

Ms. Green Gown thought that was cool, so she repeated the event, then said; "I want to marry you."

They were both very fun to flirt with. Upon reflection, I was alone in Japan on my birthday with twenty dollars in my pocket. I received two wedding proposals, friends bought me dinner, we sang "Happy Birthday" in Japanese, and I learned more about the kindness found all over the world. *A pretty good birthday*, I thought.

This experience reminded me that although I certainly ran into my share of thugs during my trip, thuggery does not define the human race. Most of us are eager to be friendly and helpful. That seems to be the true human nature, even though it's the thugs that often get the news coverage. I was so pleased that my trip gave me a balanced look at human nature around the world.

I rode to Tokyo and found a BMW shop near the Haneda airport. Takao Sato, the owner, met me at the front door. He was very accommodating and offered me help with anything I needed. He extended my Japanese insurance and started work on shipment of Andiamo to Kuala Lumpur, Malaysia. He then excused himself to gather all his employees in the showroom for tai chi. Takao and his employees formed a circle, all doing tai chi movements. I felt uncoordinated joining in, but it was fun to mimic their coordinated movements. I asked Takao about it.

"We do this twice a day to relieve stress, increase fitness, and help focus," he said.

I could appreciate the practice and wished Americans could adopt the activity.

Tokyo is a city built on mutual respect for humanity and pride in appearance. Each person I interacted with would bow and continue bowing until I was out of sight. Hotel clerks would bow, and as I walked away from them, occasionally I'd turn around to see them continuing to bow. If I turned a corner, I would glance to see them respectfully bending at the waist, head down, hands clasped together, gesturing their appreciation for my presence. When handing an item to me such as a room key card, they would use both hands as if they were handing me good fortune in life. The cultural equivalent was to use both hands to receive whatever the person handed me. I liked the exchange of respect.

The Tokyo streets were immaculate, revealing to me the pride everyone took in their city. Modern tall buildings were washed by men strapped to scaffolding hundreds of feet in the air. It didn't matter—from window washers to brain surgeons—respect was shown to everyone for their contribution to the world. Tokyo became one of my favorite cities, and Japan became one of my favorite countries while I experienced their culture.

A few days of planning and running around Tokyo and Takao had the crate for Andiamo built and the paperwork complete, so all I needed to do was sign the documents. Takao took great pride in helping me. Without him, I would have been stranded.

Dear Takao,

Thank you for helping me and handling the shipment of Andiamo to Malaysia. I know you did more than I asked and incurred unexpected expenses. I hope my gifts for you and your employees were delivered as well as Andiamo was delivered to Kuala Lumpur. Thank you very much.

Sincerely,
Robert

I planned to meet Andiamo in Kuala Lumpur, Malaysia, in a month.

Southeast Asia

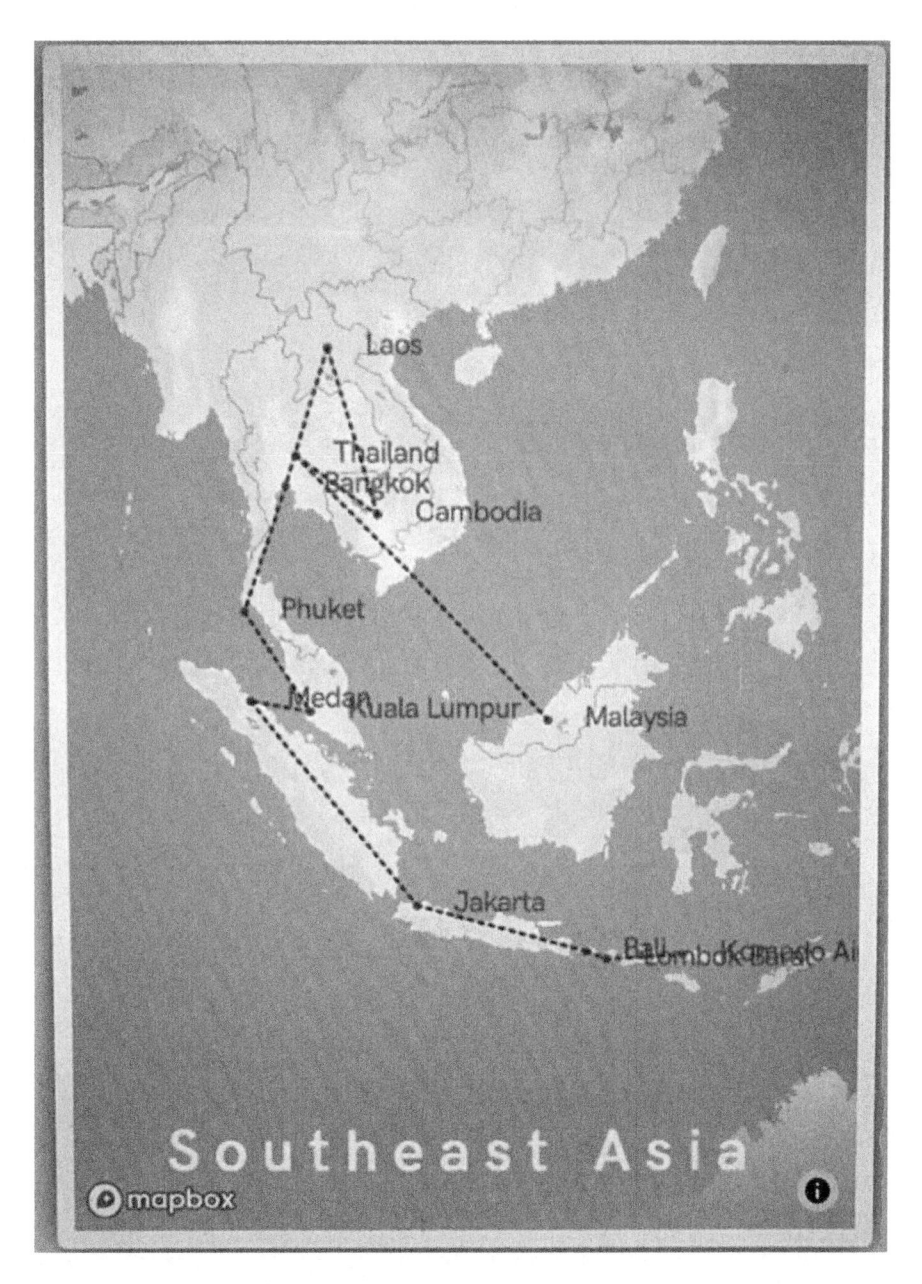

Malaysia

Northbound 2016, Southbound 2017

Mileage: 72,000

Ingredients: one Thanksgiving dinner, one group of family members

I entered and exited Malaysia many times, one of the entries being February 15, 2017. I had just missed Kim Jong Un's brother, Kim Jong Nam, being killed at Kuala Lumpur's main international airport on February 13, 2017, in a bizarre scheme believed to have been organized by Kim Jong Un himself. Two Southeast Asian girls were told they were part of a reality TV show prank. One had a bottle of lethal liquid favored by North Korea's government when killing someone. The other had a washcloth. They marked their target, Kim Jong Nam, covered his mouth with the deadly washcloth, then ran out the airport entrance.

Hours after the event, four North Korean nationals fled Malaysia, bound for North Korea, and couldn't be questioned. The two girls hired for the alleged hoax were released. No convictions were made, but it's probable Kim Jong Un ordered the hit to maintain his control of North Korea.

In Kuala Lumpur, I stayed at the Premiere Hotel, near the customs office where I was to complete arrival paperwork for Andiamo. Across the street was a restaurant named Garam Masala. It became my favorite place to eat in Kuala Lumpur. The garlic naan was sensational—fresh, hot, crispy crust layer, inside slightly gooey, topped with garlic butter and chunks of shaved roasted garlic. I could be happy the rest of my life eating nothing else but that. I had to compliment the owner, a tall, dark-skinned, handsome Bengali man named Jasbir. I mispronounced his name.

"It's Just-Beer, not Jasper," he said.

We hit it off well and became friends. I enjoyed the garlic naan everyday. I even skipped the free breakfast at the hotel to eat at Garam Masala.

Recipe: Set the table for Thanksgiving dinner, the bowls of each food item absent utensils. Allow the group of family members to eat directly from each bowl with their hands. Builds a close connection, right?

One night, Jasbir invited me to a family gathering at his brother's house. Jasbir picked me up right on time. He had made dinner at his restaurant and packaged the delicious-smelling items to go. My mouth watered in his vehicle. I hadn't eaten all day, and the smell was outrageously tempting. I threatened to rip open one of the containers and devour its contents.

The food intact, we arrived at a tall apartment building where his brother, Dr. Sharanjit, and his brother's wife, Jagjit, lived on the twenty-second floor, their apartment nicely furnished, with great views of Kuala Lumpur and a nearby lake. We had in-depth conversations about the world, travel, cultures, and their Sikh religion. They said Indians were second-class citizens. The new Muslims discriminated against them. These "new Muslims" would only eat things blessed by an imam called halal, similar to Jewish kosher food, but had no idea what it meant.

At the dinner table, there was no silverware. They asked me if I would prefer to use utensils instead of joining in their normal way of eating and serving with their hands. Wanting to experience their real culture, expand my horizons, try new things, think outside the box, I went palm-deep in a bowl of chicken tikka Masala. The practice of everyone intimately sharing food made our bond stronger. I had a feeling of being connected with my gracious hosts.

Thank you, Dr. Sharanjit and Jagjit for hosting several wonderful evenings while I was in your beautiful city. I hope your world four-wheel drive adventures continue. All my best.

Sincerely,
Robert

Around 2:00 a.m., Jasbir drove me to my hotel through the trafficless streets of downtown Kuala Lumpur to see the Petronas Twin Towers. We stopped, and I flew my drone up to the top of the towers to film the amazing night light of the tall downtown buildings. The drone was at 1,200 feet above the ground when the cops surrounded me.

"Bring it down," the angry officers barked.

My drone has a maximum descent rate of 10 feet per second. At an altitude of 1,200 feet, it takes roughly two minutes to descend.

The cops kept badgering me. "Bring it down. Bring it down."

Jasbir tried to calm them as the time ticked like a bomb. The drone came to a smashing halt near us. They demanded I delete the footage. Cooperatively, I did, but they didn't specify "all footage," as it automatically downloads to the iCloud. The next morning, I did feel a little bad, but their unjustified hostility made me rationalize keeping the hidden file.

Thank you, Jasbir ("Just-Beer"), for your kindness and hospitality and for taking time from your busy schedule each time I was in KL. I hope you and your family are well. I always look forward to our conversations via the apps. Take care of yourself, buddy.

Sincerely,
Robert

P.S. Send garlic naan!

Back on the road riding toward paradise, I took a ferry out to Langkawi, an archipelago among ninety-nine other islands surrounded by a temperate turquoise sea, rice paddy fields, and jungle-clad rolling hills. I booked a water villa on stilts, built over the water at the Berjaya Langkawi Resort. The pool was a tropical experience, with waterfalls and private coves with dangling palm fronds touching my head. My villa had all the amenities, including a secluded balcony jetting out over the water to watch the sun set over my private piece of the Andaman Sea.

I enjoyed an authentic Malaysian meal for dinner at the open-air restaurant built on bamboo stilts over the sea. Loose-fitting linen clothing was the dress code at this formal/casual dining experience, with candles and tiki torches providing romantic light. The gusty sea breeze was soul-soothing. When my cocktail arrived, served in a coconut, I put my camera on the railing for a self-timer picture. I activated the self-timer countdown: ten, nine, eight… I hurried to sit down at my table to toast the event with a smile and a coconut. As my butt hit the chair, a gust of wind hit the railing and blew my camera into the deep seawater below. I was completely devastated. All my photos were on the camera. The water beneath the restaurant was deep and churned up from the wind. A recovery attempt would require a scuba diver.

The next day, I called local dive shops to hire a diver to salvage my camera.

Without delay, the scuba diver arrived and laid out his gear at the table I had eaten at the night before. Hatti was his name, a short, jovial Malaysian gentleman with a scuba flag tattooed to his heart. "No problem, man," he said. "I'll find your camera. Where is the exact railing your camera fell from?"

"Right here," I said, as I pounded my fist on the railing.

He dropped a weighted line to the bottom of the twenty-foot-deep water to mark an approximate location of the camera and to prevent him from drifting off that spot. Hatti's oxygen tank strapped to his back created huge bubbles as he submerged. Five minutes elapsed and Hatti's head rose from the depths. His regulator was in his mouth, preventing me from seeing a smile or frown.

I had to know if the mission was successful or not. "Did you find it, Hatti?" I yelled.

No response as he swam closer to the deck.

"Come on, man, did you find it?" I yelled again. The drama increased as my anticipation overtook me.

Hatti climbed emotionless and answerless up the ladder onto the deck, where I awaited the results like an Oscar candidate. Thank goodness, it was a waterproof camera. When I was going through the pictures that evening, I burst into laughter to find one of Hatti and his scuba-masked bug eyes. He had snapped it when he found the camera still on. Epic shot.

One of the coolest things I did on Langkawi was a "Jet-Ski safari."

Zed, my guide, had thick dreadlocks and spoke with a reggae drawl. "Haaaay, maaaan, tiss beeee coooool, gunnna beee fuuuunnnn," he said as he briefed me on the operation of my rented Jet Ski.

Safety was third for Zed, not first. Number one and two were fun and weed. Zed took me on a tour of the ninety-nine islands by Jet Ski. We rode through caves with travertine stalactites hanging to the seawater and rock formations creating different shapes and colors, causing both of us to say, "Wooooow, maaaaaan, cooooool." We swam at isolated beaches inhabited only by monkeys howling and running from us. We hiked up a volcano to a freshwater lake and jumped in the cool, clean water. Legend has it that the water is so fresh and clean, anyone who jumps into the fertile water will become pregnant. Ever since my jump into the mythical water, my EPT strip (early pregnancy test) has been negative. Must be a false legend.

Zed smoked a joint while I drank a beer on an island with only sea gypsies. Sea gypsies are a culture without a nation. They live at sea on boats or on islands. The three I ran into on this deserted island sold beer and soda from a tiki hut to make money. One played guitar and sang for entertainment. The vibe was pretty chill, with a burned-cannabis odor. It was a day exploring the sea I will never forget.

BMW Langkawi agreed to work on Andiamo and store him on the small island for a month. See you in a month, Andiamo.

~~~

I arrived in Langkawi a month after I had left. I was lucky to book another water villa at Berjaya Langkawi Resort. A very happy and friendly concierge named Vino helped me each time I was there.

I snuck up behind him. "Hello, Vino, how have you been?" I asked.

His eyes popped wide open with surprise behind his stylish silver glasses. "Hello, Mr. Dolven," he said. "I am so glad to see you back. I want to book you a tour on the SkyCab and SkyBridge. When can you go?"

"Let me stow my gear and change clothes, and I'll be ready in ten minutes," I said.

He booked me an afternoon on the SkyCab (gondola) up to the Sky-

Bridge. The SkyCab takes you up the steepest cable car ascent on Earth to Malaysia's second-highest peak. At the top of the mountain, I had panoramic views of the ninety-nine islands scattered in the sea. These lush mountain islands meet the blue water with unusual shapes, beaches, and lagoons, inspiring dreams within me.

I walked the SkyBridge and made a film capturing the beauty and unique construction of the aerial bridge. There are a series of long cables suspending the walkway, giving the impression you're walking on air.

> *Thank you, Vino, for treating me kindly and guiding me to one of the best tourist attractions on the island. I hope you are well.*
>
> *Sincerely,*
> *Robert*

With Andiamo well and recovered, we hit the road. Malaysia is very motorcycle friendly. At the frequent tollbooths, cars were backed up twenty deep at each of the twelve lanes. Motorcycles have bypasses around the tollbooths. Some have fresh pavement, landscaped gardens, and rest areas alongside. As a motorcycle rider, it was a wonderful feeling of priority rarely felt elsewhere in the world.

Crossing the border into Thailand was like "but-ah."

Thailand

Northbound 2016, Southbound 2017

Mileage: 73,000

Ingredients: four different foreign currencies, one time bomb

I rode up the west coast of Thailand to Phuket. Offshore from Phuket forty-five kilometers are the Phi Phi Islands shrouded in steep-cliffed vegetation outcrops surging from the turquoise-tinted water. These are magnificent islands and my favorite in the world. They have only three-wheeled motorbike rickshaws called tuk-tuks to cart tourists around the island interiors. The roads are sand paths winding through groups of thatched hut cafes and barbecue joints. I love the laid-back style and hippy-type atmosphere.

After two nights, I escaped the Phi Phi islands back to Phuket and Andiamo. I pointed him toward Ko Samui, another tourist destination with island beauty. Then the rain started and didn't let up. Another ferry delivered Andiamo and me to the island of Ko Samui, a sensational island paradise, where it was still raining.

I rode the island perimeter five-eighths around to find shelter from the rain at an open-air hotel on the beach. My room was made of glass, with views of the rain-soaked waves.

In the morning, I enjoyed a hot breakfast at my hotel's open-air buffet. It was still raining, and the wind blew in clouds of mist as I ate.

On a ride, I just gotta ride. I can't wait the weather out. I have no choice but to get on the bike and continue.

I was under a covered parking area, sheltered from the rain. I packed Andiamo, thinking, *This rain hasn't let up all night. I'm dry now, but soon I'll be saturated.*

My boots felt nice and dry on my feet, my shirt wasn't sticking to my skin, and my underwear wasn't wedged. I finished strapping my gear, and off I went. It was three minutes before I felt the rain slowly penetrate my jacket, touching my skin like tiny hummingbirds pecking. The quickest drips reached my dry skin through worn areas of my jacket and pants.

Suddenly, the road was flooded and diverted to the shoreline, police directing traffic, knee-deep in the crashing waves. The winds howled. The rain poured. The water level had risen overnight, covering the road and entering the cafes along the beach. The ocean waves submerged the gift shops, washing their inventories away. Instead of waves and sand, it was waves and postcards. T-shirts floated by my feet. My boots were funnels to my sloshing toes. The water washed sand inland. My rear wheel spun. I was stuck.

One of the traffic-director cops, dressed in a long fluorescent raincoat, tried to pull me backward out of my hole. Andiamo and I were too heavy, so another florescent-coat cop joined, and the three of us dislodged me from the sand. The water was up to my cylinders. Two cars floated out to sea like unanchored boats. The road was being washed away as I escaped in search of Seatran, the ferry operator.

There was a festival planned that weekend with all sorts of bamboo built-canopies that had flags hung from each. One two-story bamboo structure collapsed as I went under it, creating a Vietnam War bamboo snare that almost stabbed my gut.

I located a woman manning the booth for Seatran Ferry and snuggled in under her awning out of the rain. "How do I buy a ferry ticket?" I asked.

"The port is closed," she said. "There was a ferry accident."

The water was too high and the seas too rough.

"Maybe tomorrow," she said, "but who knows?"

I quickly calculated the time for making it to Bangkok and when I needed to return to work. My internal pressure meter pegged, giving me an overpressure warning. I needed off the island that day.

I parked and talked with locals about their own bikes and how they thought it was cool that I was riding around the world. They confirmed there was a second ferry operator nine kilometers south in a town called Raja. It was a dicey operator but the only way off the island.

Riding in the rain completely soaked, I found the alternate ferry operator. I ducked under the awning of another girl's booth to get out of the rain. My dripping self caused her printed documents to bleed onto her desk. She handed me a ticket to Don Sak on mainland Thailand. I had two hours before the ferry left, so I plugged in my route to Bangkok and verified my GPS micro images were correctly downloaded for the rest of my ride. I needed those micro images to navigate the streets of Bangkok, where motorcycles are prohibited on some streets.

A guy approached me and said, "Nice bike." This guy seemed more interested than other curious types. Then he started rattling off terms known only to adventure riders, and I realized he was on a GS like mine. He introduced himself as Ment and invited me to join him and his friends. Ment was a Native American Indian-looking forty-year-old who had a long ponytail braided down his back. He seemed to know all the people in town.

"I'm drinking my own alcohol, so we need to go over to another cafe because the owners of the first cafe were Muslims and wouldn't let me drink my own hooch from my pocket." With social etiquette, Ment introduced me to his three friends, also on motorcycles. "I'm an engineer. This is Sam, a professional guitarist. This is Peter and Tang. They're farmers."

"I'm a pilot," I told them. "Nice to meet you all." That concluded our introductions.

Later, I found out Ment was an engineer who specialized in explosives. "I'm not a terrorist," he said.

I wish I would have asked more questions about him. I searched YouTube and found Sam the guitarist's videos. Good music. We rode to the front of the queue for the ferry, as motorcycles are easier to maneuver. The surf was high, and huge waves made riding onto the ferry very challenging.

Once on the ferry, leaning over the railing, I discovered Ment was also a farmer, of what he would not say. I surmised an explosives engineer and questionable cultivator with a $45,000 motorcycle could be involved with suspicious activities. I should have asked more questions.

They shared "leaves" with me, similar to the coca leaves Bolivian coca farmers chew for energy. Ment gave me a bottle of water to chase them down. The guys all had matching tattoos of some kind of farming symbol with sun and rain. In hindsight, I think they grew drugs and made bombs. I shared my "blue man," menthol crystals from Morocco. They seemed to like the homegrown style of it.

I stretched out in a chair on the upper deck. Next to it was a chain sectioning off an area and a metal sign stating, *Crew only. No entry.* Slightly out of sight, the crew was sharing a joint. Stoned crew? I can understand how the other ferry operator had an accident.

When the ferry docked, high waves smashed us into the pier, shifting it from its foundations and almost collapsing the entire dock. Then we hit the approach area, threw the mooring lines out, dropped the car ramp, and started the disembarkation process.

Walking down the stairway to the car deck below, I saw an American-looking guy and Ment standing next to Andiamo.

"When we hit the pier, your bike tipped over," the American guy said. The two of them picked Andiamo up, injuring the hand of the American, who was from Aurora, Colorado. His name was Gary, and he was visiting Ko Samui for two weeks. "My brother went down on a rented scooter. He slid under a guardrail and severed both femurs. He's been in the hospital for three weeks with three surgeries, and I've been by his bedside, but now I need to get home."

It was a terrible accident that left me with a cautious mind-set.

Each of my new buddies took turns taking pictures of them holding my jacket with my flags on the back. I gave Ment a bandana from an American tequila company. He seemed to honor it as he tucked it under his jacket for safekeeping. We took final pictures, and we were off into the faint afternoon sun.

On the nine-hour ride from Don Sak to Bangkok, the sun dried me out. Finally, my riding gear wasn't sticking to my body, and air circulated between my jacket, shirt, and skin. It was more comfortable. I was loving it, one of those EARs that leaves me feeling the ride is worth every bit of sacrifice I make. Great music playing in my helmet made it heaven.

I found a quaint hotel on the beach with dining tables in the sand and told the hotel clerk, "I'm in the mood for Thai food."

"You're in Thailand," he said. "You've come to the right place."

I planned to spend the evening writing and having some good Thai food with a beer. Showered and clean, I headed to the beach bar and planted myself at a nice table overlooking the stunning white sand beach for a perfect end to a wonderful wet/dry day.

The next morning greeted me with good weather. It was fun dodging traffic on the shoulder or any space I could fit around the slower-moving cars. I had EARs, dancing with the traffic to great music blasting. I stopped for roadside street food at a pop-up outdoor café and went to each vendor and tried everything they were selling. Great barbecue Thai chicken, pork meatballs, fried fish shish kabobs, sweet Thai pancakes with coconut and fresh fruit. My taste buds were satiated with regional flavors.

Recipe: Set the time bomb for thirty seconds. Lay four different foreign currencies on a table. Calculate the value of each currency into US dollars before the time bomb explodes. The pressure is on.

Several days prior on Ko Samui, Ment and I had plotted my course to Bangkok BMW on my GPS. I needed to use the bridge that allowed motorcycles. Bangkok has a myriad of bridges, with only one bridge allowing motorcycles to cross. There's a reason for this. The Thai people earn modest wages, so motorbikes are their affordable means of transportation. In fact, Thai roads become swarms of motorbikes that create chaos. The government prohibits motorbikes on certain bridges and roads to reduce the chaos and keep traffic moving.

It was difficult to determine which bridge I needed. Ment and I zoomed in on his phone and my GPS, comparing the two, sure we had the correct bridge and route. I had two waypoints stored on my GPS, Correct Bridge and Bangkok BMW.

No problem, I thought. *I'll make it.*

I saw tons of signs with pictures of a motorcycle and Thai writing, no English and no red *X* through the motorcycles, so I thought I was on the right course. Eventually, I was the only motorcycle on the road in a country of millions of motorcycles, which caused me concern. I had a bad feeling. I knew the Bangkok cops were terrible. When a tan, uniformed one jumped out and gave the arms-crossed *X* sign, I knew there was something wrong. He waved me to a stop at a tollbooth between lanes, where huge trucks passed on either side of us, belching diesel dust and using their thunderous Jake Brakes.

I waved my arms in defiance, yelling, "This is the bridge I was told to use!"

He laughed. "Ticket. You very bad. Driver's license, driver's license!"

I reached for my real one but came to my senses and unzipped an access zipper where I readily stow a not-so-valid driver's license reserved for these situations.

He appeared angry and happy at the same time, knowing he had a fish on the line. He was more legit than others making casual bribe attempts. He wrote out an official carbon copy ticket, circling 2,000 baht (about $54) as the cost of my offense. He handed me the ticket and said, "Pay at station." He continued waiving trucks past, their horns honking. "The motorcycle will be kept at the station for seven days."

My heart sank. I feared the worst as I calculated my time left, work, and flights home. I was under pressure.

"Two thousand baht!" he yelled.

In between two lanes with trucks rushing by, I reluctantly pulled out my money clip. I only had 490 baht, but I had several other currencies.

He said, "*No, no, no!* Moto seven days jail."

The pressure increased. I had to get going. I didn't have time to negotiate. The trucks started honking in anger. I thumbed through all the currencies. "Russian rubles?" I asked. "Mongolian tenge? Malaysian ringgits?"

"Ringgit, ringgit, ringgit!"

I had 400 ringgits in my wallet. With all the commotion and currencies I carry, I didn't do a good job calculating the value of the ringgit, because the Thai baht's value was so low. He wanted 2,000 baht, so 400 ringgits sounded relatively okay. I jumped to conclusions and was happy that he was happy with 400 Malaysian ringgits. I was still unsure as to the correct value of 400 ringgits.

Later that evening with the pressure off, I wondered how much 400 ringgits was actually worth. I knew 2,000 baht was $54, and that was the price of the ticket, but 400 Malaysian ringgits was $94. No wonder he was happy. Another "currency confusion" on my part.

At that pressurized moment, I did wonder why he had become more jovial as he returned my driver's license. Oh well, I was on my way, thinking it was the correct way. The cop steered me down a road that had the same motorcycle and Thai writing signs as before, but my GPS was directing me on that course. Trusting it and the happy cop, I continued to yet another identical tollbooth and a cop waving me over in between lanes with the trucks honking, coming within inches of me.

"No, no, no," the cop said. "Wrong-way ticket now."

I protested with anger. "I just paid another cop a mile back. He told me this was the correct way!"

This cop was laughing, and I thought perhaps they carried walkie-talkies and I was the talk of Bangkok's police department. I was getting upset with this whole "bridge crossing" thing, so I said, "No, I'm not paying."

"Seven days impound motorcycle," he said.

I couldn't accept that.

"Baht, baht, baht," he said.

"I only have four hundred ninety baht," I said. "I just paid the other cop."

He laughed. "Five hundred baht take you across bridge."

I protested, but with the pressure rising, I gave him 400 baht, which seemed to satisfy him. The unpleasant exchange complete, I followed him across the bridge.

On a slight downhill portion of the bridge, a white car in front of us suddenly stopped. The cop swerved his light, nimble motorbike to the right of the car. I slammed on my brakes in horror. The ABS braking system faulted. No brakes. I had three immediate options: rear-end the cop on the right, rear-end the car in front, or try to swerve left into the curb. I chose number three. Using the curb for braking, I wedged my front wheel against it to a full stop. My head dangled over the railing of the bridge, looking down at the dirty river water below as I caught my breath.

The laughing cop's arm waved straight ahead. I saw the welcome sight of thousands of motorbikes riding the street up ahead. Ahh, home with my people again.

The cop did a U-turn left with my 400 baht.

I was riding reluctantly on crazy "no motorcycle" roads and possibly with no brakes. My head was not in the game. I navigated to Bangkok BMW. Kevin, the service manager, greeted me with clean and combed hair.

As I sprawled out on the front steps of the dealership calming down, a silk-dressed secretary brought me a tray of sweet Thai treats, tea, and a bottle of water. "Welcome," she said.

Ahh, the BMW brand once again confirmed this was the motorcycle for an around-the-world ride.

I took a tuk-tuk to my hotel, but the traffic was so congested, I got out and walked the last five hundred yards. I checked into a nice Holiday Inn Express and hopped on a flight home the next day.

Cambodia

2016

Mileage: 74,000

Ingredients: one million fellow citizens, one warehouse, one thousand sticks of dynamite

Exit procedures from Thailand were painless after taking photocopies of everything and paying 200 baht. Just prior to the Cambodian border, touts selling visas hounded me for business. They were relentless. They make a few dollars per visa they sell. I followed the most professional-looking guy to an office inside a shack he called the "embassy." He needed an extra passport photo of me. I didn't have one at the moment, so for 200 baht, they took a photo. Twenty minutes, and I had my visa on arrival.

The immigration guy said, "I'll stamp your passport for 200 baht."

That was so I wouldn't need to go inside and wait in line. I looked inside. There was no line, so I avoided paying this guy.

The Cambodian customs official in Poipet said, "You don't need any additional papers. Your carnet is sufficient to prove motorcycle ownership."

The carnet was expired.

He did a brief check of the VIN number with the bike. "If you get stopped," he said, "tell them customs at Poipet let you in with just a copy of the carnet."

I was a bit apprehensive about the lax procedures, but what the heck? I was free to explore Cambodia.

The roads near borders are usually acceptable. I was headed for one of my most anticipated attractions in Cambodia, the Bamboo Train. A "must see" in Battambang, the region's most visited tourist attraction, it's a train made from salvaged tank and truck parts left over from the war, powered by a go-kart engine attached to a bamboo platform hand-carried from car to car. The bamboo platform serves as seating for tourists and villagers traveling the seven kilometers from the main station to the end of the line in a remote village. The platform rests on two axles, not bolted, so it can be dismantled quickly.

The platform gave huge jolts at every track section, shocking my body with metal-on-metal jolts. The scenic twenty-minute ride took me through rice paddies and fields to a small village in the jungle where locals sold cold drinks, art, and T-shirts. I used the "follow-me" function of my drone to capture the small train traveling through the rice paddies and bamboo trees surrounding the area. If we met an oncoming bamboo train, the conductors would lift the platforms and swap axles with each other, then continue the journey. It was amazing how ingenious these villagers were, crafting discarded spare parts into a thriving means of transportation.

> Recipe: Gather one million of your fellow countrymen, enticing them with promises of wealth, prosperity, and perfect ideas for society. Assemble the loyal citizens in the warehouse. Place the one thousand sticks of dynamite under the warehouse. Light the fuses and run. "Hello, Pol Pot, that's what you did."

After the Vietnam War ended, Cambodia struggled with a bloody civil war. Pol Pot, leader of the Khmer Rouge, seized power with promised peace and prosperity that he never provided. He won favor with his loyal subjects with unfulfilled hypocritical promises that led to their murders.

The Communist Khmer Rouge controlled Cambodia between 1975 and 1979 and were responsible for murdering millions of their fellow humans. Two very important memorials to the mass murders are the Choeung Ek Killing Fields and Tuol Sleng (S-21 Prison). They serve as monuments to those who died and as an educational tool to ensure these horrors are never repeated.

In Phnom Penh, I walked the Killing Fields, with their mass grave sites. I felt death surround me. There were thousands of graves spread out over acres of land. Bodies and bones of innocent humans once filled the graves. As I walked the site, a stick "cracked" under my foot. Shocked, I thought it could be a splintering human bone. A thick feeling of repugnance filled my throat. Not since visiting the Nazi prison camps had I felt such disgust.

The S-21 Prison detained "political prisoners" at a former elementary school Pol Pot converted into a prison. Struggling fingerprint smudges on the walls of tiny cells made me look away to see a table with shackles used for coercing confessions. I could not escape the horror. Leaving this gruesome site was a pleasure.

Dear Pol Pot,

May you receive exponential karmic revenge for eternity. I hope Satin's sledgehammer pounds you beneath his flaming prison, because hell is too good for you.

Sincerely,
Robert

Sambo, my tuk-tuk driver, wore a large white smile that stretched his lips continuously. He drove me to the Killing Caves with his three-wheeled motorized rickshaw, outfitted with a canopy and small bench seat covered with sticky vinyl, powered by a small 125cc engine. To prevent the engine from overheating, Sambo had attached a water bottle that slowly dripped water through a straw onto the hot engine, like a baby's sippy cup.

The Killing Caves were fifteen bumpy kilometers from town, with the last two kilometers up a steep mountain path on a scooter Sambo borrowed. At the top of the mountain, vendors sold bugs piled onto large tin trays. The beetle was crunchy and sweet, with a burnt-sugar taste, as I swallowed the body and legs. Doctor's office posters of digestive systems flashed through my mind. Images of stomach pains from ingested germs concerned me. Like taking the jump off a cliff, I bit into another burnt-sugar-covered critter.

Sambo led me to a Buddhist temple at the summit. He explained how the Khmer Rouge had used the temple to house prisoners, forcing them to confess to untrue crimes. After getting a signed confession, the soldiers made the prisoners jump off the cliff into a vertical cave a hundred feet deep with a pile of bodies at the bottom.

Sambo and I hiked down to the bottom of the vertical cave, where bodies would survive a few agonizing hours. Sambo explained a Khmer Rouge shrine depicting Satin torturing the soldiers for all their sins in life. The cave contained a massive stack of human bones and skulls piled to show the immensity of the mass genocidal murders. It was a graphic sight. I could not imagine humans treating humans that way, forcing someone to confess to crimes they didn't commit, then making them jump to their death. My horror pushed me out of the cave.

We coasted the borrowed scooter down the mountain path to the next site.

Nearby, at precisely 5:30 p.m., millions of bats exit a horizontal cave for the night in search of food in the rice fields, to return at 5:30 a.m. the next morning. This happens every day. I took photos of the bats with my telephoto lens, capturing the veins of their wings and fangs in their mouths.

I navigated to Phnom Penh International Airport to see what hotels were convenient. In horrific traffic and chaos, a scooter weaved between a truck and SUV, sandwiched and crushed by the large vehicles. The scooter rider could not move. The vehicles diverged, dropping the limp scooterist in the filthy street.

There were enough hotel options near the airport for me to leave Andiamo. I had four days before I needed to head back to America, so I rode south.

I wanted to check out the south coast of Cambodia, where the wealthy French had built vacation properties in the nineteenth century. It was a three-hour ride, but with the traffic, it took me five hours.

I was riding on a two-lane country highway when a white Honda SUV passed me, driving foolishly. Fifteen minutes down the road, traffic was backed up. I filtered to the front of the line to see a crowd of people gathered around an accident. As I slithered through the crowd, I saw the white Honda had smashed head on into a motorbike with two Cambodian teenagers, who now lay in a pool of their own blood, surrounded by a hundred locals. No ambulance, no emergency help, and no one doing anything but staring at the two kids, who most likely had perished on impact. The scene haunted me. Witnessing the dangers of the road so fresh and so close made me want to ride safe, drive safe, and be safe.

I eventually arrived in Kep, Cambodia, a pleasant coastal town. The coast road had hundreds of abandoned beachfront French villas. I scanned them, painfully considering the once-prized properties that had fallen into such neglect. It's interesting to see the evolution of societies. Kep was once "the place to be" in Southeast Asia, but in the '70s, the residents fled due to the atrocities being committed by the Khmer Rouge. It became an abandoned ghost town. Some of the properties have been renovated or repurposed. I stayed in one that had been turned into a boutique hotel.

The restaurant served me dinner at one of the most unusual tables I've ever eaten at. A giant rock in the water had been shaved off flat, and they had put a king-sized four-poster canopy bed with curtains atop the rock. I watched the sun set, sipped wine, and enjoyed delicious Cambodian cuisine while the waves gently curled onto the rock with rhythmic sequence. *This is paradise*, I thought, convinced.

The next day's ride was a long, hard one northbound back through the congested Phnom Penh traffic, bound for quintessential Cambodia: Siem Reap, featured on their currency and beer brand. Andiamo's oil temp redlined, and I was dehydrated. I had ridden ten hours to the Sofitel in Siem Reap, where I spent two nights of fine dining and relaxing in the gigantic tropical swimming pool with an island oasis.

Angkor Wat in Siem Reap is the largest religious monument in the world. It was originally constructed as a Hindu temple honoring the god Vishnu. When you visit religious sites, bare skin should be covered to show respect. I purchased two sarongs to cover my legs and arms.

I initiated my tour, crossing a bridge like a walkway up a few flights of stairs into a series of sectioned-off areas like ancient swimming pools once used by monks. The covered walkways had stone pillars and archways. The central tower represents a mountain at Earth's center, pointing toward heaven.

After two hours of walking Angkor Wat, I needed water. I spotted a shop selling everything, including cold bottled water. The door to the shop had a rusted handle and was hard to open. When I squeaked the door open, a Buddha head statue five feet high flicked a switch in my subconscious. Carved from wood and aging from the years of service in an old Buddhist temple, it seemed to stand out from the other works of art for sale. I wanted it, but there was no way I could carry a large statue with me. I asked the price and shipping costs. The huge Buddha head statue evoked a profound feeling, so I agreed to the terms. It's currently a prominent feature in my home.

My days dwindled, and I needed to start the return proceedings to show up for work on time in America.

I rode back to Phnom Penh and checked into the Dara Airport Hotel, where Pierre, a gray-haired Frenchman and general manager, met me in the lobby. He found a parking spot for Andiamo that was air-conditioned and secluded. He joked about it costing a hundred dollars per day, but later, he said, "I love what you do, Robert. Don't worry. There will be no charge for the parking."

Dear Pierre,

Thank you very much for providing a safe and comfortable place to keep my motorcycle. I hope you received the gifts I sent.

Sincerely,
Robert

I had a few birthday surprises planned on my way back to Cambodia. This was a three-week trip that took me literally round the world (RTW) one full revolution of Earth. Basically, I walked out my front door and continued eastbound until I entered my backdoor. First was a fifteen-hour flight on Emirates to Dubai. I watched *The Choice*, the movie made from the book of the same name by Nicholas Sparks. It was a tearjerker. Then *Whiskey, Tango, Foxtrot*, with Tina Fey. Good Afghanistan movie.

Dubai was built by a king with five names behind his title. He was interested in creating the world's best everything. It seems he didn't want just a horse. He wanted the world's fastest. He didn't want a tall building.

He wanted the world's tallest. He knew his country would run out of oil in the next few years, so he attempted to build a tourist industry to sustain revenue beyond his oil supply. The buildings were often vacant examples of projected growth built on hopes of occupancy, kind of a "if you build it, they will come" philosophy. The labor force was comprised of foreign expatriates, often treated as slaves and discriminated against by native Emiratis. I like Dubai in small doses.

I booked a nice room at a Holiday Inn in Dubai using my phone app. They upgraded my room to a suite. I did the hop-on, hop-off Big Bus tour around Dubai and photographed all the sights. I snow skied indoors at Ski Dubai. Then I arranged a late night 11:00 p.m. hotel checkout for my flight to Male, capital of the Maldives.

~~~

The Emirates flight to Male departed at 2:30 a.m. Arrival and immigration procedures were easy that time of the morning. At Male International Airport, I changed out of my travel clothes into beach attire.

It was a spectacular seaplane ride over the atolls, with their unique shapes and shades of turquoise, bound for the Constance Halaveli Resort with my private island and water villa. The seaplane splashed into the water and water-taxied to a floating dock. The plane's propellers still turning, I jumped out onto the dock and into a traditional boat that took me the rest of the way to the isolated atoll.

Clean white Indian Ocean sand and palm trees inhabited the tropical retreat. A welcoming committee waited with drinks and fruits. I sat down with them for a briefing of the service and amenities before an electric golf cart took me to my water villa.

I snorkeled right off the deck of my villa, walked the small island, and had outstanding buffet breakfasts and dinners on the beach. It was an exceptional birthday experience. After four days in the Maldives, I hopped a seaplane back to civilization. Then I grabbed a flight to Colombo, Sri Lanka, to explore for a couple days.

~~~

Sri Lanka is an awesome country, like India without the chaos. I paid Tri, my tuk-tuk driver, to show me the sights. A super nice guy intrigued by an American visiting his country, Tri took me to an herb garden where an interesting fella gave me a tour. He grew all sorts of herbs that he claimed remedied anything, even "big belly." Next Tri took me to a fish market with fish smells so strong they clouded the air. A guy with a wooden-handled machete, chopping tuna on a tree stump, gave me a chance to whack the carcass. After a few chops, I was inclined to count my fingers.

After I had traveled United States-Dubai-Maldives-Sri Lanka, I arrived in Cambodia. Pierre, the general manager at the Dara Airport Hotel, met me in the lobby. I bought him a coffee while we chatted.

Andiamo's battery was completely dead. I connected my battery charger for an overnight charge.

In the morning, Andiamo's battery was charged, but his tire pressure was dangerously low, making it difficult to steer. My air compressor runs off my battery, and I didn't want to sacrifice what little charge I had, so I rode with low tire pressure in search of service. Thank goodness, on the first corner, there was a street-side tire shop with an air hose to the curb. Three nice Cambodians aired up my tires and checked the pressure with my gauge.

I headed toward Laos through Siem Reap and stayed at Sofitel again. This time through, I toured the Floating Village, a highlight for me.

A cute little barefoot Cambodian kid came up to me. "Hi, I'm Wan," he said. "I'm captain." He was an adorable captain of the makeshift boat, powered by a car engine welded to the deck and a long pipe extending out into the water with a propeller at the end. Wan had an even younger first mate. They took their jobs very seriously on the tiny vessel, which I appreciated.

"The captain's word is law," I told Wan.

All the palm and bamboo structures appeared to be floating in the water. There were hundreds connected to form a village. We stopped at a floating cafe built on bamboo stilts and palm fronds. I wanted to buy Wan and his little mate something to eat. A dollar covered their desired menu items. I ate in front, and the two boatsmen ate with the family of the floating restaurant in back. They were all hovered around a big bowl of rice shared by five people. While I lay in a hammock and ate French fries, the two boys took off in another boat, stranding me. I trusted they'd be back eventually, so I chilled in the hammock.

Fifteen minutes later, they returned from helping another friend dislodge a boat from the murky waters. We went back to the mainland.

Wan,

I hope you are well and your boat is trouble-free. You were a very competent captain.

Thank you,

Robert

Back on Andiamo the next day, I rode to the Cambodian exit. No docs, no problem. Ready for Laos.

Laos

2016

Mileage: 74,000

Ingredients: one minefield, one playground, one school clock, one metal file, one African Makonde tribe person

I crossed the Friendship Bridge over the Mekong River into Laos, tracing the historic footsteps of war victims. Visa on arrival cost 700,000 kips. The ATM didn't work, so I dipped into an emergency stash of cash hidden in my tank bag. Don't tell anyone, but I also keep emergency money sewn into the epaulettes of my riding jacket. In case of a dire emergency, I can rip out the seams and forfeit the cash.

My GPS led me to the Landmark Mekong Riverside Hotel, a beautiful five-star establishment. President Obama rented the entire grand hotel during his visit to Laos. At the front desk lobby area were several clerks and lots of Russian tourists, all wanting pictures of me and my jacket with the flags. I used what little Russian words I knew to make them laugh.

Constantine, the front desk supervisor, greeted me.

"I'm riding my motorcycle around the world and need to return to the United States tomorrow," I said. "Could you please keep my motorcycle somewhere at the hotel, perhaps in a garage?"

"This is a question for the general manager," he replied.

From the back office, a forty-something man approached me and said, "Hello, I'm Mike, the general manager." He spoke with a French accent.

"Bonjour," I said, and used what other French words I knew to make him laugh.

Mike was a fellow adventure rider. "No worries," he said. "I will find a perfect spot for your motorcycle."

After showering and relaxing, I met Mike and Constantine in the lobby, and they led me to the basement. In the basement, I pushed Andiamo through a hallway, past empty storage rooms cleared out for Obama's security equipment. At the end of the hallway was a large room.

"Here is perfect," Mike said.

Great spot and good temperature in a five-star hotel. Be back in a month or so. I booked a flight out of Vientiane to Bangkok, then to Narita, then to Dallas, then to Phoenix.

In summery, this month's ride took me around the world: Phoenix-New York-Dubai-Maldives-Sri Lanka-Cambodia-Laos-Thailand-Japan-Dallas-Phoenix. Home in early October.

~ ~ ~

I returned to the Landmark Hotel on November 9, 2016. Mike, the general manager, had a chauffeur waiting at the airport for me with a sign: *Dolven*. The chauffeur opened my door, and I settled into the leather seats, opting out of a cocktail from the provided bar. I felt important, almost like Obama, when my limousine drove up the formal circular driveway where Mike and Constantine were rigidly positioned at the grand entrance to the hotel. They led me down to the storeroom where Andiamo was comfortably resting. I turned the key to attempt a start. Andiamo's headlight shone as his engine came to life.

Confident I would depart in the morning, I toured the city.

Vientiane has a depressing history, rich with war and corruption. The present government is trying to attract foreign investment. New businesses are offered two years free from tax, along with reduced operating expenses. The influx of commercial investment has boomed the economy, and new buildings are popping up throughout the city. The prosperity made the locals happy and healthy. Everyone was eager to interact with me. It made me feel good they were succeeding after the United States had a controversial relationship with Laos during the war in Vietnam.

In the capital city Vientiane, I released sparrows at the Golden Stupa for good luck. Legend says that if you make a wish and set the tiny caged birds free, Buddha will grant you good luck. I've been pretty lucky, so it must work.

I got an early start heading north. My destination: the ex-CIA secret air base named Long Tieng. Other names are Lima Site 98, LS98, or LS20A.

"It's hard to find," Mike said. "Don't waste your time."

I think that warning got lost in the translation.

After the road changed from asphalt to gravel, then to rocks, I started to wonder. My GPS led me to a small path over a mountain where the two tire tracks became one. The other had washed down in a mudslide, plunging two hundred feet. I didn't want to tempt fate. There were no humans for miles. If I fell down the cliff, I would never be found. U-turn time. I went back to a fork in the road and took the other fork.

The extreme mountainous conditions required riding in first gear most of the day. The sun dipped below the mountain peaks, leaving only shadow light. I was alone in the middle of the Laotian mountains, searching for a hidden place: the ex-CIA secret air base called Long Tieng. I was lost, with no signs of civilization. I hoped something would catch my plummeting spirit.

Finally, a small group of huts appeared. I stopped for directions, but nobody spoke English in the hut village. A girl trying to help me called someone on her mobile phone to translate. The call failed. No signal.

"You sleep me," she said. She gestured to a larger hut, which I took to be her home, featuring four equal-sized front doors, like some kind of grass hut commercial operation. It was a puzzling dwelling.

I opted to ride down the road a hundred meters further to check out more of the hut village. There were many of the same four-doored structures, all with women hanging around them. Girls were everywhere, except for one thin man selling water and soda at a little shop with a picnic table out front.

"Can I hang my hammock between these two trees on your property?" I asked him.

He said yes. The two perfectly spaced thick trees not found elsewhere in these treeless mountains were my only option for hammock suspension. The sun extinguished, and it started to rain.

Naively, I connected the dots as to why this hut village had strange four-door motel-like structures and only women present. A dam was being built nearby, and this tiny mountain hut village served as the male workers' recreation.

I had a Beerlao at the picnic table with the thin shop owner and a couple of greasy truck drivers, all eating rice from a central bowl on the table. Each man would respond yes to any question I asked.

"Which direction to the ex-CIA air base?" I asked. I pointed to my right. "Long Tieng?"

They responded yes.

I pointed left and asked, "Long Tieng?"

They responded yes.

I doubted either direction led to my elusive destination, Long Tieng.

One of the truckers then stuck his hand in the basket of rice, rolled a chunk into a ball, handed it to me, and said, "For you."

Noticing his greasy, unwashed hands, I just couldn't do it. I patted my belly and said, "I'm stuffed." Actually, I was starved and hadn't eaten the entire day.

The eight-year-old daughter of the thin shop owner was unusually curious with this greasy trucker. She climbed onto his lap and showed childish affection in a niece-to-uncle way. I just tried to be kind and ignored the odd cultural behavior.

Ready to sleep in my hammock, I thanked the thin shop owner, gave him 100,000 Laotian kips ($10), and said; "Thank you. Good night."

"Wait," he said, grabbing me. He reached down to his eight-year-old daughter's shoulder, nudging her forward. "You want?"

My eyes rotated in circles of disgust. I could not imagine a father selling his daughter.

Not a wink of sleep did I get, disturbed by the unfatherly treatment the little girl had received. I arose at 6:00 a.m., defeated. I was determined to complete my mission and backtracked to my last-known position.

Still in the remote mountains, I tried to find someone who could give me directions. I asked several men along the road, some carrying automatic weapons and some with muskets. None would allow me to take their picture. I later realized these were the remaining rebels who were holding out for their beliefs. I encountered them at a roadblock restricting access to

Long Tieng, the ex-CIA secret air base. After riding most of the mountain passes, I aborted my mission and returned to Vientiane, where I had started.

I encountered road construction and traffic. With the sun beginning to set, I found a relic of a once-grand hotel with guard gate and waterless fountains, all no longer in use and overgrown from neglect. My room cost six dollars and had air conditioning. The lizards that crawled the walls were included. Slept well though.

Speaking of unique bugs, one accomplished an incredible feat. There was an expanse of twenty feet between a tree, Andiamo, and the hotel. In the morning, I discovered that in that twenty-foot expanse, a spider had spun his web from the tree to Andiamo to the hotel. It was thick, like a trampoline. It could have caught birds. I considered the amazing work this little fella had done, spinning a twenty-foot web strong enough for a small bird.

As I exited the hotel, I noticed another bug on my windscreen that had fashioned himself to look like a huge green leaf. He wasn't afraid of my hand, so he climbed onto my glove. He was an amazing little guy, but something scared him and he flew off.

At one of the roadside markets, I noticed something for sale that I had never seen before: hairy dried buffalo hide, cut into thin strips like jerky—yes to eat. I was starving but had my limits. Hunger continued.

Another unique thing on the Laotian roads was men riding scooters with long bamboo poles tied to the back with no trailer, dragging the bamboo on the pavement. I admired the fortitude of the scooterists.

My retirement dream was driving on the road ahead. Passing it, I nodded in envy to the driver of a huge overland expedition vehicle. I accelerated as I passed, distancing myself from him and his passengers to allow time for a photo as they passed by me. A mile ahead of them, I positioned myself with my tripod, ready for a picture of my retirement dream as it drove past. I was overwhelmed when the massive white truck's tires stopped next to me.

Out stepped the driver, with a big smile and extended arm. "Looks like you've ridden a long way," he said.

"I have," I replied. "But enough about me. Let's talk about you and your fabulous vehicle."

He introduced himself as Steven. Then out came his wife, Gilly, and two daughters, Alicia and Lucy. They were a fine English family, on the road for two years at the time of our meeting. The version of school the children attended was called "world schooling," like homeschooling but traveling the world studying the Roman ruins by actually visiting them and learning firsthand. It sounded like a perfect way to educate their daughters.

The heavy-duty truck carried their life with ease. Self-sustained with solar power and water purification, the four-wheel drive could access secluded locations. I dream of obtaining a similar truck for my retirement and traveling the world.

We exchanged numbers and itineraries and planned to meet down the road.

Hello, Steven, Gilly, Alicia, and Lucy,

It was so nice to spend time with you. Hopefully, we can meet again! www.overlandingfamily.com

Sincerely,
Bob

Finally, I arrived in Phonsavan. I toured the plain of jars, which is the most significant prehistoric site in Southeast Asia. It's a collection of thousands of large stone jars used for burial rituals in 500 BC. It was like a forest of stone jars and made me imagine how they were celebrated long ago.

Recipe: Install the minefield at the school playground. Observe the children watching the school clock, waiting for it to strike "recess time." Understand when those children run out to play on the minefield playground, they may step on a mine. Now you know how Laotian parents feel.

Next, I stopped at the UXO office. It's an office dedicated to the massive identification and removal of unexploded ordnance in Laos. Phonsavan is a town filled with bomb remnants. It has a restaurant called Craters, with bomb shells and memorabilia throughout. It's eerie to think we dropped more bombs on Laos than in all of World War II. Laos is a tiny, peaceful, landlocked country with wonderful people.

I found a three-star hotel, where the front desk guy said, "We have no rooms." When I asked for the presidential suite, he said, "Hmmm, I think I have one."

Good room, hot shower, and off to Craters for dinner, where I wrote in my book and had a beer

Riding out of town the next morning, I stopped to learn how rice is processed. I parked Andiamo at a huge rice paddy and walked out to a group of hardworking farmers. They had a gas-powered machine processing the bundles of stalks. There were fifteen small-framed men and women wearing conical hats to shade them from the sun, all working in silent concert to separate the rice from the dusty stalks.

Without words, I expressed an interest in helping them. I worked with them for thirty minutes, trying to experience what it was like to be a hardworking Laotian farmer. They brought me stalks, and I lined them up, then pushed them into the machine. None of the wonderful people spoke English, and none of them judged my sanity. They all just kept working.

That day, I rode for hundreds of kilometers, always in a turn, never straight, through marvelous Hmong mountain towns with lots of potbellied pigs, chickens, and roosters crossing the road in front of me. I never hit one.

I met a group of three German riders. One of the Germans went down around a shaded, mossy, wet turn. They were on rented bikes touring Laos for three days. We chatted about riding in Laos, and they asked about my world ride. From the side of the mountain, we all dunked our hot heads under a cold mountain stream directed through a bamboo trough. It was refreshing.

A few hours later, I arrived in Luang Prabang and found a hotel on the night market street. The restaurant out front was great for people-watching, enjoying great Laotian food, and writing in my book. I sat at a table on a wagon-wheel bench perfectly tilted for eating and typing.

I strolled the night market in search of bomb fragments. Villagers had collected bomb fragments and recycled them, melting them into useable items. I bought bomb fragment spoons, bracelets, and chopsticks. After shopping, I jumped into my king-sized bed, but the noise from the night market kept me awake.

I was tired the next morning, but a wild tuk-tuk ride of twenty-nine kilometers to Kuang Si Falls woke me up. The hike to the falls started at a bear conservation park. Cute little Asian black bears had been rescued and given care. I hiked another five hundred meters through the lush bamboo forest to the start of the spectacular staircase of cascading pools. One of the most beautiful waterfalls I've ever seen, Kuang Si Falls is a multitiered waterfall spilling emerald-green water into smaller lower successive pools with white misty clouds floating above.

Back at the hotel with slow Wi-Fi, I got an email from Steven and Gilly, the English family I had met a few days prior. They were driving their white expedition vehicle around the world. They invited me for an Indian-food dinner out. Gilly's sister, Claire, and her husband, Noel, were traveling Laos and joined us. We all had wonderful stories to tell about past and present travel adventures. It was a great evening with Steve, Gilly, Alicia, Lucy, Claire, and Noel.

The girls and kids went back to their "truck" early, so Steve, Noel, and I had another beer. We talked about world politics, travel, religion, and how Steve retired at a young age from an accounting firm in Moscow and was "world schooling" his kids. Noel lived on a small budget and was traveling for two years with Claire. Noel called it quits for the night. Steve and I talked more about success.

"What is the book?" he asked me, meaning what did I think the book I was writing would mean to the world? "Answer that, and you'll have something."

It was a titular question that I've pondered since.

I woke with a hangover. Thankfully, riding fast with my face shield up forces air/oxygen down my nose, curing a hangover very quickly.

I was worried about the border crossing back into Thailand. Steve had told me that procedures had changed in July. "Now preapproval is needed, with insurance and more bureaucratic red tape, to ride or have a personal vehicle in Thailand," he said.

I suspected they may have been under different rules than I was.

My route: Laos, quick transit of Thailand, then back into Malaysia, where I would search for a boat to take Andiamo and me across the Malacca Strait to Indonesia. There was a rumor Mr. Lim's "onion boat" provided motorcycle transport to Indonesia. The problem was Mr. Lim's onion boat had had an accident and had sunk a few months prior.

The past two days were the best two days of riding I'd had, coming out of Laos on the mountain roads, then on to the beautiful Thai roads: smooth pavement, markings, no potholes, and no homemade tractors around every corner, no stalled trucks with the drivers spread out on the pavement working, no continuous oil spills from truckers with huge oil capacities creating an oil line that my wheels would slide on.

I rode very fast on Thai roads to Wat Rong Khun, the White Temple. A privately owned art exhibit made to resemble a Buddhist temple, it's rich in symbolism. I entered the temple, crossing a bridge over water. In the water were hundreds of cement arms and hands reaching upward, meant to symbolize unrestrained desire. I passed by two statues of Buddhist gods that decide the fate of the dead. The exterior of the temple was all white, with embedded mirrored glass fragments making it glisten in the sunshine. It was built in traditional Thai architecture style, with a three-tiered roof and abundant use of naga serpents. Inside was a collision of Thai style, Buddhist symbolism, and Western idols, all combined to represent the negative effects of materialism.

The ride had given me time to reflect on life. Sometimes I felt like an elephant with the strength of a mouse. When I was overheated and sweating in my riding gear, after riding ten hours, then faced with simple tasks, I felt I had no strength. When you're at your breaking point, you've just got to hold it together and realize it will get better. Sometimes I felt like a shark in a school of sunfish. The point is, don't get too down and don't get too up. It always changes. Slow and steady wins the race.

~~~

Andiamo Full Circle

The Thai Elephant Conservation Center is the only elephant facility officially recognized and approved by the Thai government as dedicated to the humane treatment of Asian elephants.

A guard who didn't speak English signaled to me that everything was closed. After a few hand gestures, he understood I was inquiring about spending the night and touring the conservation center. He took me to an office where a tiny Thai woman came out speaking perfect English. She pushed her coworker out of the way to demonstrate her abilities. She was very helpful and explained everything I needed to see and do. She escorted me on her motorbike to my private cabin within the huge elephant sanctuary. I asked where to eat dinner. She offered fried rice that another girl delivered to my cabin ten minutes later. It was only rice in a plastic baggy, but so delicious.

In the morning, the staff girl delivered breakfast (pad Thai) to my cabin on her motorbike. It was delicious too.

For their breakfast, I fed the elephants sugarcane. Their massive trunks breathing heavily like a hot air balloon burner and curling around the sugarcane stalks made me aware of the sheer size and power of these beautiful creatures. I bathed in a cool lake with them. They showered me with water from their trunks like a fire hose. Then I went to a show where the elephants were excited to paint pictures. Yes, the elephants actually painted pictures. They grasped a paintbrush with their trunk and painted a rudimentary image of scenes practiced over and over with sugarcane incentives.

I bought several to bring home. Proceeds go directly to the care of the elephants. I also visited the elephant hospital. The conservation center treats sick elephants on-site or with their mobile clinic that will travel anywhere in Thailand to care for elephants in need. They also have an area dedicated to the care of old or terminally ill elephants. It was like a tranquil first-class resort dedicated to the welfare of elephants.

Recipe: Observe the smile of the African Makonde tribe person, with teeth filed to a sharp point. This is beauty to that African culture. Use the metal file to file your own teeth to a sharp point. Wait, don't actually do that. This is for illustrative purposes only.

I needed face to face contact ever since I read a National Geographic feature story about an oppressed cultural tribe of indigenous woman with stretched necks. I googled where to find the Long Neck Karen tribe. I found them thirty miles outside Chiang Mai in a jungle village. I wandered their village for an hour. This Burmese tribe fled Burma after military strife, seeking refuge in the mountains of Thailand. Not having an official citizenship in either country, the only way they can make a living is to weave and sell their handicrafts. Tourists are attracted to their cultural oddity. They believe a long neck is more beautiful, which is the sole reason for the tribe's custom of stretching a woman's neck as tall as possible. Female babies are adorned with brass rings around their necks. Each year on their birthday, they're given another ring. This custom looks severely painful and unpleasant. Ming was a twenty three year old mother of four, holding one baby while she spun yarn on a wooden spinning wheel. She could not twist her head independently of her body. "How do you sleep?" I asked. Ming said; "I am accustomed to my rings, I couldn't live without them". Her neck was wrapped with nine inches of brass rings, while her young daughter had only five inches stretching her head above her shoulders.

Back in Chiang Mai, Thailand, I needed a place to park Andiamo and return to work for a month. My hotel app located a ritzy high-class five-star hotel nearby that had rooms available.

I approached the front desk, attended by smartly dressed staff members. "Do you have a room available?" I asked.

They looked me up and down. "Perhaps you can find a hotel down near the bus station," they said.

I had never felt so embarrassed by my appearance. In stark contrast is how passengers respect me when in uniform while acting as captain of their aircraft. This respect and repulse I have received in life rounds out my personality.

Thank goodness I found the hotel across the street with non judgmental staff had a room and allowed me to park Andiamo for a month.

Now let's go island-hopping through the islands of Indonesia.

Oceania

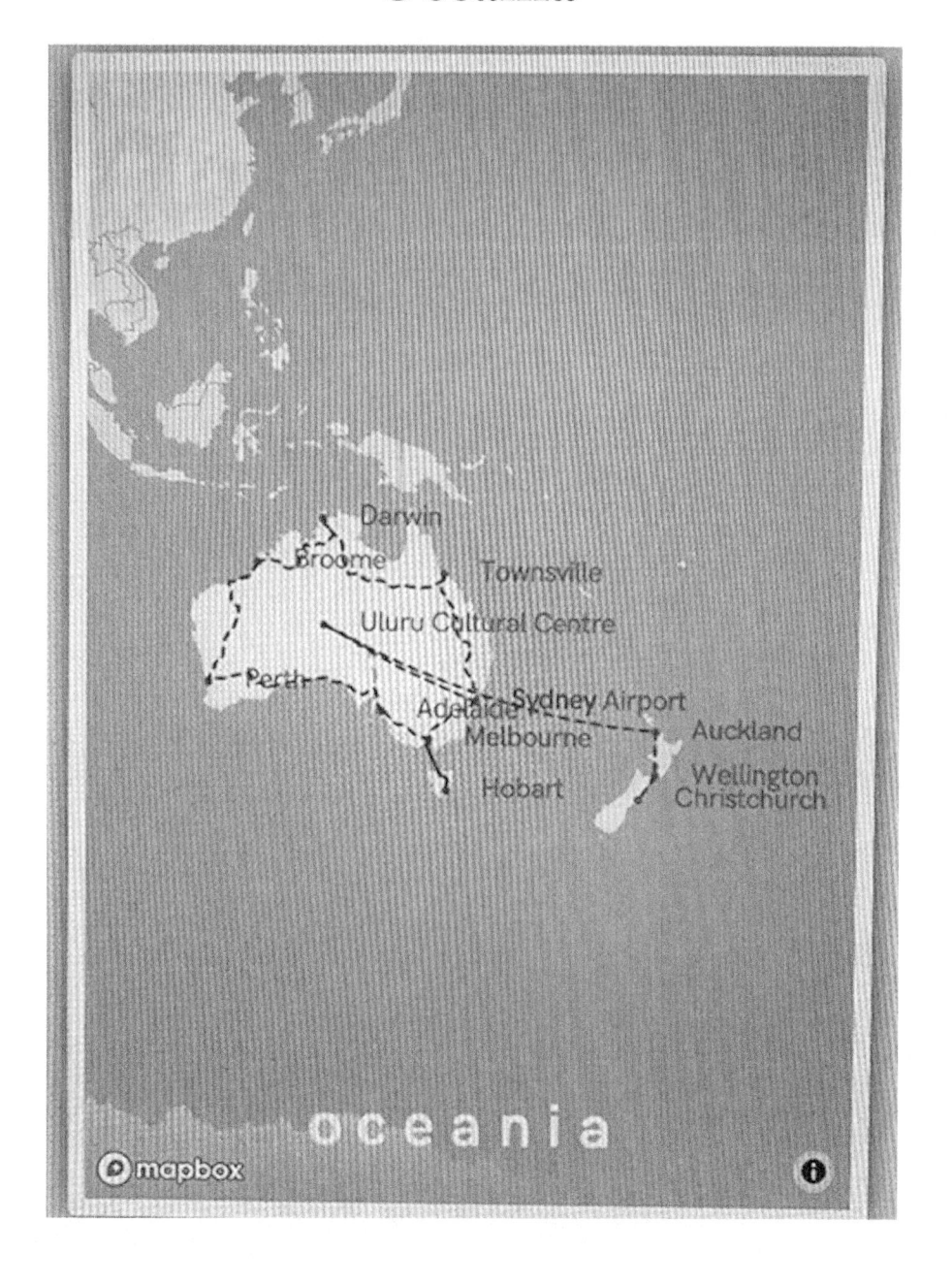

Indonesia

2017

Mileage: 74,000

Ingredients: One hundred yards of rope, one milk crate

Since Mr. Lim's onion boat had sunk, I needed an alternate means across the Malacca Strait. The only ships capable of carrying Andiamo ran sporadically.

My contact at the ferry office, a perky redheaded young woman named Shirley, called my burner phone. "I found a ferry, and the captain has agreed to carry your motorcycle," she said. "It leaves tomorrow. Can you be at my office in fifteen minutes?"

"Yes," I said. I ran out of my hotel room down to Andiamo and sped and dodged traffic to Shirley's office at the port. Shirley's brother, Steven, measured Andiamo with his tape measure and weighed him on an improvised scale to make sure we could lift my heavy bike through the passenger door of the small ship.

The next morning, after complications with my carnet and passport successfully taken care of, I rode to the end of the pier, where the passenger ship waited twenty feet below on a lower dock. The ship was small and didn't have a gangway to ride on, only a narrow passenger door which Andiamo would need to be manually lifted through. It wasn't designed for vehicles, but I had tickets for him and me.

Three port policemen, four dock workers, and I worked together to get Andiamo down a steep twenty-foot cement stairway. The narrow stairs had a flimsy metal railing preventing us from falling into the water and Andiamo from becoming a BMW boat anchor. I needed the ignition on to use the brakes. The problem is, when the ignition is on, the ABS system is active. Any signs of skidding, and the brake pressure is released, forcing me to roll further. With each step the ABS activated, thinking it was skidding, and released the brake pressure, gravity forcing me down. The men grabbed whatever they could on Andiamo—the weak turn signal assembly, the fender, the windshield—anything they could grab to stop me from falling down the stairs and into the water.

On each step, I had to stretch my legs, searching for the next step. This created balance problems. The men had to exert more strength with each step. It was a tense situation, but I made it with the help of the strong men.

At the bottom of the stairway, I had to ride over a narrow plank bridge with no railings, only water on either side. The bridge was roughly the width of my foot pegs, meaning I had to balance vertically with little lateral support, teetering in fear.

Under intense pressure to keep from tipping over, I made it across and to the entryway. All the men lifted Andiamo from the dock into the ship's small entry area, where Andiamo was then tied down. As the final passengers boarded the ship, they had to crawl over Andiamo, who blocked the entryway. Andiamo looked funny as little Indonesians slid their luggage over his panniers, seat, and tank. I didn't worry about scratches or broken parts. That stopped years ago in Mexico. However, I did worry that if we needed to evacuate, the exit would be blocked.

We crossed over to Medan, Indonesia, on the island of Sumatra. Getting Andiamo out of his tomb was equally as difficult.

It was a three-hour ride to picturesque Lake Toba, the largest lake in Indonesia at 62 miles long by 19 miles wide and 1,657 feet deep. There I found a traditional Indonesian resort. The individual cabins were built in the style called rumah adat. Made of fiber, bamboo, and timber with sloping roofs, atop stilts, they were able to withstand shock waves. The most striking feature was the roof, called a Minang roof. They looked like a simple pup tent pulled excessively high on the two roof points. I loved the unique style.

I met a joyful Indonesian man named Efendi who lived in Boulder, Colorado. He was touring his homeland for a couple of weeks. He let me sample his locally made tuak (palm alcohol), contained in a water bottle. One sip put me on the floor, it was so strong.

Andiamo Full Circle

Hello, Efendi,

I hope you are well. Maybe I'll see you in Colorado sometime.

Sincerely,
Robert

Sad to leave the beauty of Lake Toba, I headed for Bukit Lawang in search of the Sumatran orangutan. I entered the river valley road and followed it upstream to a canyon where the people had settled in a little village. I found a unique accommodation cliffside, with a waterfall running through my room. It was natural and exotic, furnished with Indonesian antiques and a king-sized four-poster bed with mosquito netting draped over it. On my private balcony was a view to the other side of the lush mountain river gorge, echoing the sounds of the rushing river below. Within my room was a private area where I could sit under the waterfall as it raged down the mountain. I sat under the waterfall with my riding gear on, since the only washing it gets is the wet rain, followed by the dry sun. The water cleansed my gear and soul for an hour.

I heard the orangutans' surreal mating calls resonate throughout the canyon, the large mammals not visible, sheltered in the vegetation but hauntingly audible.

The next day, trekking with my guide, Unwar, in pursuit of the orangutans, we crossed a cable bridge and climbed a sheer, muddy cliff. They were elusive barbarians but could be heard for miles. A large male engaged in fornication filled the jungle with bursts of pleasure, like a freight train on the outskirts of a city. Avoiding voyeuristic embarrassment, we trudged deeper into the jungle.

Various species of curious monkeys clung to my backpack. Their dexterity enabled one to unzip and pilfer my "ride the world" hat. I imagined him back in the trees telling his buddy, "Hey, look at this cool hat I stole."

Several orangutans interacted with me. They swung from tree to tree, scoping me out. Their weight bent the trees as they swung. Inquisitively, one climbed down to examine me with a closer look. In her wrinkled hand was a tree branch. She held it like a bouquet and reached out as if to offer it to me. Her humble gesture infused my heart with love. Getting that close to her shrouded me in her untamed power and strength.

This larger-than-me, humanlike animal seemed to have an understanding of our places in the world. Her large brown eyes said, "I'm content with my world. I hope you're content with yours," as she intentionally blinked.

It was a profound moment of peace and connection. Then she scaled the tree, using both hands and both feet in alternating unison back to the thick forest canopy. I watched her climb like I had just received a Dear John letter.

Two days later, I left Andiamo with Rahmat at BMW Medan. Rahmat was a young Indonesian man who was service manager and point of contact at the shop. I went home for a month, leaving Andiamo to be serviced.

~~~

I planned to ride farther south on the island of Sumatra, Indonesia. My goal was a thirty-five-hour ride from Medan to Lampung. That's a long time estimate for one segment of my ride. I arranged my work schedule and plotted my course in preparation for the next month.

The destination would be Lampung, the last big city before I'd need a ferry to Java, the next island in Indonesia. The strategy was to leave Andiamo in Lampung and return the following month so I could handle the crazy traffic in Jakarta on the start of that segment fresh and clean. My ultimate goal was to "island-hop" through Indonesia and get Andiamo over to Australia.

My buddy Randy, who had ridden Morocco with me, wanted to ride part of Indonesia. I was excited to ride with him again. Rahmat at BMW arranged a rental bike for Randy.

~~~

Randy and I met at San Francisco International Airport April 2, 2017, to hop a flight to Medan, Indonesia.

We arrived in Medan and spent the entire day sorting out Randy's rental bike. It got complicated, especially since he was going to leave it at a different location from where we picked it up. Rahmat had to organize a pickup vehicle, insurance, and price for all this. We did get it done and were on our way the next day.

Randy and I were like bacon and eggs. We just worked well together. However, back in Morocco, as I went into turns, I would wave an "okay ahead" signal to Randy.

"Dude," he said, "I hate that. You look like a dork."

I never did it again.

Sometimes our banter left people wondering, "Are they enemies or best friends?"

One thing was for sure: when Randy was around, we were laughing. Wherever we rode in Indonesia, people would gather and want to ask questions and take pictures. We had the fame of temporary celebrities.

One night at our hotel in the small town of Tarutung, Jambul, the hotel owner, invited us for a ride in his old Willys Jeep. Since it was stripped down and bare, I put my Kermit Chair (best camp chair) in the back for a third seat. We drove around town and waved to people like we were in a parade.

Randy had once owned an identical Willys Jeep. From the chair in the back, he said, "Hey, Jambul, I'll send you a new steering wheel from America."

Jambul's was weathered and cracked. It was a fun night.

The crisp morning air energized us as we rode the dirt roads. This area of Sumatra was infested with cute vintage Vespa scooters. Vespa means "wasp" in Italian, named for its shape like a wasp's abdomen. Hundreds of old Vespas patched together and running daily filled the streets. I once dealt in Vespa scooters and admired these old machines buzzing down the dirt roads, all from the '60s or '70s, providing reliable means of transport for villagers. They're great scooters. People are still using them fifty and sixty years later. The local dealer must have done excellent sales and service through the years. I rode past them with nostalgic pride.

Ten miles down the road, a wobbly jungle suspension bridge hung above a violent river. The bridge captured my adventurous eye. We stopped on the side of the road.

"Randy," I said, "I want to film crossing that bridge."

"No thanks, Bobby," he said. "I'm gonna have a cup of coffee at the cafe across the street."

Randy is smart. It was a railing-less footbridge, with narrow wood planks, able to support the weight of scooters and people. It was taunting and enticing me. On the other side was thick jungle and huge palm trees alluring me like an exotic dancer. I wanted that epic selfie Instagram video, riding in some unique location over a rickety bridge.

My front tire hit the first plank, and I rode slowly, single-handed, with my camera pointed at my unsuspecting face, filming a selfie video. It was fantastic, with lush tropical jungle, a raging white river below, palm tree huts in frame. I smiled for my epic video.

The problem with this picture was that suspension bridges start to swing. They move as you move. If you aren't in sync with the opposing forces, balance problems threaten your safety. As the bridge started to sway left and right, I needed balance right and left. My balance teetered, and the bridge swung wildly, risking me, my bike, my gear, and Randy's hopes of an enjoyable ride. Plunging into the deep, raging river would end my around-the-world journey. Adrenaline burst my veins. I regained balance and made it across.

Later, Randy and I rode Kelok 9, also known as Kelok Sembilan, which translates to "nine sharp turns." It's 2.5 kilometers of curved bridges and rising concrete that looks like an amusement park roller coaster. Leaning our bikes to the limit, we skidded around the corners. At the top, we stopped for lunch to relax after the EAR we both experienced.

We needed gas for our bodies and bikes. I could ride all day without eating. Randy liked to maintain a full tank. At a gas stop, he bought a bag of potato chips. An oversized smile as wide as the bag was pictured on the front to advertise "big flavor." As Randy gobbled, he held out a chip to a young Indonesian boy with huge eyes. Instead of taking the chip, the boy snatched the bag. Randy, being a kind, selfless soul, smiled and allowed the young boy to offer the bag to his little sister. The boy handed the now-empty bag back to Randy, who held the huge smile printed on the bag in place of his actual smile. I snapped a hilarious photo of Randy with a massive-lipped smile to immortalize our laughter.

Andiamo Full Circle

Randy had scheduled to leave his motorcycle in the next town. We found the prearranged location and left his bike there. As we sat on the steps of the building, I filmed our goodbye in black and white. We agreed it was great to ride together and vowed to do it again in Australia, when I made it there.

Randy's parting words were, "Throw a shrimp on the barbie, mate."

Dear Randy,

You were the first friend I made at our airline when we were in new-hire flight training together nineteen years ago. We have laughed nonstop since then. I want to thank you for the great times we've had together over the years. I admire your integrity, your sense of humor, and your positive outlook on life. I wish you all the best.

Sincerely,
"Little Bobby"

After Randy left, my emotions and I rode in pouring rain most of the day. My goal was to make Bengkulu in two days of riding. My GPS directed me over the mountains instead of along the beach. It was a whole day of winding mountain roads in terrible conditions and tons of traffic. I felt I was "street fighting," battling the vehicles like opponents, weaving around tractors and potholes. I rode late into the night with no suitable locations in sight, and I didn't have any food or water.

After dark, I eventually found a market that was open to ask if there was a hotel in town. Two boys on motorbikes motioned for me to follow them. I followed them a few kilometers to an old Dutch colonial house converted into a guesthouse. I was starved and hadn't eaten all day. I hoped to get a warm home-cooked meal, but they didn't have food available so I unloaded my gear into a single room and returned to the market to purchase two bags of chips and water for dinner.

An early morning start headed for Bengkulu began with a mountain ride, then as I rode along the beach… *bang*! It started to rain and rain. Large raindrops like millions of Dixie cups fired on my face, penetrating my jacket, then my base layer, then my skin, and into my mind. Everything was soaked. Opposite-direction vehicles splashed huge waves like speedboats as they passed by me. I had to duck my head to avoid it being sprayed off. I may have been riding too fast as a dual-wheeled dump truck shock-waved water into my face. The impact was so intense, my sunglasses split in two pieces. It was like diving face-first into a swimming pool with my eyes open. I felt as if water actually went behind my eyeballs. Luckily I carry extra glasses.

One hour before sunset, I stopped at a house where a short man stood in his front yard under an umbrella. I lowered my new fogged glasses to see him and asked if there was a hotel in town.

He pointed back where I had come from. "Three kilometers."

"Three kilometers?" I asked.

"Yes."

I had just come from that direction with complete nothingness. I pointed ahead and asked, "That way?"

He laughed and held up all fingers and doubled gestured them, indicating a number greater than ten fingers.

"Twenty?" I asked.

He shook his head and held up more fingers.

"Fifty?" I asked.

He held up fewer fingers to confirm a still unknown amount. It was a definite maybe there'd be a hotel ahead.

I hadn't ridden many miles that day, with slow roads and rain. Reluctant to turn around, I decided to press on and started the climb up the muddy mountain road. Then the "real rain" began. I slowed my speed and lowered my fogged glasses to see three feet forward. Darkness set in, and I slowed my pace further. At ten miles per hour, I could identify the gigantic potholes up the mountain grades and switchbacks. Semitrucks not yielding an inch blinded me with racks of off-road high-beam lights.

Still thirty-five kilometers out of Bengkulu, at this rate it would take at least 3.5 hours. There were no suitable places to stop and sleep in the jungle. I contemplated sleeping in my Kermit Chair. My hammock would be too hard to set up in the pouring rain, and I would freeze since I had climbed back up into the cold mountain air.

I just bit the bullet and kept going. Ladened with saddle sores in my saturated gear, cold and hungry, I just plugged away and decided, like the *Memphis Belle* captain said, "If we don't complete the mission, someone else will need to tomorrow." I didn't give up. I kept going, telling myself to be strong and just do it. It would end eventually.

Cold, wet, and hungry, I made my goal. I stopped outside town to check my GPS for hotels nearby.

A young man appeared, wearing a Honda shirt and helmet. "What do you need?" he asked.

Exhausted and with no patience left, I mumbled, "Just a hotel."

He ran off. One minute later, he returned with his motorbike and girlfriend. "Let's go," he said.

This was a common occurrence for me: a huge motorcycle being led by a little motorbike like a mouse leading a cat. A group of motorbikes had accumulated and were now riding with us. I saw the hotel. One rider held his arms up, forcing oncoming traffic to stop so I could turn into the hotel parking lot. I felt like I was in a presidential motorcade. A room and open restaurant fulfilled my dream. I showered and headed down to eat and write.

The next day, I made Lampung by 2:00 p.m., my final destination for the month. My first attempt to find a parking spot was at the Novotel Hotel.

"We can't keep your motorcycle here," the manager quickly said.

Up the road at the Aston Lampung City Hotel, I was greeted by a friendly staff of veiled young Muslim women. One smooth-skinned girl named Asera told me, "Yes, we will accommodate you and your motorcycle." Asera was leaving on a camping trip the next day.

"I have a gift for you," I said. "It's my Kermit Chair. Enjoy it on your camping trip."

She loved it. "The general manager would like to talk with you," she said.

I ate at their restaurant, and he sat with me and asked all sorts of questions. They had an underground loading dock where I thought I could surely find a place to park, but that didn't work out. I left Andiamo outside, wrapped in his cover.

Next morning, I bought a ticket from Lampung to Jakarta to Hong Kong to LAX to PHX. In Hong Kong as I waited to check in for my connecting flight, I saw Randy in line. I snuck up behind to surprise him. He was shocked I had made my goal and was on my way home. It was a comforting feeling seeing him.

The month home passed quickly as I prepared for my return to Indonesia with new camping and riding gear.

~~~

When I arrived at the Aston Lampung City Hotel, the staff greeted me with huge smiles and high-fives, as they had anticipated my arrival. Andiamo's battery was dead. A nice hotel worker gave me a jump start with his big diesel truck. Unfortunately, this overheated my tiny jumper cables, smoking them into a melted mess. I daisy-chained my computer's auxiliary power supply to my trickle charger to slow-charge Andiamo's battery. After five hours of this questionable charging technique, the battery was able to start Andiamo's engine.

The staff had gathered around me as I prepped my gear for the next day's departure. I gave my old tool kit and rolltop yellow Ortlieb dry bag to Raman, the security guard who helped me get a drill to fix my boot buckle. I wanted to do something nice for him, so I said. "I'll buy you lunch."

"I'm starving," he replied.

"Perfect," I said. "Let's go." I had misunderstood. What he meant to say was that he was fasting.

After I realized it was Ramadan, he and the front desk girls invited me out for an evening feast. I was exhausted from flying for two days but attended their cultural feast with all the fixings. Asera at the front desk was so cute and helpful. I really enjoyed bantering with her.

Andiamo Full Circle

Dear Asera and Raman,

I hope you are well and your careers are advancing. I wish you the best in life.

Sincerely,
Robert

The next day, I made the port town of Bakauheni easily, with no traffic and good roads. On the ferry, I met local people who wanted photos sitting on Andiamo. They held up my jacket with the flags of every country I've ridden sewn on the back like some kind of prize. I handed out my wooden coins and flashlights. I felt like a celebrity.

The ferry dropped us off in West Java. I had to avoid the motorbike-prohibited expressway toll roads in Jakarta. The side streets were overcrowded, where everyone uses any available space on the poorly maintained roads. I had a few close calls in tight quarters. One guy on a motorbike kept edging his way in front of me. He used his sacks of potatoes attached to his rear rack to push me forward. Andiamo's engine began overheating. His oil and air-cooled engine needs wind to cool. Passing on the left side, using the sidewalks with all the other motorbikes, became my only option. Cars touching cars, motorbikes touching motorbikes—it was a wonderfully overcrowded experience. I had a few off-road experiences where the front wheel would not climb the lip of the curb back onto the street. It was hot-honking chaos.

The seventy-seven miles from Bogor to Bandung took seven hours. That's an average speed of eleven miles per hour.

Consider that. Constant traffic congestion, with full riding gear in the hot Java sun. Diesel dust and thousands of motorbikes all jockeying to get down the road. The stark contrast with even the worst Los Angeles traffic made me thankful for our infrastructure and cooperation. Indonesia traffic is by far the worst traffic in the world, with everyone inches from each other at the stoplights. I was off the road by 4:00 p.m., completely exhausted, but I had made my day's goal.

Bandung to Borobudur was 234 miles, twelve hours of riding with an average speed of 19.5 miles per hour. I got an early start at 7:00 a.m., skipped breakfast, and rode all day without eating, and I only drank one liter of water.

Yogyakarta was my goal. As the day passed, I didn't know if I could make it or not. Three o'clock came, then four o'clock, and still three more hours of riding, which meant two hours in the dark, which slowed me further, adding more hours. So I plugged in Borobudur into the GPS. It was thirty minutes closer to my position. It became my new destination. Of course the sun set, then it started to rain. The high beams of oncoming vehicles created star vision on my face shield and glasses. It became very dangerous. Add kamikaze motorbikes and wild taxi vans, and you have street warfare.

Tired and ready to call it a night, I located a guesthouse. The nice owner invited me in to look at the rooms. One for ten dollars had a squat toilet. His best room had a toilet bowl but no running water. I apologized for wasting his time and got back on Andiamo. Tired, hot, and hungry, I followed my GPS to a gate. The guard came out and opened the gate to a jungle oasis with a wonderful and very trendy Buddha spa hotel inside. There was an open-air pillared meeting hall with candles, quiet Zen music, Buddhist statues, and incense burning. A nice room and a hot meal made the day's struggles vanish.

Borobudur to Pacitan was ninety-six miles and took twelve hours at eight miles per hour, with a detour to Timang Beach. I started the day at 5:00 a.m., following a scooter guide to a hilltop viewpoint to photograph the sunrise over the grand sight of Borobudur, the largest Buddhist temple in the world, but ranked behind Angkor Wat in Cambodia for combined size. There are nine stacked platforms topped with a central dome. The central dome is surrounded by seventy-two Buddha heads encased by perforated stupas, each Buddha head housed in its own private perforated stupa with different meanings. Buddhists on pilgrimage walk the stairs past each Buddha, praying for its meaning.

Borobudur looked great from afar, and the fog gave the photos a soft, textured look. I hiked back down the hill and rode to the temple itself. Then I hiked the temple stairs and found the Buddhas within the perforated stupas. They appeared so peaceful, in an eternal meditative state. Alone on the monument, a perfect opportunity for self-reflection, I realized how fortunate I was to "ride the world" and experience all these historic destinations.

Recipe: Anchor one end of the hundred yards of rope to a mountain cliff. Extend the rope out over the ocean to an island and anchor it. Attach the milk crate to the rope and propel yourself out to the island. Now you know how the "Lobster Gondola" feels.

I had breakfast at the Buddha spa hotel and checked out. Three hours past Yogyakarta is Timang Beach. The "Lobster Gondola" was my goal. It was a one-hour ride on a rocky, hilly road and hard to find, although well worth the effort. I had it stored in my GPS database. My GPS directed me to the exact entrance, using off-road routing. I parked Andiamo and walked the rest of the way. The gondola itself was an exhilarating twenty-meter ride from the mainland to a rock island in a boxlike contraption originally built for lobster fisherman. Suspended by several fabric ropes, the cart rides on metal pulleys and is hand-propelled. What could possibly go wrong? Waves crashing below serve as a reminder: certain death if the ropes give way.

Pacitan-Malang was 151 miles, eight hours of riding at 19 miles per hour. Wonderful weather. Not too hot. Some towns had Saturday markets with vehicles, mostly motorbikes, parked in a line stretching two full kilometers out of town. It was anarchy. The traffic directors waving flags served little purpose. The police were standing around texting on their phones or waving flags in no particular direction. They needed standardized signs and signals to organize the traffic. It would be a very easy fix to make things run smoother.

Whenever or wherever I stopped, people gathered and watched what I was doing. They would stand inches from me and observe my every move as if I were a magician performing sleight-of-hand tricks. At first I didn't know what to think, but soon it became an endearing experience. It was nice to feel so special.

When I stopped on a remote mountain road, a young Indonesian man on a black motorbike also stopped and was very curious about me. "Can I take photo of you?" he asked.

He was more curious than most. We talked about our love of motorcycles and how we could live on our bikes. I gave him a wooden coin and flashlight. He searched his weathered fanny pack for a special gift. He pulled out a small screw pin anchor shackle used for a keychain and gave it to me. It was a memorable moment and a connection of the human spirit. I started to fully embrace these small exchanges in life.

I made it to Malang and inquired at the Shalimar Boutique Hotel if they would allow me to keep Andiamo there for a month.

The attending front desk staff rang Ita, who spoke perfect English. "Seventy-five thousand rupiah per day okay for the parking?"

That was equivalent to five dollars. "Perfect," I said, and we had a deal.

Home for a month.

~ ~ ~

I returned to Malang a month later to the Shalimar, where Andiamo was parked outside. I packed him and rode to the ferry from Java to Bali, a short and sweet ride.

Bali is a world-class exotic island destination. Riding Andiamo on it was a privilege.

In Lovina dolphin watching, I took the early tour for more "dolphins than boats." The later tour has more "boats than dolphins." It was fun being in a traditional outrigger boat as we sailed alongside dolphins porpoising in the water. I loved being up close to the "ocean's golden retrievers."

Back in southern Sumatra, I had to jump-start Andiamo from a big diesel truck, causing an over-voltage situation. I believe this, combined with the days spent on the Bolivian salt flats, had rendered Andiamo's electrical system compromised.

In Bali, anytime I turned the handlebars beyond twenty degrees off-center, the engine would cut out. During one U-turn on a corner of an uphill portion, his engine stalled in the middle of the road as an oncoming car sped toward me. I twisted the handlebars straight and quickly restarted him in the nick of time. I'm not sure I've conveyed my point with enough emphasis. This could have been fatal. Definitely, it risked my manhood.

I researched potential causes and determined he had a faulty ignition switch. I located the cracked portion of the switch inside the handlebar assembly. BMW Bali couldn't locate a new ignition switch, so I ordered one online and would bring it back next month in September. I continued to ride the duration of the month, knowing any turns would stall me.

Below are some interesting experiences I had in Bali.

~~~

In David Bowie's will, he requested his body be cremated in Bali in accordance with Balinese traditions. I saw many such ceremonies throughout Bali in country villages and larger cities. The Ngaben ceremonies are amazing spectacles that combine celebration and sorrow. They arrange parades in the streets with hundreds of attendees dressed in traditional attire, carrying floats emblazoned with scaled serpents and dragons with long tongues spitting fire. Traffic stopped for the walking processions of colorfully dressed people. Drums beat, symbols clanged, and people chanted messages for eternal happiness. I loved them.

~~~

Built in a shallow area in Lake Beratan, the Ulun Danu Beratan Temple serves to bless the water from the lake before it flows downstream to irrigate the entire region. A shrine of multitiered roofs, it's large at the bottom, progressively smaller above. The Hindu design fascinated me. It looked like umbrellas stacked on top of each other.

~ ~ ~

In a small town in a shaded work area, a squatting man chiseled a large piece of stone with no safety glasses. Small fragments flew by his eyes. Unconcerned for his safety or distracted by my presence, he blew dust from the statue. Carved stone Balinese statues filled large outdoor courtyards of the artists' carving shop. I examined the unique features of each. Among a large inventory, I purchased one of Vishnu riding the Garuda carved from limestone. Featured prominently in my home today, it represents the ever-protecting, ever-present god protecting Earth. It weighs three hundred pounds.

I shipped an equal-sized Buddha statue from Cambodia. I figured the cost and logistics would be similar. There were many email threads between the shipper in Bali and the receiving agent in Los Angeles and myself. There were customs, forms, fumigation certificates, taxes and duty fees on both ends. One email I received requested more fees. Otherwise I'd be fined $5,000. Finally, DHL was able to clear their own customs, and nothing more was necessary. It took five months to arrive in Phoenix, but I love the statue and what it represents.

~ ~ ~

The canopy of trees shaded the walkways as I entered the Sacred Monkey Forest. Monkeys climbed my legs onto my shoulders, clinging to my hair. I had a cluster of bananas ready for their salivating mouths. Their little fingernails were just like mine as we exchanged ownership of bananas. The babies washed them down with suckles of mothers' milk. Mothers watched their babies roll around, kicking their bowlegged feet and swimming their arms. Some looked like little punk rockers with monkey mohawk hairstyles. One operated a drinking fountain with familiarity, pushing the button to watch the stream of arched water, then sipping like an old man in a public park. I spent the day enjoying monkey business.

~ ~ ~

Cute, cuddly, furry honey bears sat on my lap as I fed them carrots. Little brown eyes surrounded by lighter-colored hair and longish snouts concealing sharp teeth gave them an uninviting look. Docile and sweet as they were, I wanted to wrap my arms around them. Their five-inch claws embedded in paws larger than my head, the putrid smell, and their untamed strength conflicted with my desire for a hug. I knew as soon as I ran out of carrots, they would quickly eat my hand. They were not Mr. Teddy in my crib.

~~~

On the edge of a two-hundred-foot cliff, two ropes were suspended from large tree branches, and a wooden seat swung out fifty feet over the canyon below. At the apex of the swing's motion, the perspective is this: a swinger becomes the only object in the world, with nothing but the swing's ropes and occupant in view. It didn't look as alluring as the Instagram girls dressed in long flowing red robes and hair wistfully blowing in the wind.

~~~

The world's most expensive coffee, kopi luwak, is coffee made from beans that have passed through the intestines of an animal called the Asian palm civet. Similar to a mongoose, the civet eats coffee cherries, the excrement is collected and separated, and the beans are roasted. As the coffee cherries pass through the civet's intestines, a fermentation process occurs, giving the beans their unique flavor.

I questioned the origin of this process. How did the first person come to discover its flavor? Did the person inspect a dropping and say, "Let's make this into coffee and drink this stuff?" It's mentioned in the movie *The Bucket List*. When Jack Nicholson has a coffee machine delivered to his hospital room, Morgan Freeman laughs, knowing the process. I saw the process on a plantation in Bali. It's good coffee, but I didn't pay the $700 per kilogram.

~~~

At an afternoon workshop to learn how to make my own cologne, I was walked through the entire process: identifying, quantifying, and mixing my personal custom fragrance. It was a unique thing to try.

~~~

Back to the States for a month.

I packed the ignition switch under the shirts in my carry-on luggage, since BMW Bali couldn't obtain one. I rented a room near the shop. The next morning I brought the part to them. They installed it and delivered Andiamo directly to my hotel. He seemed to be running rough, but they said it was no problem. I suspected a bit of a problem, but I wasn't going to press the issue. I was on a tight ride schedule. The next morning, I packed up my gear and headed for the Ghost Palace.

My spine scraped the barrier as I ducked under the access gate of the grand entrance, overgrown with years of neglect. The circular driveway led to a staircase, cracked with moss, flanked by fearsome Balinese dragons. Flying my drone down the haunted hallways flexed the cobwebs like a bedsheet on a clothesline. Chandeliers framed the front desk where never had a clerk checked guests in for their honeymoon retreat. Civil war broke out before the grand opening of this ghostly resort.

My dusty footsteps were visible on the mosaic tiled floor. I seemed to hear eerie echoes of music never played, baffled by thick velvet floor-to-ceiling curtains hanging from partially fallen rods. Pillars in the grand ballroom struggled to support the rotunda roof with peeling cupids shooting arrows. Through the shower room, following the direction of the rusted pool sign, porcelain fragments waiting at the urinals filled with sharp mirror slices led me to the swamp pool. The terraced lounge decks crumbled in molded concrete, with serpent fountains spitting air into the dreams of splashing swimmers. This was someone's vision evolved into vapor.

~~~

I rode Andiamo onto the ferry, bound for Lombok, the next island in Indonesia. Ferrymen tried to convince me to get a cabin, but after looking at the filthy space, I decided to spend the five-hour trip sleeping on a wooden bench on the upper deck.

As I left the north coast of Lombok and climbed the secluded mountain road near Mount Rinjani, Andiamo was having problems. Inches from the top of the mountain, Andiamo quit and would not start. A group of uniformed Indonesian men and boys gathered. They knocked on my fuel tank, and I agreed. It did sound empty. I explained I should have close to 100 miles left in the tank. The trip odometer read 235, not my normal 320-mile range.

"You're out of gas," they yelled.

Since Andiamo wasn't starting, rather than argue, I asked, "Where can I buy gas?"

One older man replied. "You can coast down the mountain to a woman selling gas out of plastic bottles."

So I did. The first kilometer went great, coasting at a decent pace. Unfortunately, on one uphill portion, a truck in front of me putzing along exhausted my remaining momentum, and I stalled near the top of the slight uphill. Two Bali boys on a motorbike pushed me to the crest, and I coasted five more kilometers with ease to where the woman was selling gas out of plastic bottles. I purchased four liters and tried to start him, to no avail. I turned on my global hot spot. It wasn't working either. My phone had no signal.

My anxiety increased. "How far can I coast?" I asked the woman.

"You can coast two more kilometers to a small town," she said.

So I did. In town, I came to a stop in front of a hardware store. I troubleshot the problem and identified it as a blown fuse for my fuel pump. I changed it, and Andiamo started fine. I was on my way again.

The next morning, he ran fine until about twenty miles from the ferry I had planned to take to Sumbawa, the next island. Then he completely died again. I pulled over near a small house, where I checked the fuel pump fuse. It had blown again, so I changed it, but with no priming of the fuel pump.

A woman suggested I get some boys to push Andiamo a few blocks to where another boy worked on motorbikes. Two ambitious Indonesian boys pushed me as I steered. The ground of the makeshift mechanics' hut was filled with random nuts and bolts. The boy wasn't familiar with big BMWs, so I was on my own. The horn was working, so I switched out the fuel pump relay with the horn relay, since they're identical. That didn't work. I removed the fuel pump to check the wiring. It looked fine. I put direct current to it, with no response. I needed a new fuel pump. It's the same fuel pump used in some Subaru cars. Unfortunately, there was no auto parts store on the tiny tropical island.

As the sun was setting, I needed a place to spend the night. Everyone in the crowd that had gathered offered their homes. I loved the warm hospitality, as I was truly stranded and in need. I had planned to hang my hammock at the small roadside mechanic shop between two posts in the driveway. Then a nice woman invited me to come stay at her house with her family.

A bunch of Indonesian boys pushed Andiamo and me across the street to the backyard of the family's house, where I hung my hammock and camped for the night. The husband's name was Anwar. He wore a traditional Balinese batik udeng hat and a colorful sarong. His wife, Gita, wore a similar sarong and silk blouse and carried their one-year-old daughter in her arms. The cute couple had been married six years and had two children. They also had calm, peaceful spirits. Anwar and I lounged in our sarongs on an elevated wooden platform covered by a thatched canopy serving as an outdoor family dining area. He was young and flexible, while I struggled to crisscross my legs.

Gita served a delicious meal. We sat on pillows in our sarongs, eating with our hands from a large community bowl of rice.

"Is there any possible way to drive me and Andiamo back to Bali using your pickup truck?" I asked Anwar.

He considered my question. "Yes, I would be happy to help you."

But Gita expressed concern. "Darling," she said to her husband, "I don't want you to leave. The volcano is going to erupt any day now." They worry about volcanos erupting like we worry about driving in rush hour traffic.

Anwar placed his hand over his heart to show regret. "I am sorry, Mr. Robert," he said. "I cannot drive you, but I do have an idea." He opened his flip phone and made a call to his cousin, who agreed to take me to the port of Lombok, where I could ride the ferry back to Bali.

The next morning, we were off to the port. Using a splintered wooden plank as a ramp, we unloaded Andiamo with the help of porters at the port.

We pushed the bike onto the ferry, and I was off, back to BMW Bali for a new fuel pump. It was a nice ferry ride. I worked on my book and video for five hours.

Once we were on Bali, the porters were aggressive and not accommodating, only concerned with making money for themselves. One did help push me off the ferry to a parking area for a few dollars.

I needed another pickup truck to drive me and Andiamo twenty-five kilometers to BMW Bali. As the sun set, I became desperate. I paid a guy one million rupiah, which is about seventy-five dollars, for a ride to BMW Bali using his pickup truck. I had arranged a late-night arrival at the BMW Bali shop. The night security guard helped me unload Andiamo off this guy's pickup. I booked a room at a nearby bungalow and planned to return in the morning to verify there was no possibility of fixing it without a new fuel pump.

The next morning, they confirmed the fuel pump was bad. I got online and searched for the cost of a fuel pump in America. I found an original BMW one for $400. It would've been $800 if I had ordered it through BMW Bali via Jakarta, so I planned to bring a fuel pump back to Bali next month, again in my carry-on luggage.

Home for a month.

~~~

The flights back to Bali were fine.

I left the new fuel pump with BMW Bali. They worked on Andiamo while I toured Upside Down World, the Trunyan Cemetery, and an abandoned amusement park. BMW Bali texted me that the turn signals and fog lights now didn't work (more electrical anomalies), and they couldn't figure it out. I had no choice but to take the bike and hope for the best.

I paid BMW Bali for their service, and I was on my way to attempt Lombok and continue my Indonesian island-hopping.

Andiamo stalled as I was riding up the gangplank of the ferry to Lombok. He barely started again. When the ferry arrived on Lombok, he wouldn't start at all. Disappointed, I left him at the ferry port near a guard shack and went to a hotel to sort things out. I stayed at Cocotinos Sekotong on Lombok while I searched for a shipper to Australia.

The next day, I rented a scooter to ride around Lombok Island looking for shipping companies. I got a flat tire with the rented scooter on a country road. Thankfully, a scooter mechanic was nearby. I pushed it to him, and he had it patched within twenty minutes. Amazing work.

I found a shipper who took Andiamo to his office. He built the crate, handled the customs, and shipped Andiamo to Sydney, Australia. I planned to receive the shipment in Sydney in a couple months.

I took a taxi to the port and hopped on a banana boat to Gili Air, a small footpath-only island between Bali and Lombok. From the port, I walked barefoot to a small resort with a swimming pool out front. I strolled the sand streets and ate dinner at an open-air Italian restaurant. Cool vibe on a laid-back island.

I took a flight to Flores Island, then a boat to Komodo Island to see the Komodo dragon. The Komodo dragon is the largest lizard in the world and venomous by means of biting and infecting its prey with rancid saliva. It prefers meat that is rotting, which makes its saliva deadly. I witnessed one stalk a deer. As the dragon lunged with his mouth open, the deer jumped over a log, stopping the dragon's lunge.

Mount Agung volcano did erupt that week. I had left Bali just before the eruption that closed the airport and stranded people in Bali for a week. Another narrow escape.

Home for a month. I'll see Andiamo in Australia.

Australia

2018–2019

Mileage: 75,000

Ingredients: one-mile-long oven, one liter water, one hydration vest

A shipping agent on the island of Lombok, Indonesia, built a crate for Andiamo and shipped him to Sydney, Australia, for services unavailable on the remote islands of Indonesia.

After twenty hours of airports and flying, the plane touched down in Sydney. I took an Uber to Procycles Sydney. Andiamo had arrived okay, but he was not fixed. They claimed the mirrors and windshield had been lost in the shipment. The wooden crate created customs fumigation problems. I had a certificate of fumigation from Indonesia, but Australia is very protective of their fragile ecosystem, so they conducted another fumigation of the wooden crate. That cost me another $450. My service adviser at Procycles Sydney advised me there were "bigger problems" with Andiamo, and it was too hard to communicate them via emails.

I had wasted a trip to Australia. Not all bad, because Sydney is my favorite big city in the world with its diverse activities, architecture, and cultures. I let Procycles work on Andiamo while I hopped on the Big Bus tour of Sydney.

First stop: Bondi Beach, where businessmen opened their office-building door wearing loafers and closed it wearing flip-flops, only steps from the sand, with surfboards in hand. The waves rolled in like tubular turquoise bursts of freedom.

Second stop: Darling Harbor. I sipped wine and strolled the boardwalks, which had a plethora of trendy bars and cafes, all with sexy, accented staff.

Next stop: Harbour Bridge. I walked across the bridge where Paul

Hogan worked as a painter. The iconic bridge provided great views of Sydney Harbor.

Next stop: I visited Fortune of War and had a pint of lager at Sydney's oldest pub. I sauntered the streets of the Rocks District, formerly the red-light district, with century-old buildings, cobblestone streets, and laneways with open-air markets.

Next stop: I bought a day pass to the water taxi and visited all the stops for a unique way to see the city.

That night I attended a production at the Sydney Opera House, one of my favorite buildings in the world. A UNESCO World Heritage site and one of the world's most recognized structures, it's made to look like a ship's sails. Usually, I'm happy with a couple days in a big city. Sydney, however, calls for longer.

Andiamo needed more service, and I needed to get back to the States. I hopped a flight home via the island of Fiji, where I took the one-hour boat ride out to Cloud 9. The two-level floating platform bar in the middle of the South Pacific Ocean had been on my radar for a long time. They played great music while I relaxed on an oversized bed and soaked in the sun. I jumped from the second-story deck into the warm water. It was a fantastic day.

I received an email from Procycles in Sydney that said, "The fuel pressure regulator was bad, producing one bar, then four bars and should maintain a steady three bar."

Andiamo also had a cracked frame and bent center stand. They fixed the fuel pressure regulator. I planned to fix the other problems later.

I wound up with twenty-five days off in March, which allowed me to use vacation in a very effective way. With such a great schedule, I focused on doing five of my bucket list items in my almost month off.

1. I hiked the Great Wall of China.
2. I visited the Terracotta Warriors.
3. I hiked Mount Huashan, the world's deadliest hike.
4. I flew into Lukla Airport in Nepal.

5. I chartered a helicopter and got a close-up view of Mount Everest from base camp.

I made a video titled *Bucket List*, detailing each item, and posted it on my Facebook page.

After a whirlwind tour accomplishing five of my bucket list items, I made it to Sydney to pick up Andiamo. He ran perfectly.

I headed south for the island of Tasmania on an overnight ferry. I wanted to see a Tasmanian devil, an illustration of how Australians kiddingly stereotype Tasmanian people. Compare Americans' stereotype of Appalachian people.

I stopped at a park specializing in the care of Tasmanian devils. I walked through the gates of the Tasmanian devil refuge, expecting some kind of cartoon character spinning in circles, eating everything in sight with needle-sharp teeth. The owner kept the devils in an area with two fences, four feet high—not to prevent them from escaping, rather to keep a guest from falling into the fenced area where the vicious creatures resided. They looked like a bear but were sized like a domestic cat, with teeth like white needles, jaws that would lock on to prey, and translucent red ears that seemed to light up in a devilish way. Typically the female is dominant in the Tasmanian devil world.

There was a male and female in the corral. The male had scars and bite marks covering his body. As the guide tossed bits of meat to the two, the female chased the male away from the food. The squeals were a deafening high-pitched alarm, signaling an attack. The two devils squealed continuously and sunk their sharp fangs into each other, splattering blood everywhere. The guide dangled a football-sized hunk of beef over the fence. As the female lunged for it, her teeth locked on to the meat, and he lifted her up in the air, dangling her like a dog playing tug-of-war. She would not let go of her dinner. I pictured the spinning Warner Bros. cartoon character and thought he was tame compared to this true devil.

A few hours ride south in Port Arthur, Tasmania, and I walked the Convict Trail in the footsteps of Australia's first citizens, who were criminals.

The first fleet of British ships arrived in Australia in 1788 with 1,000 to 1,500 convicts, seamen, and civil officers to establish a penal colony. Britain sent more than 165,000 convicts to Australia. They sent the more serious convicts to Tasmania and the worst of those to Port Arthur, where I saw the terrible conditions they lived in, kept in cells unfit for a body, fed scraps of bread and splashes of water. The convicts were used as free labor in logging, mining, and roadbuilding.

Returned home for a month.

On my way back to Tasmania, I stopped in Ghana, West Africa…

~~~

A bucket list deviation in my story… Back at work, bucket lists were on my brain.

I was flying with Walt, and I asked him, "What's the first item on your bucket list?"

"I want to visit the 'slave castles' in Ghana, West Africa," he said.

"Now that's something I need to do!" I replied.

We planned to do it together and researched and prepared for the trip. There was a nationwide shortage of the vaccine for yellow fever, which is required for Ghana. I found a clinic that had two injections for Walt and me. We received the injections together and scheduled our trip the next week. The night before we were to leave, Walt had to cancel for work obligations. I went alone.

Dear Walt,

Thank you for the inspiring conversations about your ancestry and tracing your roots to Africa. I wish we could have experienced the "slave castles" together. It was an adventure in emotions for me. I can't imagine how dramatic it would have been for you. When you eventually visit them, I'd like to hear about your reactions. I hope you are well.

Sincerely,
Bob

Andiamo Full Circle

My first stop in Ghana was Elmina Castle, which President Obama had just visited. I walked through the entryway imagining what it would have been like to be taken from my home by local tribesmen, forced into a prison, then shipped off to some strange land. I stood in the dungeons where twelve million humans had been sold and sent away against their will. The walls and floors were stained with body matter, but what a story they could tell…

~~~

Ben, my next first officer, said, "My first item on my bucket list is to try caviar."

We landed in Cleveland, Ohio, and I took an Uber to a fish market that sold caviar and bought a half ounce of white sturgeon caviar for Ben.

"It tastes salty," he said when he tried it.

~~~

Next I flew with Justin. "My first bucket list item is to visit the great wine regions around the world," he said. Not surprising for a wine enthusiast.

"I'm riding Australia at this point," I said. "Do they have good wine?"

"Australia produces some of the world's best wines," he said, "and you're headed for the heart of it in the McLaren Vale region."

"Pick the best wine of the region and buy a bottle," I said. "Then I'll visit the vineyard itself, and we can do a comparison."

He chose Mollydooker's 2016 Shiraz. I went to the vineyard in McLaren Vale, Australia, and bought a bottle. We tried them together virtually via FaceTime and both agreed it was delicious wine, plus it was a fun tour with Liza and Todd giving me VIP treatment and samples of all the fine wines.

Hello, Liza,

Congratulations on your wedding. I hope all is well. Hello, Todd. Thank you for putting me in touch with Doug Pitman to work on my bike. He did a great job,

Sincerely,
Robert

The most exciting overnight ferry trip from Tasmania to Melbourne featured a romantic singer onstage with thick, long black hair, wearing a tight red dress, that made the trip fly by with groovy music warming my heart. The rhythmic sea combined with great music made my dreams come true.

West of Melbourne, I rode the most beautiful coastal route I have ever ridden. The Great Ocean Road was a stretch of 151 miles of continuous amazement. The highlight for me was the Twelve Apostles, a collection of limestone-stacked pillars offshore. The wind and waves create a salty mist in the air, making them appear heavenly with their unusually precarious steeplelike rock formations.

I needed a new set of tires and an oil change. Todd from Mollydooker Vineyard suggested Pitmans Motorcycles in Adelaide, Australia. He said the owner was an ex-business partner and would do a good job. I rode to Pitmans, where I was greeted by Doug, the owner. In addition to normal service, I asked Doug if he could fix the subframe and center stand.

"No worries, mate," he said.

I asked if he could have the frame painted yellow.

"No worries, mate."

I left Andiamo and my gear with Doug and returned to the States to work for a month.

~~~

I stopped off in Papua, New Guinea, on my way back to Australia, for the largest indigenous event in the world. It was a stunning display of native cultures. I made a video of the visually stimulating costumes and posted it on my Facebook page. More details there.

Doug couldn't locate a reasonably priced subframe in Australia, so I sourced one from a salvage yard in Florida and shipped it to Australia for powder coating in yellow and installation. Within the month, Pitmans Motorcycles had repaired the subframe and powder coated it yellow to match the accents, and had changed the tires, center stand, and oil, all for $827, when $800 was a standard price for just the new Metzeler Karoo 3 tires in other parts of the world. A shoutout to Doug Pitman! Pitmans

Motorcycles in Adelaide, Australia, is by far my best motorcycle repair experience of this around-the-world motorcycle ride.

> *Thank you very much, Doug. You did great work and completed the service on time at a fair price. The frame has worked well, and I love the color.*
>
> *Sincerely,*
> *Robert*

The next day at Border Village, a small town before crossing into Western Australia, I met two off-duty police officers filling their motorcycles at the gas station/motel. "Looks like you've ridden a long way," they said. "We'll buy you a beer at the bar."

I brought my Bucket List Banner to the gas station/motel/bar and swapped bucket list dreams with everyone gathered at a table. Terry wanted to hike the Kancoona Trail. Mike wanted to ride his bicycle down the bike path alongside the Danube River in Budapest. Hearing their bucket list ideas, I sincerely hoped they'd accomplish them and live happy lives.

They told me how the police systems worked in Australia. I had one beer and a burger and needed rest. We shook hands with great admiration for each other's goals and said our goodbyes. It restored my faith in cops. They were motorcycle riders who understood my situations around the world with bad cops.

The next morning, when I was crossing the border from South Australia to Western Australia at an agriculture checkpoint, a heavy uniformed lady wanted me to unpack my gear to look in my side boxes while she was waving huge semitrucks, vans, and cars through.

I pleaded with her. "It takes me twenty-five minutes to unpack and pack the gear."

After reviewing my documents and giving me a stern warning not to carry agricultural products into Western Australia, she hastily conceded and waved me through her checkpoint.

Exasperated, I accelerated rapidly, rounding a corner into an oncoming police car that lit up the red and blues. I pulled off to the side of the road.

The police car drove up next to me. The passenger-side aging male cop said, "Don't stop here. Keep it going around the corner."

"I wanted to show immediate compliance," I said.

The muscular female cop had something to prove. "It will be a violation."

I asked for a warning.

"No way," she quickly said.

My patience was tested as she forcefully administered a breathalyzer sobriety test at 9:00 a.m. I had had one beer with my burger the previous night and had shown no signs of intoxication to the cops.

"It's regulations," she said.

Guilty until proven innocent is the way most other countries' legal systems work. In Australia that morning, I was considered drunk until I could prove I was sober. God bless America.

The next night was spent in Esperance, where ten kilometers out of town, my tank ran dry at 250 miles, again not my normal 320 miles. I suspected a fuel oddity and had my two-gallon gas bag full. I coasted into an animal rescue farm and accessed the gas bag. Pouring from it would be a problem, so I drank my full liter of water to make a makeshift funnel.

At that very moment, a pickup truck stopped. "Do you need anything, mate?" the driver asked.

"Yes, a funnel," I said.

He reached into the back of his truck and produced a big funnel, which worked so much better than the small makeshift water-bottle funnel. Bad luck followed by good luck again, full circle.

From the beginning, my fuel gauge had been inaccurate, virtually inoperative, so I track fuel use with my odometer and gas pump gallons added. This is a historic problem with Andiamo's model year, a 2004 BMW 1150GS.

Once in Esperance, I looked for a hotel. At the Best Western, the front desk gal called every hotel in town. They were all full. It was a holiday weekend. Finally, she called the campground and reserved a campsite for me. Bad luck turned good luck again. Full circle. Serendipity.

Recipe: Preheat the one-mile-long oven to 150 degrees. Soak the hydration vest in water for five minutes. Put it on. Guzzle the one-liter bottle of water. Ride a motorcycle through the oven ninety times. Feel the hydration vest cool you for only a few minutes. Then it's dry and ineffective. After the extreme heat, the liter of water is converted to only sweat, not urine.

I rode the "90 Mile Straight," Australia's longest straight road, 146.6 kilometers across the Nullarbor Plain, a semiarid region with no trees, just unrelenting nothingness. It has no towns, no service, no vegetation, no animals—just heat. Every twenty miles on the pavement were runway markings for aircraft landing on the road to provide rescue or emergency evacuation of accident victims. I imagined landing an airplane on a highway, taxiing up to an accident, collecting the victims, and flying them to safety. That would be the only way to save a person from this wasteland. I prepared for the crossing with extra water, extra gas, extra stamina, and a hydration cooling vest.

Before I set out on the Nullarbor, I had soaked the vest in water, the theory being that as I rode, wind would pass through the vest with an evaporative cooling effect on my body. It's a cheap way to stay cool for a short bit in extreme heat. Then the vest dries and is useless. The windless portions of my body where the vest met my hips remained saturated, creating a moldy clamminess after a full day of riding. Upon completion of the Nullarbor, the red heat on my face arrived minutes before at the "roadhouse." Inside the roadhouse, of course they sold *I SURVIVED THE NULLARBOR* T-shirts. Roadhouse is Australian for gas station in the outback, mate.

I made it to Perth and found a BMW dealership to store Andiamo and look into the fuel anomalies. Home for a month.

Life is short and I have a list of things I need to accomplish. On my way back to Perth, I had extended vacation days and planned on a trip to Israel, then down to South Africa for a three day safari, then a flight to Perth. At that time, our pilot group was in contract negotiations with the company. It got ugly when the company canceled all vacations for several months. With all vacations canceled, I had to cancel my plans for Israel and South Africa. I had a short time off, so I planned a short ride. Time enough to ride Perth to Broome, Australia.

Perth BMW cleaned out the fuel lines but didn't do anything more. The charge was $250 but no motorcycle storage fees. The bike seemed to run okay as I rode up the west coast of Australia.

I camped on a secluded beach with a beautiful Western Australia sunset, totally isolated and private. The waves broke at my feet, soothing them. I toasted the sunset with my stainless steel wine glass. That night I left my tent doors open for an ocean breeze. In the morning, I had huge red welts over my entire self where ants had spent the night chewing on my body. The itching continued throughout the day.

The ride up the west coast was tremendous but very hot. I poured water over my head to avoid overheating. Beautiful hotels, swimming in the pools, and camping on the beaches made it a wonderful portion of my journey.

One morning after I packed up camp on the beach, my rear wheel spun in the sand deeper and deeper until the axle was buried. There was no way for me to get out of this soft, deep sand. I was stuck. I hiked a kilometer to find five Australian men ready to surf. I didn't want to interrupt their day, but I was stranded and needed their help. We used their four-wheel drive ute to pull me out of the sand to a hard surface.

When I offered compensation, they said, "No worries, mate."

I needed a parking spot to leave Andiamo in the small town of Broome. I rode to RV parks and hotels to no avail. Finally, I found a trucking company that had a warehouse with an available corner where I could park Andiamo and leave him for a month.

The fourteen-and-a-half-hour flight home in economy was grueling, but I made it. Jet-lagged, I was glad to have a few more days off to reset my body clock.

After my return, in Broome I found a villa with a private pool. I relaxed for a day in the paradise residence. Nearby was an elevated restaurant overlooking the ocean. An exquisite romantic dinner while enjoying the smooth sun-orange ocean invigorated my soul. Camel trains walking the beach cast long shadows as the sun sank into the Indian Ocean.

It was terribly hot riding in midsummer in Western Australia. The boab trees intrigued me. They were along a stretch of highway in the Kimberley region of Western Australia. They looked like wine bottles with twigs at the top. They were eerie and dry but fascinated me.

I crossed the border of Western Australia to the Northern Territory, where the speed limit increased to 130 kilometers per hour, the highest I had seen in Australia. The rough roads, an overloaded bike, and extreme heat ripped a few tread knobs off Andiamo's rear tire down to the fabric core. The tire was fairly new, but a softball-sized portion was missing, worn to dangerous limits. I was 66 kilometers outside the nearest town of Katherine, Australia. My options were to hitch a ride with a truck, hop a train, or cross my fingers and hope the tire stayed together until I made it into town. As the tire rotated, I would feel a slight sink when the bare portion hit the road. It was 66 stressful kilometers, wondering if the tire might burst.

Rolling into Katherine, I saw a Honda dealer. Perhaps they had a tire that fit. Sure enough, in a dusty corner, the mechanic found an aged replacement. He had the old tire off and the new tire on like a NASCAR pit crew. Again, bad fortune followed by good fortune.

On my way to Darwin, Australia, Andiamo's engine started to sputter. I slowed and pulled into a vacant roadhouse to ponder what could be wrong. The problems appeared to be fuel-related. I had been questioning the fuel system operation for a couple of months. Water in the tank is what I suspected, since the gasket on the fill cap was old and cracked. Water must have seeped in overnight when it rained heavily.

BMW Darwin allowed me to keep Andiamo there for a month while they worked out his issues.

On my way back to the States, I stopped off in the Philippines for some island-hopping, including an epic tour of Coron Island on a catamaran, snorkeling, and lunch at a hut on stilts in a private alcove. Coron Island is a collection of small mountains growing out of the water, with dots of lush vegetation that my drone filmed from above. I feature a video on my Facebook page to show the true beauty. Then I rented a motorcycle and toured the small island.

After two days, I hopped a flight to Bohol Island. I saw the tarsiers, the smallest mammals in the world. They were so cute with their tiny bodies and huge eyes like saucepans.

Hopped a flight back to Cebu for canyoneering and cliff jumping.

I caught a flight home from MNL (Manila) to HNL (Honolulu) on Hawaiian Airlines, then to Phoenix.

~ ~ ~

On my way back to Darwin, I rented a car in Alice Springs and drove to Uluru/Ayers Rock, the "Red Center" of Australia. It's a single mountain, 1,400 feet high, sacred to the Aborigines of Australia. I attended a sunset dinner and didgeridoo performance, in traditional Aussie outback style.

I flew to Darwin and paid 3,500 Australian dollars to Cyclone Motorcycles to fix the fuel system and brakes and rear shock. Phil, head of the service department, was short on patience but long on details.

Hank, the mechanic, said, "Keep an eye on the rear bearing. There's a little play in it."

I worried and wondered why he hadn't fixed it, but I needed to get going to make Townsville on the east side of Australia.

Eastbound out of Darwin, riding a desolate part of the Australian outback, I noticed a small seep of oil from the rear drive. I checked the level. It was a bit low. At an auto parts store, Slick 50 (gear lube) was $130 for an 800-milliliter bottle. They had lube additive for $10. That would get me to Townsville. I bought two tubes. I kept the wrench available and checked the level each stop for two days. I'd crawl on the dirty pavement, wrench open the access port, and top off the level. The seep became a drip. The drip became a leak. Running low on gear lube, I calculated the distance to my final destination of Townsville.

Twelve miles out of Richmond, Australia, the bike shuddered. I thought it was the road surface, like riding on road vibrators embedded on the shoulder to wake you up. I steered to a smooth portion in the middle. The vibration continued. My mind raced through possible causes.

Then came an up-and-down motion like riding a pogo stick. I thought maybe another flat spot on the tire. I pulled over on a wide portion of road and crawled in the dirt to inspect the source. Lube was gushing out of the rear drive into a mixture of lube and metal shavings, indicating ball bearings being churned up. Lube was not going to get me to Townsville. With no option to continue and inevitably be stranded further from civilization, I tried cell service for a rescue estimate. A weak cell signal got me through to a tow service and a 1,100 Australian-dollar estimate to take me to Townsville.

Wanting more than that option, I bounced twelve miles back to Richmond, where there was a one-pump roadhouse. The only vehicles traveling this part of the Australian outback were huge Australian road trains, massive trucks towing sometimes four semitrailers like a train. They fascinated me.

I parked in a spot where road trains could stop alongside me in hopes of bumming a ride from one. The first guy driving a string of empty trailers stopped.

From his window up high, he yelled, "What ya need, mate?"

"I need a ride to Townsville," I yelled over the engine noise.

He shook his head. "Sorry, mate, I'm picking up a full load in the next town."

"No worries," I said, and headed for the roadhouse across the street.

The door to the little roadhouse squeaked open as I entered. It had a fried-food-under-heat-lamps smell. Inside, stretched out in a plastic chair, was a handsome trucker dressed in a ripped T-shirt, baggy shorts, and flip-flops, talking on his mobile phone and eating a meat pie. I acted like I was shopping for something he had, with subtle gestures toward him to display interest. I waited for him to finish his phone call and take a huge bite of his meat pie.

"Excuse me, sir," I said. "My name is Robert. Where ya headed?"

"Rodney," he replied. "Townsville."

"Could you give me and my motorcycle a ride?" I asked.

He answered with a smoker's voice. "Yes, if you can hoist the bike onto my flatbed trailer. I don't have a ramp."

I was delighted I had a potential ride, dejected I had no way to lift Andiamo six feet up to his flatbed trailer.

Then like a surfboard on a rainbow, I noticed a construction site across the street that had a forklift puffing away. I ran over to the foreman. "Hey, mate," I said. "I'm stranded with my motorcycle. Can I use your forklift to lift my bike onto that flatbed trailer?"

With a warm smile, the busy Aussie foreman nodded. "No worries, mate." He whistled to the forklift driver and explained my predicament.

Like paramedics rushing to the scene of an accident, we ran alongside the forklift to where Andiamo lay unconscious in a pool of gear lube. The foreman threaded a strap sling through Andiamo's body like a medic on a battlefield. The forklift driver hoisted Andiamo six feet in the air and swung him onto the flatbed trailer as if on a gurney. Rodney and I cinched Andiamo to the trailer, like paramedics in an ambulance. The prospect of making Townsville made Andiamo's vital-signs monitor beep with a spike of hope.

I was surprised how many steps up were required to bounce into the air suspension of the passenger seat in Rodney's truck.

A kind and wonderfully famous truckie (Australian for trucker), Rodney was known in the area for his ambitious twenty-four-hour nonstop trips. He had four cell phones in his truck, two glued to his ears. I'm not sure how he did it, but he conducted business on one cell phone and chatted with his girlfriend on the other. Oh, and he had a cigarette hanging from his mouth, dropping ashes in his lap. Oftentimes, he set aside those distractions to steer our road train. My destiny was in Rodney's hands as he would toss one cell phone onto the dashboard to retrieve another.

I took comfort, thinking to myself, *This massive road train outweighs and sits higher than anything in the region, so we'll simply plow over or go through any obstacles.* I asked Rodney, "Have you ever hit a kangaroo?"

With sarcasm, he replied, "I'm not sure. Kangaroos are like bugs to a

Andiamo Full Circle

windshield. Cows will dent my massive bull guard, but if a herd is on the road, they can cause some damage."

Australia has "cattle stations," where cattle roam freely on millions of acres. Ranchers called "drovers" often use helicopters to drive their cattle.

Cell phone #3 rang. It was Rodney's wife scheduling a pickup in a town nearby, so we deviated. I wondered what cell phone #4 was used for. Was it like the Batphone or something? Was Rodney some kind of superhero? He was to me.

Periodically, I saw road signs with a picture of a CB radio.

Rodney keyed the microphone of his CB radio. "Road train eastbound approaching Danners bridge," he said. Another announcement: "Road train eastbound approaching Fredrick's corner."

The Australian outback has thousands of one-lane bridges around blind corners.

"If we meet another opposite-direction road train," Rodney explained, "neither can stop to avoid a head-on collision, so we announce our positions as we approach the hazardous areas marked by the CB radio signs."

I rode for two days and five hundred kilometers to Townsville with Rodney in his Australian road train. It was fun getting to know Rodney and to get a feel for the trucker life.

"How long ya been drivin', Rodney?" I asked.

"Thirty years," Rodney said. He and his wife owned their own trucking business, which kept Rodney on the road twenty-five days a month. His children were grown. His youngest daughter was a flight attendant for Qantas, and his son took care of the sugarcane plantation he owned.

In Townsville, I stayed at Rodney's house, where he showed me a collection of vintage Holdens. Rodney and his son had made one into a race car and raced locally. Holden was an Australian car company.

The next morning, we drove his road train around Townsville to find a loading dock near the BMW shop so I could roll Andiamo off the flatbed trailer. At a gas station truck stop, we found one. It was 9.7 kilometers from BMW Townsville. We placed boards to compensate for the difference between the loading dock and high trailer. I pushed Andiamo off onto the loading dock and said goodbye to Rodney.

Bob Dolven

Dear Rodney,

You saved my life and extended patience and generosity. Thank you so much for the entertaining conversations and experience. You are without a doubt living life on your terms. I wish the best for you and hope your wonderfully positive outlook on life continues.

Sincerely,
Robert

The problem now was that I had another 9.7 kilometers to BMW Townsville. I needed another good Samaritan who had time and an empty trailer to take me and Andiamo the remaining distance. After three hours of me assessing capable vehicles at the truck stop, a nice pickup truck towing an empty trailer pulled in.

I introduced myself and explained what had happened. "Now I need a trailer to cart my motorcycle into town."

"Wow, mate," he said. "What an adventure. Sure, I can help you." Andy was the good Samaritan I needed.

I love the Aussie spirit of people helping people. I believe that's true because most of Australia is remote outback where people depend on each other for survival. Andy and I used a ramp at the truck stop to load Andiamo onto his trailer. We had to drive around BMW Townsville looking for another loading dock, since Andy didn't have a ramp. We finally found one and used cinder blocks to jack up the ramp so I could roll off Andy's trailer. I pogo-sticked the final kilometer and left Andiamo outside the closed BMW shop.

Dear Andy,

Your selflessness shone through when you took time out of your day to help me. Our conversation about karma and doing good things for others to allow good things to happen to us left me hoping you have received kindness in return.

Thank you again,
Robert

Andiamo Full Circle

I called BMW Townsville in the morning, and the mechanic rode to my hotel to get my key so he could move Andiamo into the service area. Later when I arrived at the shop, the mechanic showed me the rear bearing that had come apart. The damage wasn't as bad as it could have been.

"No worries, mate," the mechanic said. "I can fix it."

I stuffed my gear into a cardboard box and put it in their storage room. I left Andiamo in their hands to be fixed. I'd be back in a month.

That evening, I met up with Halvard, one of my Norwegian relatives, for dinner. He was in Townsville working on his master's degree in biology. To earn some extra money, he was a snake catcher. If anyone needed a snake removed from their home, Halvard was the guy to do it. He asked if I wanted to be a part of releasing a venomous snake he had rescued from a woman's home.

"Yes, of course," I said.

We drove out into the country to set the reptile free to roam in a more suitable habitat. I could sense the appreciation Halvard had for this lethal creature. I could also sense my apprehension. Out of the bag and into the woods, the snake slithered. Afterward, we had a delicious meal at a seafood restaurant on the water.

The next day, I took the ferry to Magnetic Island. I arranged rental of a vintage Mini Moke. A Mini Moke is one of the cutest windowless, doorless, topless beach vehicles I have ever seen. I drove that thing around the entire island, among other things, visiting a koala rescue park and cuddling the adorable little koala bears. After a couple days exploring Magnetic Island, I took a flight to Sydney for a performance at the Sydney Opera House.

The next day, I took a fourteen-and-a-half-hour flight home to Phoenix. When I arrived home, I got an email from BMW Townsville. The quote for repairs was 5,700 Australian dollars—about 4,000 US dollars.

I would love to know the total cost of Andiamo's repairs over the years, but I'm scared to add them up. My best guess would be that Andiamo has cost me an amount approaching 100,000 US dollars.

On my way back to Townsville, Australia, in July 2019, I stopped off to see Vivid Sydney. It's a festival of light, music, and ideas where artists create light projection exhibits in parks, streets, and on the side of buildings to celebrate Sydney being the center of creativity for the Asia-Pacific. The most fascinating and perhaps the coolest art exhibit I've seen was the projection onto the Sydney Opera House of images of colorful creatures, giving the impression that giant beings had taken on the form of the Opera House's sail-like shapes. I absolutely loved watching this.

At BMW Townsville, I paid the bill and rode down to Airlie Beach, where I had arranged a five-day sailing trip around the Whitsunday Islands as captain of my own thirty-six-foot catamaran. I hadn't sailed since I was a kid with a Hobie Cat on Lake Harriet in Minneapolis. I was not a current sailor and was nervous about being responsible for a large boat on the ocean.

It's called "bareboating," skippering your own boat. The charter company Whitsunday Escape allowed me full unsupervised use of the boat with minimal instruction. My briefer, Tim, a retired South African-born sailor, had little concern about sending me out alone since I had bought the insurance policy as well.

He gave me a two-hour briefing on the systems and operation of the million-dollar thirty-six-foot catamaran. The boat was luxurious, equipped with three staterooms, two bathrooms, a huge galley, wraparound dining table, flat-screen TV, outdoor dining area with barbecue, and a trampoline on the bow area to lie on and enjoy the sun. It also had a small-powered dinghy for shore excursions. After his brief briefing, Tim jumped out and let me loose to explore the magnificent Whitsunday Islands for five days. Tim was thorough, but how could I remember all the details of the complex craft?

The charter company required me to use the VHF radio to give status reports twice daily. The pressure of navigating in rocky harbors and shorelines with the advanced GPS required my undivided attention. It was similar to flying an airplane and made me feel like a baby pilot again.

I sailed the open water with big waves and wind, private coves with secluded white sand beaches, and narrow channels bordered by steep mountains. I used the dinghy for trips into shallower waters to explore the beaches and spent the evenings watching the sunset over the stunning island scenery. My heart was full of love for this romantic vacation and yearned for more. I took great care to operate the boat responsibly and damaged nothing. I would highly recommend doing this. It was the trip of a lifetime.

Dear Tim,

Thank you for extending patience as I asked more questions than you felt necessary. I still can't believe you were convinced I wouldn't wreck the boat. It was one of my most enjoyable experiences of my life. Thank you.

Sincerely,
Robert

My next plan was to arrange shipment of Andiamo from Australia to New Zealand and ride everywhere and experience everything New Zealand had to offer. I found a shipping agent in Sydney and left Andiamo and all my gear with the crate builder.

"No worries, mate," he told me. "I'll take care of everything, and you can pick your bike up in Auckland in a month."

New Zealand

2019

Mileage: Unknown (odometer cable broken)

Ingredients: one bottle of wine, one planned celebration

On my flight from Houston to Auckland, New Zealand, I had brought some new camping equipment that couldn't be carried on board an airplane, so I had to check my bag. I keep GPS tracking devices in my bags to locate them if lost or stolen.

At the baggage carousel of Auckland International Airport, I rubbed my eyes to wake up. My GPS tracker indicated my bag was still in Houston. Air New Zealand gave me an amenity kit and a hundred dollars to compensate for no clothing. The amenity kit contained a toothbrush, toothpaste, comb, deodorant, and one white T-shirt. I paced around my hotel room in the white T-shirt, calling Air New Zealand to confirm my bag would arrive the next day at 11:00 a.m.

The front desk called my room at 11:00 a.m. to say my bag had been delivered to the lobby. I dashed down the elevator to find the bag intact. A welcome change of clothes and I was in an Uber to Taurus Logistics, Andiamo's receiving agent. They had my two carnets and the importation paperwork completed. I had two carnets because one expired as Andiamo was en route to New Zealand. Both needed entry and exit stamps just like a passport.

Andiamo was still packed in a large wooden crate. I disassembled the crate with a crowbar, careful not to cut my feet on the exposed nails. Someone had damaged the speedometer/odometer cables in the shipment. I use the odometer to track my gas mileage. Not having it would be of great inconvenience.

Customs had gone through everything on the bike and in the bags.

They had searched pockets inside pockets and confiscated some menthol crystals mixed with black seed and wrapped in a bandana. I had purchased them in Morocco and carried them without a problem for years. They took my gas bottle that I used for my portable camp stove. They said these were hazardous items and must be destroyed. They left my gear in a piled mess.

Three hours of uncrating and preparation, and I was on the road to adventure.

I rode three hours south to Rotorua, New Zealand, to try zorbing. A Zorb is a fifteen-foot inflatable ball-inside-a-ball. It rolls and bounces down a ski hill in a trench-like track dug into the ground with you inside.

The young Zorb worker drove me in a van to the top of the hill. There was a starting gate platform where the ball was ready to roll down the hill. I dove into the ball filled with water.

The guide secured the flap door with Velcro and gave me a countdown like a rocket launch. "Three, two, one, go." He pushed me out the gate.

The ball started to roll downhill. The direction was controlled by large gullies in the grass. The water inside made it slippery. Bumps bounced the Zorb, multiplying the effects on me inside like an elastic yo-yo. I was at the Zorb's mercy. My heart raced in a screaming rage. It was like being a piece of popcorn in an air popper. In the hairpin turns, the Zorb climbed the rails, then went back down the opposite direction.

When the spinning stopped, the guide at the bottom opened the Velcro flap, snapped a picture of my still-swiveling head, and asked, "How was that, mate?"

"It was by far the most exciting ride I've ever experienced!" I screamed. Ya gotta try zorbing.

I rode back up to Auckland and left Andiamo in a space at the hotel parking lot. I left my gear with the hotel bellman. On the flight home, I had a nice window seat with no one in the middle. That was nice because passenger etiquette dictates timing potty breaks with the aisle-seat passenger to avoid waking him up. Home for a month.

The ride in September 2019 focused on unique accommodations in New

Zealand. I searched the internet for the most unusual places I could spend the night.

In Waitomo, New Zealand, I found an old cargo airplane in a field converted into a hotel room. It was a British-built 1946 Bristol Freighter once used to carry military jeeps. It had a hinged bulbous nose that allowed World War II jeeps to be driven into the belly of the plane for transport to the battlefield. The large cockpit had been converted into the master bedroom, with flight controls, instruments, and a king-sized bed behind. I pretended I was the pilot in the left seat, advancing the throttles for takeoff. I flew in my dreams all night.

Next, I stayed in an old fire watchtower in downtown Auckland repurposed into a boutique hotel with great views of the city. The top of the tower had cushy couches around the perimeter in which to relax and gaze over the city while I enjoyed a sunset cocktail. Parked beneath, Andiamo looked like a fire truck ready to save lives.

I spent the next night in a tree house overlooking the ocean from the thick forest. It was like a huge children's playhouse with all the comforts and amenities of home. I sipped wine on the balcony overlooking the ocean, pretending I was a kid.

The next night, I stayed in a lighthouse on the shore of a rocky island inlet. I climbed the interior circular staircase to the top terrace with its massive signal light, and pretended to alert ships entering the harbor as the waves crashed against the rocks.

On to a shipping container set atop rolling acres of green. One side was a wide sliding glass door opening up to a tranquil, elevated deck. It had an outdoor shower and toilet surrounded by a draping, vine-covered lattice and river-rock floor. It made me feel one with nature.

I anticipated the night in the yellow submarine. It's an artistic expression of Beatles memorabilia down to the smallest detail in a life-sized yellow submarine. I pretended to dive and look through the periscope while Beatles music played on a vintage turntable.

The best unique accommodation was the Nest, a podlike container perched on a cliff overlooking the Tasman Sea, with a hot tub on a large wooden deck. It was self-sustaining and off the grid, miles from civilization. This remote cliffside dwelling allowed me to detach from reality, immersed in a fantasy as sole occupant of the world. Unique accommodations at night followed by adventures in the day.

I hiked one kilometer into a cave to see glowworms, insects that glow a blueish-green light. The dark grotto ceiling looked like a star-studded sky.

I Blokarted on a three-wheeled go-kart powered only by a colorful sail, like a windsurfer on wheels. Back and forth, I rode the wind. Strong gusts sailed me to Happyland.

Next I drift-karted on an electric tricycle with slippery back wheels, skidding around corners left and right on a cement track. The object was to maintain the skid in a controlled manner.

Roads in First-World countries are generally well maintained. However, in New Zealand I rode the state-recognized highway, Ninety Mile Beach, open only during low tide. When the shoreline recedes out to sea, the sand is left hard, able to support vehicles with no sinking effect. The New Zealand government uses this route in lieu of rebuilding an aging alternate route. The route shaves off forty-five minutes from the poorly paved route ten kilometers inland.

I checked my watch. The tide was one kilometer out and had left a wide damp-sand roadway. From a soft-sand access road through the dunes, I rode onto the beach with trepidation, knowing that if suddenly the tide rolled in, I would be stranded with no way off the beach to the alternate road ten kilometers inland. Like an unbroken boulevard of green lights, I chose the speed. For ninety miles, tiny, salty waves splashed off my tires. I was surfing on the sand, able to cut turns and ride freely with nothing but sand dunes on my left, and on my right, shallow shoreline on the sun-drenched horizon. I inhaled freedom to the end of this wonderful ninety-mile experience.

As the tide rolled back in, my rear wheel narrowly escaped being submerged in the advancing water. On solid pavement, I headed south, back to Auckland.

I had a day to explore Auckland, so I set my sights on adrenaline.

Auckland's Sky Tower is over a thousand feet high and the tallest freestanding structure in the Southern Hemisphere. I wanted to jump off it—

attached to a bungee cord, of course. I took a high-speed elevator to the top floor. Wearing only a jumpsuit and harness, I stepped out into fresh winds on the top platform overlooking New Zealand. A tattooed young man hooked a carabiner to my harness. I inched closer to the ledge of this skyscraper. On the horizon, I longed to be in the left seat of the airplane departing Auckland International Airport bound for elsewhere. My eyes darted down to the sidewalk a thousand feet below, filled with bystanders holding cell phones. The cars looked like ants on the streets.

Mr. Tattoo said, "Put your toes over the ledge, mate."

My eyes locked on to his for confirmation.

"You're ready!" he exclaimed. "Jump!"

My conscious, mature mind was already in a taxi to the airport as my hands let go of the railing. Freehanded and able to flail, I allowed my toes to let go of the ledge. My breath remained there while my body plummeted faster than the pit in my stomach and my entire being was scattered like a dropped eggshell. A few milliseconds later, everything regrouped like a star cluster shooting toward Earth. Finally, my breath caught me as the carabiner was unclipped. Not until I was off the landing pad did my mature mind reenter my head. I felt like some kind of flying circus performer. With a downtown-sized smile, I lusted for another adrenaline fix.

Fortunately, on the next block was the Sky Screamer, a human slingshot into the sky.

As I was belted to the chairlift-type apparatus, the operator yelled, "Three, two, one, go!"

I was sprung into the sky like a catapult, spinning so fast that vision was impossible. Up and down like an elastic yo-yo I went. That was my last adrenaline fix for that month's trip.

My flight home the next day was the opposite of adrenaline adventure, with a comfortable seat and movies to watch for fourteen hours.

～～～

BMW Wellington took care of Andiamo and wired my new GPS unit, since the old unit went to GPS heaven. A bill for 1,900 New Zealand dollars, and I took a ferry ride to the South Island.

I disembarked the ferry to ride through the steep fjords of the South Island of New Zealand. Frequent road closures slowed my pace. On a wide, flat portion of the valley, I camped on the beach, absorbed in nature. I pulled the cork and poured a glass of local wine. The fresh air cleansed my lungs. The green fjords soothed my eyes. The blue water made me thirsty. I swallowed the setting.

After I had packed up my campsite, I rode south to meet up with a fly-boy buddy. Dave is a Kiwi who happened to be in New Zealand at the same time. He recommended we meet at a famous fish market considered to have the best fish in New Zealand. We ate fish-and-chips right out of the water into the fryer and wrapped in newspaper. Steaming-hot flavor filled my mouth.

Thanks, Dave,

It was great to see you and your homeland. I wish we could have spent more time together, but I had to ride.

Sincerely,
Bob

The ride over Arthur's Pass in torrential freezing rain chilled my bones. Parts of the road were washed out, diverting traffic. To each side of me were steep mountains lush with misty waterfalls slicing vertically. The scene was very Norwayesque, which made me think of my heritage.

That night, I slept in a grain silo converted to a chic hotel. Ian, the owner, used large corrugated grain silos as individual apartment hotel rooms. He designed each detail made with items available at the local hardware stores. The silo's style was functional and durable, with exposed copper pipes and garden spigots in the kitchen and bathrooms, lights made from galvanized pipe, wing nuts, and braided cable, and stairs made from welded steel with a patina coating. It was a treat to occupy this space.

Thank you, Ian, for providing a unique and restful night at your creative hotel.

Sincerely,
Robert

I rode south to Mount Cook, the highest mountain in New Zealand. Its range runs the length of the South Island.

I booked a suite at the Hermitage Hotel. Mount Cook filled my picture window with a majestic view. The peak and base, framed perfectly, made me feel small and undeserving of its intense beauty.

My alarm woke me at 5:00 a.m. in time to hustle to the airport for a helicopter and ski-plane trip to the top of the Tasman Glacier. Seated according to weight in the helicopter, I was fortunate to be up front.

When we landed atop the glacier, the pilot said, "We're on top of thirty meters of ice. It takes forty-five years for the ice to descend the mountain into the Tasman Lake."

Infinitesimal is how I felt, compared to the vastness of ice and snow beneath my feet as I walked on top of the glacier.

On an herb farm at the base of the mountain range, I ate lavender ice cream in a field of lavender on a lavender-colored Adirondack chair. The sweet purple treat was like savoring the glacier, while the lavender fragrance calmed my olfactory system into tranquility.

Interrupting my peaceful feeling was a report on the clerk's radio: an earthquake on the North Island had caused many deaths. Travel had been restricted. I thought it might be a problem for me transiting the North Island on my way home. Natural disasters seem to follow me.

New Zealand wines are world-class, and I wanted to sample some at a local vineyard. Riding twenty miles south of Christchurch, I noticed a roadside sign that proclaimed, SERIOUSLY DRINKABLE WINE, with a finger pointing to the vineyard entrance. With my taste buds tantalized, I rode along the manicured, treelined driveway leading to the Straight 8 Estate vineyard. James and Mary, the owners, were out front sipping sunshine and relaxing on the sun deck in lounge chairs at a wine-barrel table.

I introduced myself. "Hi, I'm Robert. I'm in search of some seriously drinkable wine. Do you have any?"

"You've come to the right place, my friend," James answered.

We went inside, and I sampled their varietals in the well-appointed antique tasting room. They were generous with the samples, and I loved them all. Mary served a Pinot Noir that became my favorite.

The delicious juice in my glass spilled the question. "I need to return to the States tomorrow," I said. "Can I leave my motorcycle here for a month?"

A simultaneous yes from both James and Mary sealed the deal. At the time, we had no idea how complicated our agreement would become due to a worldwide pandemic.

The estate was named after James's pride and joy, a 1935 Railton vintage race car powered by a Hudson straight 8 engine. The car had been in his family over fifty years. It wasn't just a showpiece advertising the love for their vineyard. It got driven on special occasions. An unexpected low thumping sound progressively quickened with black clouds of smoke from the tail pipe as the old race car came to life.

"Hop in," James said.

I was careful not to put my foot through the aged wooden floor of the cockpit. The rpm needle bounced as James hit the gas, spinning the tires on the gravel road. The rear wheels skidded around the corner as James split rows of grapevines. Leaves slapped my face.

He stopped to check a grape, tasted it, and said, "Perfect. This will be a good harvest."

I felt like an honored celebrity riding in the open-air sports car.

That night, James and Mary made a fabulous lamb dinner with mashed potatoes, salad, fresh bread, and plenty of their sensational wine. James was no shrinking violet. We debated all night to declare peoples' inalienable right to life, liberty, and the pursuit of happiness. I slept in one of their spare bedrooms. The next morning, James and Mary, with their infinite generosity, drove my headache to the airport.

We hugged goodbye, and I said, "I'll see you in a month."

Little did we know, a worldwide pandemic would shatter that statement.

Recipe: Open the bottle of wine and pour glasses for your guests. Smash the "planned celebration" into smithereens. Toast to "adaptability."

Extras

COVID-19

I used to say nothing would stop me from completing my motorcycle ride around the world. I never dreamed of a worldwide pandemic preventing my continuance.

As I write this in December 2020, I don't know when I can get back to New Zealand to complete the final leg of my around-the-world motorcycle ride and ship the bike to America. The borders are closed at this time. Andiamo is parked at the Straight 8 Estate vineyard in New Zealand. I am very gracious and apologetic to James and Mary for allowing me to keep Andiamo on the property for this unfortunate extended time.

I accepted a company-offered leave of absence in May, and another in July and August. I rented a condo for thirty days in Grand Marais, Minnesota, on the shore of Lake Superior with an inspirational view that surfaced my emotions. My goal was to write the first draft of the book looking out over the Great Lake where I had vacationed growing up. I typed for thirty days, fourteen hours per day, and achieved my goal. In July, I wrote the second draft of the book in my living room. For August, I rode the Amtrak trains around America, writing the third draft.

~~~

New Zealand is the last country scheduled on my around-the-world motorcycle ride. I have experienced many different cultures and ways of life, good and bad. This exposure has left me with one undeniable truth: the United States of America is the best country in the world.

I have traveled the world, observing and comparing the infrastructures, governments, legal systems, economies, cultures, and the way people live their lives to the United States of America. By far and without a doubt, the United States has the best of everything. Americans should visit other countries to solidify this fact for themselves. Don't just go for poolside cabana visits, but get "into" the country and feel what it's like to be a local citizen dealing with everyday issues.

I'm not comparing Third-World countries. I'm comparing First-World countries where travel is safe and Americans are welcomed. You will return with a newfound gratitude for what has been provided for you as an American.

Gear Guide

This chapter is dedicated to travel gear recommendations. I have used and found these items to be the best. My sponsors and non-sponsors receive unbiased equal evaluation.

Camera Equipment:

For normal shooting, the GoPro HERO8 Black is the best all around go-anywhere camera. It does everything you need to capture epic images. If you want to bring only one camera on your trip, this is the one. It's small, waterproof, has great low-light quality, great image stabilization, and is user-friendly. If you want to capture the entire environment and get creative, bring the GoPro MAX 360 Degree. The two cameras will do everything and save space in your luggage.

Travel Clothes:

ExOfficio Give-N-Go underwear is the single best piece of travel clothing I've used. It breathes and keeps you comfortable on fifteen-hour flights. You can wash it each night, and it'll be dry by morning. When you hike to that private waterfall, it can serve as a swimsuit.

TravelSmith Tropical Blazer has plenty of pockets and is wrinkle-free for packing into your luggage.

Bison Belts Last Chance Heavy Duty Belt is adjustable to your size and can be used to tie your gear in an emergency.

Johnston & Murphy men's McGuffey shoes can be worn to dinner or on a city tour, then folded into a small space in your luggage.

The Retro 1951 Hex-O-Matic pen is the best writing instrument. It's made from solid metal, with a knurled grip and tapered point to see what's being written.

The Money Clamp Geneva money clip will fit one bill to a fat stack of Uzbek soms. It's durable and small enough for front-pocket use to prevent pickpockets.

Casio Pro Trek series watches feature solar power. They never need a battery and have a compass, altimeter, thermometer, and twenty-four time zones for your local time anywhere in the world. The radio sync never needs setting. I've used three different models. The best travel watch.

Camping Gear:

The American-made Kermit Chair is the strongest, most comfortable camp chair. It has sturdy arms and folds down small. Simply the best camp chair available.

The Hennessy four-season Expedition hammock gave me the best sleep experience in the jungle I've ever had. It keeps you dry in tropical downpours, even when it rains horizontally.

GSI Micro Table. The first time I bought this table, the saleswoman said, "Buy it if it will make your life better." It's the right height and able to withstand a boiling pot of water. Folds to a compact size.

Riding Gear:

Aerostich Combat Touring Boots are the best riding boots I've ever used. They're high, and they protect you on the road and at the campsite. The leather is high quality, thick and durable over the years. The soles are grippy and solid. The lace-up closure forms to your calf and is very comfortable. These are the best-made motorcycle boots.

Wolfman Rainier tank bag is the one item that hasn't failed in some capacity or another. Zippers work well and no straps have torn. It expands to accommodate your purchases at the open market.

BMW Rallye 2 Pro riding suit. I've made enhancements to make this a customized coat. The back holds the flags of all the countries I've ridden through.

Pelican cases are the best protection for your valuable items. They make sizes for all your gear, and they offer a lifetime warranty.

This is a small sample of gear I have tried.

Airlines Flown

United
Continental Airlines
Delta
Emirates
Lufthansa
Pegasus
Croatia Airlines
Aeroflot
Azerbaijan Airlines
British Airways
LAN Chile
LAN Peru
LAN Argentina
LACSA Costa Rica
Sansa (Costa Rica)
Maya Island Air
Ryanair
EasyJet
JetBlue
Spirit
American Airlines
TAP Air Portugal
Tunisair
Alitalia
Cubana
Aerolineas Argentinas
Frontier Airlines
Copa Airlines
Avianca

Qatar Airways
Transaero
Air Astana
S7 Airlines (now Siberia Airlines)
Rossiya Airlines
Korean Air
Polar Cargo Polar Air Cargo
Japan Airlines
AirAsia
Thai AirAsia X
Malaysia Airlines
Air China
Air Koryo
China Eastern Airlines
Spring Airlines
Air KBZ
Trans Maldivian Airways
SriLankan Airlines
Lao Airlines
Asiana Airlines
Garuda Indonesia
Lion Air
Sriwijaya Air
Fiji Airways
Virgin Australia
Jetstar
Jet Airways
Nam Air
Qantas
China Southern Airlines
Yeti Airlines
Air Niugini
PNG Air
Philippine Airlines

Bob Dolven

Cebgo Airlines
Cebu Pacific Air

Parking Spots

1. Mexico – Alex's garage
2. Guatemala – BMW Guatemala, Jose
3. El Salvador – Pirelli tire shop
4. Costa Rica – Self-storage
5. Colombia – BMW Bogota
6. Ecuador – Swissotel Quito
7. Peru – Miraflores Park Hotel
8. Bolivia – Hotel Libertador
9. Chile – BMW Santiago
10. Argentina – Ruben's garage
11. England – Vines of Guildford BMW, south of London
12. Norway – Relative's house
13. France – BMW Nice
14. Spain – Underground garage of Gerardo's apartment building
15. Portugal – Louie's parents' farm
16. Portugal – Louie's parents 2.0
17. Tunisia – Kaifer's house
18. Italy – Hotel Amalfi
19. Croatia – Hilton Imperial Dubrovnik
20. Turkey – BMW Istanbul
21. Lebanon – Radisson Blu Martinez in downtown Beirut
22. Romania – Micheal's house
23. Ukraine – Hotel in Kiev
24. Russia – BMW Moscow
25. Georgia – Kopala Hotel
26. Azerbaijan – Yamaha/BMW Baku
27. Kazakhstan – Marriott Aktau
28. Kazakhstan – BMW Almaty
29. Krasnoyarsk – BMW Krasnoyarsk

30. Mongolia – Customs Office
31. South Korea – BMW Busan
32. South Korea – BMW Busan 2.0
33. Japan – Hiroshima Crowne Plaza
34. Japan – Haneda BMW
35. Malaysia – BMW Langkawi
36. Thailand – Bangkok BMW
37. Cambodia – Dara Airport Hotel, Phnom Penh
38. Laos – Landmark Hotel, Vientiane
39. Thailand – Duangtawan Hotel Chiang Mai
40. Malaysia – Premiere Hotel, Kuala Lumpur
41. Indonesia – BMW Medan, Sumatra
42. Indonesia – Aston Lampung City Hotel, Sumatra
43. Indonesia – Shalimar Boutique Hotel, Malang
44. Indonesia – BMW Bali Denpasar
45. Indonesia – Shipped from Lombok to Australia
46. Australia – Procycles Sydney
47. Australia – Best Western Hobart Tasmania
48. Australia – Pitmans Motorcycles, Adelaide
49. Australia – BMW Perth
50. Australia – Regal Transport, Broome
51. Australia – BMW Darwin, Cyclone Motorcycles
52. Australia – BMW Townsville, Pickerings Auto Group
53. Australia – Ship Sydney-Auckland
54. New Zealand – Crowne Plaza, Auckland
55. New Zealand – BMW Wellington
56. New Zealand – Straight 8 Estate, Burnham

Common Questions

Q: How much does the motorcycle cost?
A: New models $26,000. My used price was $6,000.

Q: When/where did you start the ride?
A: May 2009 from home in Phoenix, Arizona.

Q: How fast does the motorcycle go?
A: I've got up to 150 miles per hour on the German autobahn.

Q: When/where will you finish?
A: Not sure when but definitely in the USA.

Q: How much have you spent on the trip?
A: Average cost to me has been $50,000 per year.

Q: How can you manage it having a full-time job?
A: I stagger my schedule in two-week increments.

Q: What problems have you had?
A: Bike, border, health problems... so many.

Q: Have you had anything stolen?
A: Yes, small items. Nothing big.

Q: Why are you doing this ride?
A: To make lemonade out of lemons.

Q: Are you married? Have kids?
A: Not married. No kids.

Q: What's your favorite country?
A: The United States of America.

Q: Do you jump-seat or buy tickets?
A: Jump-seat if I can risk it. Otherwise, I buy tickets.

Q: Do you have a blog or website?
A: I used to but not since Algeria. Only Facebook now.

Q: Where do you park the motorcycle?
A: Anywhere I can. Do you have space?

Q: Do you get tired of the travel?
A: Not travel, but the red tape of travel.

Q: What are you going to do when your ride is done?
A: Kayak the three biggest rivers in the world.

Q: How did you come up with the title of the book?
A: One of my favorite things to do while riding was thinking of book titles. I didn't decide until it came time to publish the book. Coming up with a title prematurely would be like building a house starting with the roof, or starting a restaurant with only the name. It seems that a book title is one of the most important all-encompassing things about a book. Therefore, I didn't make a final decision until I knew what the ride was about.

Some possibilities were *Andiamo Around the World; Velocity Sub One; Clicking Kilometers; Quiet Conversations with Terrorists; Peace Rider; Moto Piloto; Sit Back, Relax, and Enjoy This Book; Nonstop, Perpetual Vacation; Perpetual Layover; Perpetual Motion; The Perfect Imperfection; Never Ends Well for da Gringo; Lemons to Lemonade; Dancing with Traffic; EARs RTW – Round the World.*

Printed in Great Britain
by Amazon